Contents

Understanding post-war British society

Edited by James Obelkevich and
Peter Catterall

London and New York

First published
by Routledge
11 New Fetter Lane, London EC4P 4EE

Simultaneously published in the USA and Canada
by Routledge
29 West 35th Street, New York, NY 10001

© 1994 The Institute of Contemporary British History.
Individual chapters, the contributors.

Typeset in Times by J&L Composition Ltd, Filey, North Yorkshire.

Printed and bound in Great Britain by
TJ Press (Padstow) Ltd, Padstow, Cornwall.

British Library Cataloguing in Publication Data

A catalogue record for this book is available from the British Library.

Library of Congress Cataloging in Publication Data

Understanding post-war British society / edited by James Obelkevich and
  Peter Catterall.
      p.   cm.
   Includes bibliographical references (p.   ) and index.
    ISBN 0–415–10939–6 : $65.00. – ISBN 0–415–10940–X (pbk.) : $17.50
    1. Great Britain – Social conditions – 1945– I. Obelkevich, Jim.
  II. Catterall, Peter, 1961– .
  HN385.5.U53   1994
  306 .0941–dc20   94-7263
                                                            CIP

ISBN 0–415–10939–6 (hbk)
ISBN 0–415–10940–X (pbk)

List of figures

List of tables

Contributors

Celia Brackenridge was Principal Lecturer in Recreation Management at Sheffield Hallam University. Since 1994 she has been Reader in Sport and Leisure at Cheltenham and Gloucester College of Higher Education. Her current research is into child abuse by sports coaches and she is lead member for Britain of an international coalition of women's sport organisations.

Joan C. Brown is an independent researcher in social policy. Both now and in her past status as Senior Research Fellow of the Policy Studies Institute her main work has been in the field of social security and poverty. She was involved in the first of the European Community poverty programmes and has written extensively on the UK social security system. Among her recent publications are *Why don't they go to Work?: Mothers on Benefit* (1989), *Victims or Villains: Social Security Benefits in Unemployment* (1990), *Child Benefit: Options for the 1990s* (1990) and *A Policy Vacuum: Social Security for the Self-employed* (1992).

Robert G. Burgess is director of CEDAR (Centre for Educational Development, Appraisal and Research) and Professor of Sociology at the University of Warwick. His main publications include: *Experiencing Comprehensive Education* (1983), *In the Field: An Introduction to Field Research* (1984), *Education, Schools and Schooling* (1985), *Schools at Work* (1988, with Rosemary Deem) and *Research Methods* (1993). He was recently President of the British Sociological Association and is currently President of the Association for the Teaching of the Social Sciences. He was a member of the ESRC Training Board and is currently a member of the ESRC Research Resources Board.

Peter Catterall is director of the Institute of Contemporary British History and Visiting Lecturer in History at Queen Mary and Westfield College, University of London. He is editor of *Contemporary Record, Modern History Review,* and *Contemporary Britain: An Annual Review.* He is also historical adviser to the British Video History Trust.

Rosemary Crompton is Reader in Sociology at the University of Kent. Her latest publication is *Class and Stratification* (Polity, 1993).

John Curtice is Senior Lecturer in Politics and Director of the Social Statistics laboratory at the University of Strathclyde and is Deputy Director of the Centre for Research into Elections and Social Trends (CREST), an ESRC research centre. He was Co-director of the British Election Survey at the last three elections and is co-author of *How Britain Votes* (1985) and *Understanding Political Change* (1991) and co-editor and contributor to *Labour's Last Chance?* (1994)

Grace Davie is Lecturer in Sociology at the University of Exeter and Secretary-general of the International Society for the Sociology of Religion. She has written numerous articles on the Sociology of Religion, notably in the field of unchurched religiosity and on the significance of the religious factor in the construction of contemporary Europe. She is co-author of *Inner City God: The Nature of Religion in the Inner City* (1987) and author of *Religion in Britain Since 1945* (1994).

Chris Harris is Professor of Sociology at University College, Swansea. His publications include *The Family and Industrial Society* (1983), *Redundancy and Recession* (1987) and *Kinship* (1990).

C. M. Law is Reader in Geography at the University of Salford. His latest publication is *Urban Tourism: Attracting Visitors to Large Cities* (1993).

Arthur Marwick has held visiting professorships in the United States, France and Italy. He was appointed in 1969 to establish the Department of History at the Open University. In 1991 he was awarded a D.Litt by Edinburgh University in recognition of his published contributions to twentieth century cultural and social history. He is currently working on a book entitled *The Sixties: Cultural and Social Change in Britain, France, Italy and the USA c. 1958–1974.*

Anne Murcott is Senior Lecturer at the London School of Hygiene and Tropical Medicine. The social anthropology and sociology of food has predominated among her research interests for 15 years. In addition to publishing books and articles, and serving as editor of the international journal, *Sociology of Health and Illness*, most recently she co-authored *The Sociology of Food: Diet, Eating and Culture.*

James Obelkevich lectures at the Centre for the Study of Social History, University of Warwick. He wrote *Religion and Rural Society: South Lindsey 1825–1875* (1976) and edited (with Raphael Samuel and Lyndal Roper) *Disciplines of Faith: Religion, Politics and Patriarchy* (1987). His current research is on the history of consumption in twentieth century

Britain. Forthcoming works include *Body Care in Britain 1950–1980* and *Consumption in Britain Since 1945*.

Edward Royle has been Reader in History at the University of York since 1989. Apart from his interest in the history of popular religion and unbelief in nineteenth century Britain, he has published several works on British radical politics as well as his textbook study, *Modern Britain: A Social History 1750–1985* (1987).

R. M. Smith is Director of the Wellcome Unit for the History of Medicine, University of Oxford and fellow of All Souls College. He is the author of a number of books, including *Land, Kinship and Life-cycle* and (with Margaret Pelling) *Life, Death and the Elderly: Historical Perspectives*. He has published a large number of articles on various aspects of family and demographic history. His current research is concerned with the relationship between welfare and demography in English history from 1600 to the present.

Penny Summerfield is Senior Lecturer in the Department of Educational Research and Co-director of the Centre for Women's Studies, University of Lancaster. She is the author of *Women Workers in the Second World War* (1989) and co-author of *Out of the Cage: Women's Experiences in the Two World Wars* (1987). She has also published numerous articles on women, war and social change, and on gender, class and schooling in the twentieth century.

Anthea Tinker has been Director of the Age Concern Institute of Gerontology and Professor of Social Gerontology at King's College, London, since 1988. She has been on the staff of City University and the University of London and has worked in three government departments. Her work has been mainly in the field of ageing in the last eighteen years. She has written ten and co-authored at least another ten books.

Diana Woodward was successively Senior Lecturer in Sociology, Head of the Department of Applied Social Studies and Dean of the Faculty of Health and Community Studies at Sheffield Hallam University. In 1992 she joined HM Inspectorate, with the brief of inspecting courses in health and social care in further and higher education. When this section was dissolved she joined the Quality Assessment Division of the Higher Education Funding Council for England, until in 1994 she was appointed Professor of Community Health Studies at Cheltenham and Gloucester College of Higher Education.

Understanding British society

James Obelkevich and Peter Catterall

British society is a complicated affair, full of loose ends and bits that don't fit. This may be a good thing for the people who live in it, but it is a source of frustration for those who study it and try to understand it. Every attempt to sum it up in a simple formula – as a 'class society' or whatever – has proved to have so many exceptions and qualifications that it was more trouble than it was worth. The first thing to understand about British society is that there are no short-cuts, no master keys.

The aim of this book is therefore modest. It makes few references to Weber, Durkheim and the other great names of the sociological tradition. It deliberately rejects the idea that British society is best understood as a giant monolithic structure; it does not try to tie up all the loose ends in a single knot of grand theory. Instead it follows a pluralistic approach, taking a fresh look at the loose ends themselves – population, the family, work, leisure, religion and so on – and tries to make sense of them in their own right, with each chapter summarising recent research on a particular topic. The authors have also tried to put their subjects in historical perspective, retracing the course and causes of change in the post-war period. The assumption is that it is better to understand particular themes in some detail, and in historical depth, than it is to bandy about vague general-isations about 'class' or 'capitalism' or 'hegemony' or whatever. British society, as it emerges from this book, is diverse and ever-changing – and incapable of being summed up in any simple formula.

The authors are a mixed team of mainly sociologists and historians and their chapters naturally reflect their individual interests and concerns. Some focus chiefly on the role of the state and on the consequences of official policies; some are preoccupied with questions of gender. The book does not lay down a party line, and the authors' findings point in different directions. But they do suggest a few lessons of a more general nature.

The first is about the role of ideology. A decade or two ago the ideology most in favour was Marxism, and it had an influence not only on the relatively small group of committed Marxists but also on the great major-ity of sociologists who politically were firmly within the Labour Party. In its time Marxism had a positive role to play. It reminded us that society was not a harmonious, integrated, organic unity; that poverty was a reality; and that class differences still mattered.

But Marxism got many things wrong. It was at a loss to account for the spread of affluence and the rise in living standards. Even on its chosen ground of class, it was unconvincing. Its master theme of class struggle could not be squared with what was actually happening in post-war Britain. It could not come to terms with the middle classes – their growth, diversity and cultural fragmentation. And it was equally baffled by the working classes, who so often voted for the 'wrong' political party – the Conservatives – rather than for Labour. This lack of fit between Marxist notions of class consciousness and the actual voting behaviour of the working class was an embarrassment, and it could not be covered up by such devices as 'false consciousness' or 'hegemony'. The fact was that most workers were not socialists and did not want a socialist revolution; their political outlook was incapable of being explained in Marxist categories. And when Marxists were faced with divisions in society other than those of class – such as gender, nationality, race, religion or age – they either tried to reduce them to class conflict or ignored them altogether. If Marxism ever provided an adequate analysis of British society – which may be doubted – it does no longer.

Our problem is that while we can see the deficiencies of Marxism, we do not as yet have an alternative set of reference points to put in its place. One possibility is the neo-liberal and free market ideas that came back into fashion in the 1980s. They propose a very different model of social behaviour, based on individual aspirations and expectations, and they have had an impact upon economic and, increasingly, on social policy. But their effect on British sociology, so far, has been limited. The two leading neo-liberals, David Marsland and Peter Saunders, have made some telling criticisms of sociological orthodoxy, exposing its leftish bias, its prejudice against the market and against capitalism, its naïve assumption that socialism offered a better way. But they have still to construct a distinctive sociology of their own.

Today the most fashionable ideology is feminism. Like any ideology, it has strengths and weaknesses, and its effects on sociology have been mixed. Its great positive contribution has been to bring women, and gender, into the centre of sociological enquiry. Sociology has at last opened its eyes to the question of gender – a crucial advance and one that was long overdue.

But feminism also has its less helpful side. Just as Marxism often degenerated into a series of crude leftist slogans known as vulgar Marxism, so feminism has its contemporary equivalent in what could be called vulgar feminism. Its reductionist catchphrases are all too familiar: 'patriarchy', women's 'common oppression', 'women's values', the family as a 'site of oppression', 'all men are rapists', 'feminism is the theory, lesbianism the practice', etc., etc. The result is a seductive but simplistic tale of evil, powerful men oppressing helpless, innocent women. Far from opening our eyes to hidden truths, this kind of sloganising only creates new myths, and prevents us from seeing women, and men, as they really are. The result is demonology, not sociology.

One of its most misleading assumptions is that women were nothing but victims. But there have been millions of exceptions, notably the working-class women who, far from being subordinate and put-upon, were the powerful, central and dominant figures in their families. Nor, contrary to the myth of 'common oppression', were all women equally disadvantaged: middle- and upper-class women were among the most privileged people in society and had vastly more in common with their husbands than with their working-class (or black) 'sisters', whom they shamelessly exploited when they employed them as domestic servants. No more convincing is the claim that women are excluded from power. Margaret Thatcher not only attained supreme power but wielded it more ruthlessly than any male prime minister in British history. And women today hold the posts of director of public prosecutions and of director of MI5 – at the heart of the state's security apparatus.

It is well known that since the end of the war the proportion of women in paid employment has increased dramatically. But the claim that *all* working women want to pursue 'careers', and are only held back by 'glass ceilings' imposed by men, is yet another myth. Undoubtedly such barriers existed and still exist, but historically working women have jobs rather than careers. The primary commitment for many women is often still not to work but to their traditional role in rearing a family – just as it was for their predecessors in the 1940s.

Another source of error has been the tendency to inflate the achievements of feminism, to assume that if women's condition improved, feminism deserves the credit. But the expansion of higher education, for example, which benefited women (especially those from the middle class) far more than it did men, came before, not after, the revival of feminism at the end of the 1960s. Feminism was not the cause of women's entry into university education: it was, if anything, one of its consequences. Similarly, the trend for married women to return to paid employment started early in the post-war period and owed nothing to feminism. Misleading too is the tendency to inflate the size of the feminist movement itself – to assume that all women are discontented with their lot and are in some sense feminist. In fact, most women have accepted their role in the family and in society and have not questioned or challenged it. Far from being instinctive feminists, most women have rejected the feminist movement and what they see as its dogmatism and arrogance.

Underlying the vulgar feminist scenario is the rather insulting assumption that women are so weak that they, their lives and their identities are controlled totally by men. But the inconvenient fact is that femininity is constructed by women just as much as it is by men – and that women also play a central part in the construction, and perpetuation, of masculinity itself. Scapegoating men as the source of all evil gets us nowhere. We have to come to terms with men as they are, and with their capacity, like that of women, for good and for evil.

Marxism and feminism can both provide powerful insights. But each also has its blind spots and its limitations. Just as Marxists had little to say to workers who preferred the *Sun* to *New Left Review*, so feminism makes a poor guide to the vast majority of women who are not feminist, who reject feminism, and who find *Woman* and *Best* more rewarding than *Spare Rib*. People have to be understood in their own terms: this can not be done by imposing on them some alien ideological agenda – Marxist or feminist – from outside.

Some of these same criticisms apply to what is probably the dominant outlook in British sociology today, which is feminist and left of centre. It tends to be highly critical of British society, which it sees as swarming with inequalities and injustices. It seeks to expose the evils of racism and sexism, the disparity in power and in life-chances between rich and poor. It is appalled by the unfairness it sees in British society. Inevitably it is disappointed by the fact that these evils do not arouse more protest, more opposition. It asks why the 'oppressed' – workers, women, blacks and others – do not challenge the system, reform it, even overthrow it.

Such a question is certainly worth asking. There is a great deal of inequality in Britain, and exposing and highlighting it is one of socio-logy's essential duties. Yet few people, even its main victims, do much about it. One explanation is to blame the media. There would be more protest, it is often said, if only the media did not conceal injustice and distract attention from a corrupt system. But this does not take us very far. The media expose faults, failings and injustices in Britain every day of the week. The real answer is that faults, failings and injustices are only part of the picture. Britain cannot be understood merely as a collection of 'social problems', as an anthology of 'oppression', whether based on class, race, gender or whatever. Nor can it be understood in terms of 'struggle' – whether between 'dominant' and 'radical', middle-class and working-class, men and women, old and young, or whites and blacks. There is much more to British society than this simple tale of goodies and baddies.

Sociology, if it is to fill in the larger picture, needs to look at some of the more positive things that have happened in Britain during the last few decades. There is, above all, the huge improvement in standards of living. Despite the widening of the gap between rich and poor during the 1980s, most people are far better-off now than their predecessors were a generation ago. Working-class people today take for granted such things as domestic appliances and foreign holidays which then were in short supply, or unavailable, even to the well-off. There has also been a great deal of upward social mobility. Many young people from working-class families entered higher education and embarked on non-manual careers; even larger numbers started work in manual occupations and climbed into non-manual ones. Women too benefited from the expansion of higher education. Indeed, the numbers of women going to university increased much faster than the numbers of students from working-class backgrounds. British society has often been described, by sociologists and others, as rigid and class-ridden. But it has also shown a remarkable degree of openness and mobility. If Britain is divided into three classes, then of the men in the top or 'service' class – professionals, managers, proprietors and supervisors – those from manual, working-class origins actually outnumber those born in the service class itself. The majority of British men have either moved into a different class from the one in which they were born, or have married a woman from a different social class. Women's mobility is comparable. Class is a reality, but it is not set in stone. British society does not consist of fixed, monolithic classes, but of much more porous, heterogeneous groupings, in which the majority of people have personal or familial links across class lines.

No one could deny that Britain has its share of conflict. But just as significant is the fact of consensus and shared values. By the standards of many advanced societies, overt conflict, let alone violence, is surprisingly rare in Britain. As many foreign visitors and observers have noted, one of the most striking facts about Britain – despite war, industrialisation and relative decline – is its sheer continuity, the absence of violent social and political disruption. In any international ranking of social stability, Britain, despite the increase in poverty, ranks near the top of the league table. Any study of British society that highlights the conflict presents a very distorted picture of the society as a whole. And with the fall in strikes and industrial disputes in recent years, it could be argued not only that conflict is *not* the most important feature of British society, but also that it is one that is in decline.

A second lesson of this book concerns the role of the state. That role still includes the state's traditional primary duty of protecting the country from external threats and of preserving law and order – which, since the end of the war, has also meant combatting communist subversion and IRA terrorism. (The growth, and abuse, of the 'secret state', with its powers of surveillance, control and covert action, is one of the more worrying developments of the post-war period.)

But no one could ignore the fact that during this period the state's field of operations has expanded enormously, and now extends far beyond its traditional role. Even in the Thatcher and post-Thatcher years, the state has carried on planning, directing, regulating, employing, subsidising. Indeed, it spends money – and collects taxes – on a vast scale. Public expenditure is the equivalent of about 40 per cent of gross domestic product. Well over half of this expenditure, moreover, is now devoted to the welfare state – to health, education, housing and so on. Social security transfer payments alone account for a third of government spending, the equivalent of (though not counted as part of) over 10 per cent of GDP. Compared with its fairly restricted range of activities earlier in the century, the state now gives the impression of intervening in just about every corner of British life. It has become a central fact in post-war society.

The question, however, is whether it is *the* central fact. And here there are reasons for scepticism. Of course, the state is ultimately responsible for the legal framework within which British society is supposed to operate; but that framework is itself a reflection of past social attitudes, as for example the laws on Sunday trading. And rarely is the law a detailed blueprint: rather, it sets limits to what people can do, and leaves a good deal of leeway within them. And as the example of Sunday trading suggests, there are also places where there is no consensus on what the law ought to be and where it is widely ignored. Where the law is out of touch with contemporary reality, people usually find ways round it.

We also need to be a little sceptical in evaluating the effectiveness of the state in its more specific areas of activity. The state may appear to have policies for everything, but that does not mean that those policies are always successful, or that they are the only factor in the situation. In the area of food and diet, for example, the policies of the Ministry of Agriculture, Food and Fisheries certainly count for less than those of Sainsbury's and Tesco. No policy or policy-maker intended the increase in single-parent families, but it happened anyway. Social policy often simply reacts to developments not of its making. And for consistent ineffectiveness and failure, it would be hard to match the record of governments in trying to manage the economy. Their policies have shown far more misses than hits, despite (or because of) the fact that they had plenty of expert advice from economists, and despite the fact that they controlled the main economic levers, such as interest rates.

The gap between what governments want and what they get can be seen in the biggest (and most expensive) policy area of all, the welfare state. The aims of its founders, after 1945, were nothing less than to liberate the people of Britain from ignorance, want, squalor, idleness and disease. Today even its most ardent champions would not claim that it has achieved those aims. While it has undoubtedly done much good, overall it has been something of a disappointment, falling well short of the high hopes expressed for it in the 1940s and 1950s. Although the nation's health has undoubtedly improved since the establishment of the National Health Service, the NHS can not take all the credit for this, nor has it succeeded in eliminating serious disparities in illness and mortality between classes and regions. In housing, tower blocks are universally acknowledged as a human disaster.

But perhaps the most striking example of the failure of government has been the steady rise in crime. Crime has gone on increasing throughout the post-war period, in periods both of high and of low unemployment, despite changes in policing, sentencing, and the party in office. Indeed, government policies have been blamed by critics of both left and right for contributing to the crime wave. Where the left argues that Thatcherite economic policies of the 1980s led to unemployment and crime, the right, meanwhile, has pointed an accusing finger at 'liberal' educational and social policies of the 1960s, which it claims have undermined respect for law and order. Both sides recognise that the effects of policy may be very different from those intended.

Society is not just a lump of clay to be given shape by the master hand of the policy-maker. Within it are interests and forces that have a life and will of their own and which, actively or passively, resist and deflect the might of the state, making its policies ineffective if not actually counterproductive. Social policy is only one influence among many on social conditions. If it is often the most publicly visible, it is only occasionally the most important. That does not stop reformers of all kinds from looking to the state to make the changes they seek. Compared with corporations and other institutions in British society, the state is more public, more accessible and easier to influence. But its frequent lack of success should be a lesson to us. The state is still the most direct and obvious way of trying to change society. But it is not the best way of understanding society.

An obsession with the state and with policy has one further bad effect. It leads to a preoccupation with causes and origins, to the neglect of results and outcomes. To turn again to the question of food and diet, what matters in the end is not the policies, whether of the government or of the supermarkets or of the food industry, but what food people actually eat and the role of food in their lives. And to understand these things we need to talk to the people themselves. The proof of the pudding is not after all in pudding policy, or in the pudding industry, but in the eating. In housing, similarly, what matters is not just the government's housing policy, or the role of building societies and local authorities, but how people actually use their houses and live in them. In the end we need to study outcomes: not just what policies do to people but what people do with policies.

A final lesson is the importance of history. Critics of British society have often despaired of its apparently invincible conservatism – its immobility and resistance to change. But what these chapters show is that it has been far from static. Since 1945 it has been through phases of austerity and prosperity, booms and slumps, of demographic booms and bulges. There have been big changes, on the whole beneficial, in the lives of women and of the working classes. Contrary to the theory of a fixed and immutable Britain, these changes have not been limited to the surface of society but have reached its deeper structures. And they are still taking place.

What this means is that present-day society cannot be fully understood in present-day terms. It needs to be seen in a deeper chronological perspective, one that goes back to the early post-war decades and indeed beyond. Sociology, in other words, is incomplete without history. The two disciplines have sometimes mistrusted each other as incompatible or opposed ways of understanding society. In fact, they are overlapping and complementary, each having something valuable to contribute to the other. Sociologists can enrich historians' appreciation of social structures and relationships, while historians can provide a longer-term perspective, an understanding of change over time and why change took place when it did. What they have in common is, above all, a respect for evidence and a commitment to disciplined empirical research: they know that the truth will never be revealed by theory alone. Sociologists and historians, working together, have produced this book; their co-operation is itself one of the keys to a better understanding of British society.

Chapter 1

Trends in post-war British social history

Edward Royle

INTRODUCTION

All ages are ages of transition and only rarely and coincidentally does history see decisive breaks at century ends or, in modern times at least, at the change of a monarch. Indeed, it would be strange if such breaks were evident in social history. The 'nineteenth century' or the 'twentieth century' are meaningless concepts, though they have some mythic power: we expect change and so to some extent we create it. In this chapter I shall argue that, in several important respects, the decisive break with what we think of as the nineteenth century, or the late-Victorian world, does not come with the death of Victoria a few days into the twentieth century, nor even with the First World War, but in the period after 1945. The major trend in this latter age of transition, has been an accelerating discontinuity with the past.[1]

Dating this watershed in modern British social history is not easy, for change occurred at different times and rates in different areas of society. One problem is that, because of the war, no national census was conducted in 1941, with the result that one of the social historian's standard sources of information is missing. Clearly there were many changes in society between 1931 and 1951: were these the products of the 1930s, or of the war, or of the immediate post-war period? The answer is, in different cases and to different degrees, all three. But if there were trends emerging in 1951 compared with 1931, these had become much more marked by 1961, which suggests that it is in the post-war period – and especially the 1950s – that the most significant developments occured to create our own period of rapid social change. As Britain recovered, not only from the Second World War but from the aftermath of the war, the deep-seated nature of these changes became fully apparent.

By coincidence there was a new reign beginning in 1952, hailed by contemporaries as 'the new Elizabethan age'. Things may not have turned out quite as those publicists of change intended to imply, but they were right to see how the cumulative effects of social change through successive periods of depression, war and austerity were now leading to a new era which those same pedlars of popular images were later to identify rather belatedly – and with a singular lack of originality – as 'the swinging sixties'.

What were these major trends? In the rest of this chapter I want briefly to introduce several of the cultural aspects of social change: the family, household structure, consumerism and its associated technologies, the position of women, class, race, religion and education. Finally I shall end with a few comments on what I see to be the political importance of studying contemporary social history.

FAMILY AND HOUSEHOLD STRUCTURE

Although demography is outside the scope of this chapter, a few pertinent statistics will help to provide a context for the argument that follows. After all, demographic change is, in part at least, itself a function of cultural change. The age of marriage began to fall after 1931, and by 1951 the number of married men and women aged under 24 was 84 per cent greater than in 1931 – an average annual increase of 4.2 per cent. The comparable annual figure for the 1950s was even higher – 4.7 per cent. Although this increase in early marriage saw some rise in the crude birth-rate, with the 1947 post-war peak in births coinciding with the demobilisation of fathers, these years nevertheless also saw the breaking of the link between the number of births and the number of women in the population of child-bearing age. Methods of contraception, increasingly in use from the 1870s, were becoming by the 1950s the principal regulator of population – a social fact which led to the quest for more efficient methods of contraception and the marketing of the birth-control pill in 1963 – one of the major technological revolutions in post-war British society.[2]

The link between marriage and childbirth also began to be broken. The proportion of registered illegitimate births in England and Wales rose only slightly, from 4.2 per cent to 4.9 per cent, between the beginning of the century and the early 1950s. But by the beginning of the 1960s it was 5.9 per cent and by the early 1980s it was 12.9 per cent. In the 1980s this proportion continued to increase at an accelerating rate and by 1991 had reached 31.7 per cent. The rates for abortion, divorce and remarriage also increased in these years, though with some levelling off in the 1980s: abortions rose from 11.9 per cent of conceptions in 1971, to 17.0 per cent in 1981, and 19.7 per cent in 1988; divorces rose from 0.6 per cent of all marriages in 1971, to 1.19 per cent in 1981 and 1.27 per cent in 1989; and remarriage rose from 20 per cent of all weddings in 1971, to 34 per cent in 1981, and 36 per cent in 1991.

Of course, to a large extent these figures reflect changes in the law, but the historian still has to ask why such marked changes in social behaviour occurred. The law is itself an expression of the attitudes and values of society: it is not simply a historical cause but also a historical consequence. What those attitudes might be can be gathered from the increasing numbers of births outside marriage which were registered in the names of both father and mother, rising from about one-third the number of registered illegitimate births in the 1950s to over three-quarters of the number of registered illegitimate births by 1991, around half of these joint registrations being by parents who shared the same address. Similarly, whereas in 1972 only 16 per cent of women who married had co-habited with their future husbands before marriage, this figure had more than doubled by 1980 and had exceeded 50 per cent by the end of the 1980s. In brief, a major cultural shift in the nature, function and expectations of the family has occurred in British society since the 1950s.

This has had many important consequences, not least for the formation of households. The older pattern, prolonged by depression, war and housing shortages, was for the relatively late formation of households – occurring even after marriage and thus acting as a brake on the birth rate. The more recent trend has been for households to be formed not simply at marriage, but before marriage. In the 1970s the number of households increased by 6.5 per cent while the population increased by under 1 per cent. In the 1980s a 10 per cent increase in households was produced by an estimated increase of only 1.4 per cent in the population. The number of households containing only one person has more than doubled in the past thirty years. A quarter of all households now contain only one person and a further third no more than two. This, of course, in part reflects the increasing proportion of old people in the population – another significant trend in the post-war years – but in part it reflects the determination of young people to form separate individual or co-habiting households on or shortly after achieving adulthood.

Cause and consequence are here, as in all social history, inextricably mixed. Changes in the family have both caused changes in household formation and been caused by the possibility of different patterns of household formation. This, in turn, has had important economic consequences for the nature of the housing market, population densities, and the growth and spread of towns and suburbs. Above all, changes in the pattern of household formation have been of enormous significance for the extent and nature of consumer spending. The latter has, in turn, been underpinned by rising real incomes for the bulk of the population and, in the critical 1950s and 1960s when modern expectations became fixed, by full employment.

THE CONSUMER REVOLUTION AND TECHNOLOGICAL CHANGE

The consumption patterns of modern society have been radically different from those of pre-war society. Assisted by such legislation as the Holidays with Pay Act of 1938, people have been able to extend and diversify their leisure-time activities beyond the hopes of all but a few in pre-war society. It was Sir Billy Butlin, just before the war, who perceived the potential of the new mass holiday market which he exploited with great success in the post-war years. By the early 1950s, some 25 million people in Britain were spending a few days away from home on holiday each year. With growing affluence this pattern then changed again. In 1951 about 2 million people took their holidays abroad; by the early 1970s this had reached 7 million; and it now stands at three times that figure. Whereas in 1971 a third of people living in Britain had been on holiday abroad, by the late 1980s less than a third had not done so.

This aspect of the consumer revolution has been made possible by technological change. Travel by air on any significant scale is a post-war phenomenon. Heathrow Airport, the busiest in the world, was not opened until 1946. The first jet-propelled passenger air service across the Atlantic dates only from 1958. Technology also affected transport services on land. When the railways were nationalised in 1948 their track mileage was scarcely below its nineteenth-century peak. Now it is half that level; and railways – those bringers of civilisation to the nineteenth-century country-side – have disappeared from many parts, especially rural Wales, Scotland and eastern England. A cul-de-sac of modern bungalows on the site of the demolished railway station in one small Lincolnshire town is charmingly named, 'Beeching Close', after the chairman of the report that led to wholesale closures in the 1960s. Such closures were occasioned by, but also gave rise to, an increasing use of road transport and, in particular, of private motor cars. Whereas before the war there had been only 2 million private motor cars, there were 9 million by the mid-1960s and there are now more than twice that number. Approaching two-thirds of households in Britain own at least one motor car, with revolutionary consequences for the individual's freedom to choose where to live in relation to work and how to spend leisure time.

Technology has had an enormous impact on consumption, leisure and culture. By the beginning of the Second World War two-thirds of house-holds had an electricity supply; now almost all do. Moreover, almost all households now have a wide range of (largely female) labour-saving devices to plug into the system. In 1950, only 4.7 per cent of consumer expenditure went on furniture, electrical and other consumer goods and motor cars. This figure is now almost 12.0 per cent. Four out of every five homes in the late 1980s had a washing machine and almost all a refrig-erator and at least one television set. The ramifications of this are numer-ous. With domestic fridges and freezers has come a transformation in the marketing and range of foodstuffs. Frozen foods have brought convenience cooking and an end to seasonality in diet, completing by extension that earlier revolution which came with the development of canned foodstuffs in the later nineteenth century.

Television has, perhaps, brought the greatest revolution of all. Despite a slight fall in viewing hours in the later 1980s, the average person over the age of 4 watches twenty-five hours of television a week – two-thirds as much time as that spent weekly (including overtime) in paid employment. In the first full year after television licences were issued in 1946, there were just 15,000 of them. By the mid-1950s there were 4.5 million; today the figure is five times as many. With remarkable faith in an electronic miracle that most do not begin to understand, almost the entire nation can be entertained, informed and brought to witness events as they happen on the other side of the world and beyond. This has given to just a few people tremendous power to shape our politics and our culture. It is no coincidence that, in political revolutions across the modern world, the first target of the insurrectionaries is the television station.

Since 1955 advertising has been permitted on television and this has had an important impact on consumer culture. Consumerism is itself not a new or even a recent phenomenon; but the power of actors to enter homes electronically and sell products from cornflakes to politicians, using all the illusions of controlled realism, is new beyond the wildest dreams of the chapman, pedlar or brush-salesman of old. Furthermore, the money generated by television has had an important effect on other forms of leisure. Fees paid for showing sporting events, for example, have transformed the fortunes of – and in some cases helped to preserve – professional sport and sportspersons of almost every description. Another consequence of television has been the targeting of programmes and products towards the younger generation. The consumer society survives economically by creating new and ever-expanding markets for its goods. In 1961 there were 22 per cent more teenagers in the population than in 1951. The 1960s were created for them by the promoters of the consumer society – special clothes, music, literature, all prone to fashion and obsolescence. In more recent times, with the decline in this age group in the population, attention has been extended on the one hand to the pre-teen group and, on the other, to the elderly retired market of 'senior citizens'.

GENDER, CLASS AND RACE

Most of the changes so far described, from the birth-control pill to washing machines, have had an even greater impact on the female half of society than on the male. Women's liberation as a cultural and political movement should be understood as part of a much wider change which has made possible and realistic the demand for alterations in attitudes and the law with respect to women. The form which the sexual division of labour assumed in the nineteenth century may have been dictated by male control of the decision-making processes, but the fact of some division of labour was rationally based in the struggle of most of the population – male and female – for survival. That struggle has today ceased to dominate the lives of the great majority of the population and with it has gone much of the basis for traditional divisions of labour. One consequence of the opportunity for liberating women from the home and childrearing has been a change in the structure of employment. In 1951 the female participation rate in the labour force was around one-third. It had not much changed in the preceding half-century but in the 1950s it began to climb, reaching 40 per cent in the early 1960s and over 50 per cent by the later 1980s – second only to Denmark in the European Union. The participation of women in the labour market has been particularly marked, as one might expect, in white-collar employment and in the service industries – expanding areas at a time when the demand for unskilled manual (and therefore male) labour has been in decline. At the same time, however, it is true to say that much female labour is still concentrated in part-time and low-paid employment. Of the 13 million men in employment in 1993, almost all were in full-time jobs but of the 11 million women, nearly half had only part-time employment. Moreover, the gap between male and female wages has not changed for the past two decades. In this respect the employment position of women is changing only slowly.

Broad social changes, especially in consumption patterns and rising disposable family incomes, led many commentators in the 1960s to start talking and writing about the demise of class in Britain. With abundant evidence of the rise of the affluent worker, able to buy his own house on a private housing estate and increasingly willing to vote Conservative, the thesis had some attractions. Certainly, Conservative policy in the 1980s was to extend the numbers of such affluent, property-owning workers, and the Labour Party, after three successive electoral disasters in 1979, 1983 and 1987, likewise felt driven to change its policies to court the votes of such people. However, what the sociologists still debate is whether the embourgeoisement of the affluent worker is more myth than reality. A major survey, by John Goldthorpe and others in the 1960s, certainly challenged the view at the height of its popularity. Since then the radical departure of the Conservative Party under Mrs Thatcher's leadership from traditional liberal conservatism somewhat confused the issue in the 1980s; and the return of economic recession at the end of the decade produced some evidence to suggest that Britain has not by the early 1990s progressed very far down the road to a classless society (Goldthorpe et al. 1969).[3] Indeed, the earnings gap between the highest and lowest paid has increased; and the distribution of disposable income has fallen for the poorest fifth of the population from 10 per cent to 6 per cent since 1979, whereas it has risen for the richest from 35 per cent to 43 per cent.

One major social division which certainly has increased in post-war British society is the racial one. Cultural and racial diversity is not new, as the presence of large numbers of Irish and Jewish immigrants in the nineteenth century confirms. Not even the presence of black people is new, for there have been blacks in Britain since the eighteenth century and earlier. What is new is that highly visible presence of non-white people which has become such a feature of post-war society, and the wide measure of cultural diversity which they have brought with them. The Irish, with their pigs, potatoes and popery, were a culture shock to nineteenth-century Protestant Englishmen; but the languages and religions of the East are even stranger to the British man and woman of the later twentieth century. Black immigration did not begin on a large scale until the late 1940s, when West Indian and then Indian workers were recruited by British employers at a time of acute labour shortages as the post-war economy began to revive. By the late 1950s, for the first time, immigration to Britain was exceeding emigration and between 1962 and 1971 governments of both parties began to impose restrictions. By the late 1980s the combined black community had reached about 4.8 per cent of the total population. However, nearly half of these were not immigrants but British born; conversely, half of those born outside the United Kingdom were in fact white – mainly Irish, who still constituted the largest immigrant group.

RELIGION

One of the most visible forms which this cultural diversity has taken is religious. Indeed, one of the most significant trends in post-war society concerns the transformation in the social position of religion. Sociologists have long debated whether 'secularisation' exists and, if so, whether it has taken place; others prefer to use the term 'de-Christianisation', which is historically speaking the more defensible concept (Gilbert 1980).[4] Although there has been a steady decline of religious observance since at least the latter decades of the nineteenth century, and although there have been temporary revivals such as occurred in the late 1940s and early 1950s, the prolonged and steep decline in religious practices that has taken place in most Christian churches since the late 1950s must stand not only as one of the most significant social trends of our time, but also as one of the greatest cultural breaks with the past. In the quarter century between the start of the 1960s and the mid-1980s, the number of baptisms in the Church of England fell by nearly half – far more than the falling number of births alone would suggest – and the number of confirmations fell by over half. The Church of Scotland and the Methodists fared even worse; the Roman Catholics did only a little better. Between 1970 and 1990 the combined membership of the Christian churches fell from 8.5 million to 6.7 million – 18 per cent of the adult population – and the age structure and sluggish recruitment patterns of the churches suggest this will continue to be the trend for the foreseeable future. Church attendance is even less – 14 per cent of the population are reckoned to be 'active' members of the Christian churches and possibly as few as 10 per cent go to church at least once a month. Though initially the major immigrant religion, Catholicism, did rather better than Protestantism, it too has experienced a steep decline in the past fifteen years, with a 23 per cent drop in adult membership. By contrast the newer immigrant religions have grown strongly. Between 1975 and 1992 the number of Muslims more than doubled to over half a million – compared with around 460,000 Methodists, the largest denomination of Protestant Nonconformists. For every hundred adult members of the Christian churches in the United Kingdom in 1992, there are almost eight followers of Islam and another nine followers of other non-Christian religions.

EDUCATION

Finally, any survey of social trends since the Second World War, should mention education. As with class, with which education in Britain has been inextricably linked for two hundred years and more, social change here has been more sluggish than many social engineers might have wished. Indeed, politicians have manipulated education in an attempt to secure social goals beyond those of pure learning – which, as a consequence, some would argue, has suffered – and they have largely failed. Nevertheless, this should not conceal the magnitude of the changes that have occurred over the past four decades. Secondary education for all was proclaimed as the aim in England and Wales only in 1944 and was only becoming a reality throughout the country in the early 1950s. Now all children receive a secondary schooling up to the age of 16 and, despite a participation ratio of only 40 per cent in full-time education and training between 16 and 18 – less than half that of Germany, Belgium, France or the United States – post-compulsory education in Britain has undergone a revolution since the 1950s.

The foundations for wider participation in higher education were laid in the later 1950s and resulted in a major expansion in institutions and student numbers in the 1960s and 1970s. Between the late 1960s and late 1980s the percentage of 18–19 year-olds entering higher education more than doubled, from around 6 per cent to about 14 per cent. Since then a further period of rapid expansion has increased the number of home full-time students in higher education from 579,000 in 1988–9 to 842,000 in 1991–2. At the same time, the proportion of females entering higher education has increased (from a lower base) more rapidly than the proportion of males. Between 1970 and 1991, the number of men in full-time higher education increased by 61 per cent and the number of women by 120 per cent, the growth being particularly marked after 1985. But though the distinction between the sexes has almost disappeared in higher education, there is still a marked difference in participation among the various social classes. Sluggish recruitment from the lower social classes and amongst minority ethnic groups suggests that the goal of equality of opportunity in education has not yet in practice even come close to realisation. In this respect, as with much welfare legislation, the first section of society to benefit from an expansion of services has been the middle class and a major social and cultural shift is yet to be achieved among the population at large.

CONCLUSION

It is always difficult for the chronicler of recent historical events to gain a proper perspective. Nevertheless, this does not mean that the contemporary world should not be a proper province for historical investigation, for the historian can bring a critical training to bear: a belief that, even in a chapter full of percentages, there are in the end no facts, only opinions; that this evidence cannot speak for itself, or if it is allowed to it will only mislead; and that much of what is often passed off as scientific truth must be suspect. This is particularly so when history is referred to by politicians whose versions of the past must be understood quite legitimately as political propaganda and not as history at all.

This has especially been apparent in recent party political controversy about the consequences of those rapid social changes that have taken place since the Second World War, not least in that political reflection of the needs and thereby the shape of society, the welfare state. There is not space here to enter the whole debate about the nature, development and future of the welfare state, the direction of social trends and their moral implications, or the future of social policy. But the historian is not surprised to find that, over the past decade, politicians have (or should have) been brought to question the policies and dogmas of 40–45 years ago in the light of the massive transformation of society which has taken place since then. To understand this debate about the future of social policy, and to assess the various programmes being put forward by the different political factions as they respond to – or, in some cases, react against – this unprecedented period of rapid social change, one needs some sense of historical development and perspective. This is what the study of contemporary social history seeks to provide.

NOTES

1 The ideas in this chapter have been worked out over a longer timespan up to the mid-1980s in my *Modern Britain: a Social History 1750–1985*, Sevenoaks, Edward Arnold, 1987.

2 The facts and figures in this and subsequent paragraphs have been taken or deduced from those invaluable compilations, *Annual Abstract of Statistics* and *Social Trends*, published by HMSO. Estimates have been made where the figures presented do not take precisely the same form or address the same questions in the different annual editions of these works.

3 John H. Goldthorpe, David Lockwood, Frank Bechhofer and Jennifer Platt, *The Affluent Worker*, 3 volumes, Cambridge, Cambridge University Press, 1969. See also J. H. Goldthorpe, *Social Mobility and Class Structure in Modern Britain*, Oxford, Clarendon Press, 1980.

4 A. D. Gilbert, *The Making of Post-Christian Britain: a History of the Secularization of Modern Society*, Harlow, Longman, 1980. The most detailed recent figures for Christian participation in England are given in *' Christian' England: What the 1989 English Church Reveals*, London, MARC Europe, 1991. For a longer-term perspective, see R. Currie, A. Gilbert and L. Horsley (eds), *Churches and Church-goers: Patterns of Church Growth in the British Isles since 1700*, Oxford, Clarendon Press, 1977.

REFERENCES

Gilbert, A. D. (1980) *The Making of Post-Christian Britain: a History of the Secularisation of Modern Society*, Harlow: Longman.

Goldthorpe, J. H., Lockwood D., Bechhofer F. and Platt J. (1969) *The Affluent Worker*, 3 vols, Cambridge: Cambridge University Press.

Chapter 2

Elements of demographic change in Britain since 1945

Richard M. Smith

One theory, above all others, has provided a framework for much of the discussion of the striking demographic changes that have occurred in the last century. This is the so-called 'Demographic Transition Theory' and there has been considerable debate concerning whether post-war British society, indeed Western society as a whole, continues to be interpretable within terms of that theory's key premises (Davis *et al*. 1987). In its essentials, Demographic Transition Theory is a type of dogma of the 'irreversible sequential change' variety. It is an evolutionary schema setting out the demographic stages through which societies are bound to move as a consequence of industrialisation and urbanisation (Woods 1982: 158–84). The initial condition in which high mortality and high fertility coexisted is stage I, and some have suggested in the English case that this ended *c*. 1750. This was followed by a phase of falling mortality in association with high fertility, creating rapid demographic growth (Stage II) until *c*. 1870; and after this there was a compensatory fall in fertility in Stage III which culminated when stationary demographic conditions were established in which very low mortality and fertility coincided simultaneously, especially after *c*. 1966. Much empirical research has shown that this model provides a problematic basis for our understanding of British demographic history in the period prior to 1900. Stage I in England cannot accurately be described as one in which high fertility and mortality coexisted in a compensatory fashion; nor can the great surge of population growth after 1750 be accurately explained by a fall in mortality (Wrigley and Schofield 1981). Nineteenth-century changes do not seem readily depicted as fertility falls occurring in the wake of prior mortality declines (Woods 1992). These matters cannot be the subject of discussion in this chapter as our purpose is to assess whether the last forty or forty-five years can be seen as the culmination of this stadial model. Do they represent the triumphant establishment of Stage III or should this Whiggish device be jettisoned and replaced by an attempt to conceptualise a post-transitional demographic regime of low birth rates (of the kind associated with below replacement rate fertility), low mortality, population ageing, stationary or negative demographic growth? The figures relating to total population numbers in the United Kingdom seem, at least superficially, to be consistent with such a view. Contrary to the predictions of Transition Theory, population grew quite rapidly in the decades immediately following the Second World War. The United Kingdom contained 50.3 million people in 1951 (compared with 46 million in 1931) and growth thereafter took that figure to almost 56 million in 1971. The last two decades, however, have witnessed much slower demographic expansion and the population estimated for 1991 is only c. 57.3 million, of whom almost 21 per cent are over 60 years (Laslett 1989: 69).

The emphasis in this discussion on the reasons for the divergence of demographic trends between the two halves of the post-war era will be on fertility and family formation, not because it is supposed that mortality has remained unchanged but because movements in fertility rates have been more influential than mortality shifts in driving the national demographic motor. Furthermore, the interpretation of fertility trends requires a linked discussion of a number of key areas of social change in post-war Britain, centring upon social and sexual attitudes, the family and the status of women. To generalise, perhaps somewhat crudely, it could be suggested that mortality has assumed a rather steady but slow course in its decline through the post-war decades. Indeed, after the dramatic falls in the first third of the twentieth century among the very youngest age groups in particular, the potential for major and rapidly expedited changes in mortality rates thereafter was somewhat limited.

None the less, certain features of mortality change after the Second World War are worthy of comment. Two age groups, in particular, have benefited disproportionately from improvements in their survivorship. Infants experienced a fall of nearly 75 per cent in their mortality rates from 1940 to 1980. The most rapid decline (a fall of almost 40 per cent from 50 to 29.9 per 1,000) occurred from 1940 to 1950 and the remaining decline slowed to reach a point now where the potential for further reductions is severely limited (Winter 1986: 153–7). Currently the infant mortality rate is about 9.0 per 1,000, with perinatal deaths (still births and deaths within the first week of life) associated with prematurity or low birth weights and congenital malformations predominant (*Social Trends* 1991: 115). Of the deaths occurring after the first week of life, almost 40 per cent are now categorised as cot deaths of 'sudden death syndrome'. Notwithstanding the significant improvements in infant life chances, Britain's place in the international league table of infant mortality has deteriorated in the post-war decades (Coleman 1988: 417).

Since 1960, the crude death rate relating to the total population has shown little change. For instance, the rate for males was 12.4 per 1,000 in 1961–5 and 11.5 in 1989; for females it rose very slightly from 11.4 to 11.5 per 1,000 (*Social Trends* 1991: 29). However, these rates are misleading indicators of mortality being so susceptible to influence from the very considerable changes in the age structure of the population over this period. While the elderly have increased their share of the total population they, along with infants, have experienced the most striking falls in their mortality. For instance, the mortality rate for females aged 75–84 fell by 30 per cent and for males of that age by 17 per cent in the twenty-year period between 1961–6 to 1981–5. These declines compare with falls of 22 and 14 per cent for females and males respectively in the same age groups over the immediately previous, and far longer, period from 1901–5 to 1961–5. The post-war period has also witnessed a continuation and intensification of the growing advantage experienced by elderly females when their life chances are compared with those of males. For instance, in 1981–5 the ratio of male to female mortality rates for persons aged 65–74 and 75–84 were 1.87 and 1.60 compared with values of 1.36 and 1.30 for the period 1936–40 (Victor 1991: 44–6).

Following the publication of the 1971 decennial estimate of mortality by social class, it was evident that the reported class differences were greater than previously recorded (OPCS 1978). This was highlighted by the report of the DHSS (1980) working party on inequalities in health which pointed to the fact that differences in standardised mortality ratios (SMRs) had increased steadily from the 1931 *Supplement* (Registrar General 1938). It was suggested by one commentary on these data that in Britain in the post-war period, 'all groups have profited from mortality declines but higher status groups have profited more than most' (Preston *et al.* 1981). These apparent trends, whose reality it should be noted has not been accepted in all quarters (e.g. Stern 1983; Illsley 1986), should be considered against the background of the growing primacy of cancer (especially lung cancer) and ischaemic heart disease as causes of death. Such developments might be thought consistent with the shift in the composition of causes of death, away from a pattern in which infectious diseases predominated to one where causes most usually associated with life-long health behaviour (which can readily be shown to vary by class) loomed large (Goldblatt 1990; Marmot and McDowall 1986).

Notwithstanding these noteworthy developments in mortality at both ends of the age-range and the disturbing growth in and intransigence of social and geographical differentials in mortality (Townsend *et al.* 1988a; 1988b), students of post-war demographic change have consistently focused their attention upon fertility shifts in their attempts both to understand and to influence the nation's demographic comportment.[1] The focus of fertility change has identified a striking watershed in 1964 – the year in which the Total Period Fertility Rate, having risen throughout the previous fifteen years, peaked at 2.94 (Brass 1989: 24). After 1964 the Total Fertility Rate fell to 1.66 in 1977 and has since crept up to marginally more than 1.8, where it currently loiters with no apparent intention (Brass 1989: 24;

Social Trends 1991: 28). A value of 2.1 for Total Fertility means that a population is replacing itself in so far as each woman would be replaced on average by one daughter in the next generation. The need for marginally more than two children per woman to provide one succeeding daughter is to be accounted for by the sex ratio at birth (fewer female than male babies) and the need to allow for those females who die before reaching the age at which their mothers gave birth. Total Fertility Rates of 1.8, such as characterised the United Kingdom in much of the late 1970s and 1980s, are below replacement. None the less, it should be noted that many parts of continental Europe experienced fertility falls in the late 1970s and 1980s below those encountered in the United Kingdom. For instance, Denmark and the Federal Republic of Germany possessed Total Fertility Rates below 1.4 which, if sustained, would lead to noteworthy demographic shrinkage (Brass 1989; van de Kaa 1987). Only the Republic of Ireland exhibited Total Fertility Rates which at 2.4–2.5 in the early 1980s were significantly above replacement level. What other noteworthy features concerning fertility-related behaviour distinguish this period?

Marriage, for females in particular, had already shown signs of taking place earlier, and fewer women were going through life as spinsters in the late 1930s. The post-war years saw even greater resort to marriage, so that rates reached a peak in 1972 (Coleman 1988: 69–75; Elliott 1991: 85–9). Some very obvious demographic factors were working to enable this change. The shift in the sex ratio, helped by improving male life expectancy and a substantial reduction in young adult emigration, significantly raised the marriage chances of young women. However, the post-war decades experienced a veritable 'marriage boom' (Hajnal 1965). Indeed, the popularity of marriage increased for more than thirty years and the 1972 peak in marital incidence occurred some years after fertility began to decline. In fact, the 60 per cent of women aged 20–24 registered as currently married in the 1971 census was probably a historic record. A similar 'rush into marriage' can be detected in the fact that in 1972 one in three spinsters marrying was a teenager (Lewis 1992: 44). Nothing like it can be found in the evidence that has been analysed for the period since the early sixteenth century and probably since sources become available for the statistical study of marriage from the mid-thirteenth century (Wrigley and Schofield 1981; Smith 1979). Before the Second World War, women in the age-group 20–24 would have shown an incidence of marriage closer to 30 per cent. Indeed, prior to 1939 in excess of 15 per cent of women would have reached their 50th birthday never having married. With the marriage rates of the early 1970s, fewer than 5 per cent of women would have remained spinsters (Coleman 1988: 71). Since the early 1970s, formalised marriage lost its popularity for persons in their twenties to a striking degree (Brown and Kiernan 1981; Kiernan 1989).

To a marked extent more recently, resort to marriage at older ages reflects a rise in cohabitation without legal marriage. In the period 1979–88 the percentage of British single (never-married) women aged 18–49 living with a man more than doubled. However, it would seem that because of these trends as much as 50 per cent of the fall in the percentage of those married between 1973 and 1980 may be due to increased cohabitation. In 1987, just over half of women marrying for the first time had lived with their spouse before marriage (Kiernan and Eldridge 1987).

How have these trends in marriage and cohabitation affected the percentage of births occurring within legally constituted marriages? Although the percentage of children born outside marriage rose in the Second World War, that proportion fell immediately thereafter and in the 1950s it was around 5 per cent – only marginally higher than it had been in 1939 (Coleman 1988: 63). The rate began to rise in the 1960s and, apart from a short-lived stability in the late 1960s or early 1970s, has risen especially steeply over the last two decades. By 1989, 28.7 per cent of all births occurred outside marriage (*Social Trends* 1991: 29). The shift towards later marriage after the early 1970s and the partial substitution of cohabitation for early marriage are responsible for part of this increase. At the same time there has been a marked increase in the proportion of births outside marriage registered by both parents, rising from 45 per cent of births in 1971 to 70 per cent in 1988. What is more, it is known that in 71 per cent of these joint registrations in 1988, the mother and father gave the same address, suggesting that births outside of marriage were not so closely associated with lone motherhood as they were in the 1950s and 1960s. Indeed, the most important characteristic of lone motherhood or the one-parent family is its association with marital dissolution. By 1988, about three-quarters of mothers heading one-parent families were previously married. In addition, as mortality declines, the number of widows with dependent children has been falling. The proportion of all families with dependent children that are lone-parent families increased from 8 per cent in 1971 to 14 per cent in 1987, largely reflecting the rise in divorce and the increasing incidence of births outside marriage. Of all lone mothers, those who were divorced increased from 24 per cent in 1971 to 44 per cent in 1987, and those who were single rose from 16 to 29 per cent. The lone mothers who were widowed fell from 31 to 8 per cent over the same period (*Social Trends* 1990: 38). .

The Divorce Reform Act (1969) made irretrievable marital breakdown of marriage the sole criterion of divorce. These easier grounds for divorce came into effect in 1971, and it appears that the act accelerated an upward trend in divorce that was already apparent. Students of post-war divorce attach special attention to the 1950s. In fact, the rate of divorce fell after the Second World War. Only 7 per cent of marriages initiated in 1951 had been broken by divorce after twenty years (Coleman 1988: 75). Furthermore, the low divorce rate coupled with the much-reduced chance of mortality disrupting a marriage combined to produced a phase of marital stability without known historical precedent (Anderson 1990: 29–30). Since then divorces have risen markedly. However, there is reason to believe that the divorce rate stabilised, or at least increased more slowly, in the 1980s than in the 1970s. None the less, at present divorce rates, about 37 per cent of marriages are expected to end in divorce. The growth in divorce has had implications for the proportion of all marriages that were remarriages. Between 1950 and 1987, remarriages as a percentage of all new marriages rose from 20 to 35 per cent – a rise that was almost entirely due to the increase in divorced persons marrying (Lewis 1992: 44). However, similar to first marriage rates, remarriage rates have fallen since 1972 (Coleman 1988: 94–6). Some of this fall reflects the effect of an inevitable decline in crude remarriage rates from the larger flows into the population of divorced persons which followed from the rising divorce rates. But, consistent with the falling rate of remarriage, is the rise in the average length of time between divorce and remarriage for the remarriers. The rising divorce rate and declining remarriage rate have altogether worked to increase the number of one-parent families, although the effect has been modified somewhat by an increasing resort to cohabitation among previously married mothers.

Some observers have doubted whether it is strictly accurate to suggest that this high proportion of families with children headed by a lone parent is a 'new' social phenomenon. Anderson (1983) has suggested that marital breakdown rates in the nineteenth century were probably not very different from those found today, the difference being that divorce rather than death is now the main cause of lone parenthood. Given the early marriage age, relatively high mortality and uncontrolled marital fertility characteristic of the late eighteenth and early nineteenth centuries, 18–20 per cent of households may then have been headed by lone parents (Snell and Millar 1987). None the less, Millar (1987) suggests that the rising divorce rate and the associated growth of lone mothers (two-thirds of whom in the late 1980s were divorced) certainly created new problems for the post-war welfare state.

It would be hard to deny that the growth in one-parent families is the most significant change in family structure that has followed from or been part of the demographic changes in the last two decades. However, a correlated development has been a simultaneous decline in the importance of the family grouping made up of married couple and children. In 1988, only 26 per cent of British households contained this configuration. Given the postponement of childbearing and the ageing of the population that has also occurred, there were more households in 1988 that contained a couple without children than there were households containing them. Single-person households in 1988 made up another 26 per cent (exactly the same percentage as families with children) (*Social Trends* 1990: 36). Later marriage, increased divorce, ageing of the population, and an increased propensity of the unmarried to live alone had caused there to be a fourfold increase in this particular household category since the 1930s.

Demographic changes since 1945, and particularly since 1939, have been highly noteworthy. Demographers differ in their attempts to explain these shifts depending on whether their intellectual and institutional links are closer to sociologists and social historians or to economists or economic historians. Those who fraternise with sociologists (although in the minority) are more inclined to focus on ideational change in their search for explanations of change. One approach that has caught the attention of social demographers places great emphasis on ideational changes that are regarded as having eighteenth-century origins (van de Kaa 1987). This is a viewpoint associated in particular with a certain group of continental European demographers, exemplified by Professor Ron Lesthaeghe (1983; Lesthaeghe and Surkyn 1988) who see the fertility fall of the late nineteenth century and the first third of the twentieth century as a product of a growing secular individualism, legitimating the pursuit of personal goals with only limited reference to a set of cohesive and overarching religious or philosophical customs. Under such conditions, parental responsibilities were redefined and a growth in concern with child quality rather than quantity became more prominent (Ariès 1980). These ideational shifts, which were in the process of creating a steady decline in family sizes from the last third or quarter of the nineteenth century, were disturbed first by the disruptions of the First World War and then by the interwar depression. Subsequent to the Second World War, the long-run secular trend was again shaken from its course in a phase during which governments embarked on economic programmes centring on full employment and the development of the welfare state.

Such phases can be readily interpreted respectively as conducive first to an exaggeration of the fertility fall, such as happened in the 1920s and 1930s, and then to an equally exaggerated fertility recovery of the type that characterised the 1950s and early 1960s. Lesthaeghe's position has much in common with that of the historian Jay Winter (1986), who sees the fertility movements between 1940 and 1964 as constituting part of a broad cultural reaction to what he terms 'the revival of family life' in the wake of the disturbances caused by the Second World War. After this generation of mothers, who had been socialised through these troubled years of the 1930s and 1940s, had completed their childbearing, the earlier decline of fertility was resumed by subsequent cohorts and given a further boost by the arrival of especially effective contraception and liberalised abortion laws.

None the less, distinguished demographers have argued with considerable plausibility that the availability of superior contraception from the late 1960s affected fertility without a necessary alteration in the value system. Serious consideration has to be given to the view that the reduction of unwanted fertility was probably a major factor in the decline in marital fertility between the 1960s and the 1980s. Samuel Preston (1987), for instance, has remarked that monogamous marriage provided an opportunity for licit sexual activity; the social logic of this arrangement would be undermined when contraceptive techniques became largely coitus-independent. Consequently the risks attaching to pregnancy were, so this argument suggests, no greater in stable than in unstable unions. The birth-control pill enables a world to crystallise in which sex is no longer confined to marriage and, as a consequence, rates of entry into marriage fall, rates of exit rise, cohabitation surges. What is more, the reduced commitment of partners to each other makes having children an increasingly risky affair, especially for women.

As a consequence of these changes, Preston (1987: 186) suggests that marriage took place later and women accumulated more work experience and earning potential prior to marrying. This increased earnings potential enhanced the cost of children in terms of forgone earnings, serving still further to lower fertility (Joshi 1987). In addition, higher earnings potential enabled women more easily to divorce when marital strains arose. Another technological development is, as John Ermisch (1990: 8–9) notes in a broader sense, the changing composition of employment as the service industries and occupations expand causing a growth in the types of jobs that women have generally taken, leading to a rise in their real wage and hence encouraging women to spend more time in employment.

John Ermisch (1990: 9) also seems convinced that British women from large families are less likely to begin childbearing in their twenties and that they also end up producing smaller families. This is a view conventionally associated with the American economic demographer and economic historian Richard Easterlin (1980) to account for the high fertility and early marriage of those small birth cohorts from the 1920s and 1930s who created the baby boom of the 1950s and early 1960s. Such an approach would also be consistent with low fertility displayed by women in the larger birth cohorts of the 1950s and early 1960s when they reached their twenties in the 1970s and 1980s. This has reflected the increased potential for consumption and leisure pursuits, and a concomitant decline in activities requiring a great deal of time, such as childbearing and spouse-attending. As Preston (1987: 184) perceptively notes, the last twenty or thirty years have seen considerable growth in personal interactions and joint consumption of goods and services among people sharing similar tastes, who do not have to be one's children or parents or even one's spouse.

Arguments of the kind we have just considered make it easier to see how child-rearing has become an increasingly risky activity relative to many other elements of the adult experience. They do not, however, perhaps with the exception of the theory associated with the impact of cohort size, readily translate into highly convincing explanations of the rising fertility trends of the period between 1945 and 1970. As Lesthaeghe and Surkyn (1988: 36) interestingly observe, rising levels of female labour force participation, much favoured in certain quarters as a framework for under-standing fertility fall, occurred in the period from 1945 to 1965 against a trend of rising marital fertility. In fact, it has been acknowledged that increases in female employment opportunities can have different fertility effects: it can induce earlier marriage and childbearing followed by a return to the labour force – a pattern that would seem to have characterised the 1950s and the 1960s; it can also induce a 'work now' effect with post-ponement of family building which seems to be much more characteristic of the 1970s and 1980s (Ni Brholchain 1983). Lesthaeghe and Surkyn (1988: 36) wonder whether the availability of the pill may have stimulated the change in timing of work and childbearing, but they are ultimately inclined to give it a rather limited place in their account. They prefer an ideational argument for early childbearing and part-time work in the labour force after children have reached secondary school age. They believe that this derives from what they see as an 'embourgeoisement' of British lower-middle- and working-class life; a cultural model which accentuated the qualitative aspects of domestic life, and a division of labour between the sexes which they regard as a *sine qua non*. Perhaps it is here that Winter and Lesthaeghe come close together in so far as they might both see this cultural model or ideal inhibited in its development by the Second World War, but strongly supported thereafter by the social security schemes and the considerable redistribution of income in Britain in the immediate post-war period. These changes made this behaviour affordable to many, notwithstanding the postponement of wives' earnings and the probable accrual of benefits disproportionately to husbands in the so-called new 'companionate marriages' that sociologists believe they found in the 1950s and 1960s (Finch and Summerfield 1991).

The empirical basis of this view has been strengthened by the statistical exercises undertaken by Michael Anderson (1983; 1985; 1990) who has calibrated a homogenisation of family and life-cycle experiences which reached its apogee in the 1950s and 1960s and displayed a social ubiquity that had not been apparent earlier in the twentieth century. He also tentatively suggests that these features were beginning to be lost again in the late 1970s and 1980s. However, to emphasise the specificity of condi-tions immediately following the Second World War would be to disregard the fact that the roots of this homogenisation undoubtedly predate 1945. For instance, it can be argued that after the First World War there was a narrowing of class differentials in both mortality and fertility, age at marriage and mean household size. Furthermore, there came to be an increasing similarity across the population in the age at which major life-cycle transitions occurred. In the 1940s, 1950s and early 1960s mar-riage and childbearing were experienced by women within a narrow age band. The small family became the most frequently encountered family unit; retirement occurred to men increasingly at a specific age that involved all social classes. Indeed, society became increasingly age- rather than class-banded (Anderson 1990: 66–70).

Obviously much more work needs to be done on comparable data sets for the quarter-century after 1965 to see whether increasing heterogeneity of experience is really detectable or whether it was related to economic difficulties of that period. If such a growth in the variance of behavioural patterns proves to be detectable, Lesthaeghe would no doubt account for it as a consequence of the incessant march of individuals 'doing their own thing' in the absence of strong social sanctions reining them in. But such an all-embracing thesis rooted in Demographic Transition Theory and dependent upon ideational changes set in train by the European Enlightenment cannot readily account for many of the shifts of demographic behaviour between 1940 and 1965. However, it has to be acknowledged that there are few alternative theories as systematically comprehensive that derive from sociology and social history which can be said to act as effective competitors to Lesthaeghe's own position.

NOTES

1 It is perhaps significant that the series of seminars jointly sponsored by CEPR and the British Society for Population Studies and published under the title of *The Changing Population of Britain* (Joshi 1988), should have resulted in a book, excellent in all respects, in which mortality changes were largely disregarded (except in a brief discussion of the demographic attributes of ethnic groups).

REFERENCES

Anderson, M. (1983) 'What is new about the modern family; an historical perspective', in Office of Population Censuses and Surveys, *Occasional Paper* 31: 1–16.
—— (1985) 'The emergence of the modern life cycle in Britain', *Social History* 10: 69–88.
—— (1990) 'The social implications of demographic change', in F. M. L. Thompson (ed.) *The Cambridge Social History of Britain 1750–1950 vol. 2: People and Their Environment*, Cambridge: Cambridge University Press, pp. 1–70.
Ariès, P. (1979) *Centuries of Childhood*, Harmondsworth: Penguin.
Ariès, P. (1980) 'Two successive motivations for the declining birth rate in the West', *Population and Development Review* 6: 645–50.
Brass, W. (1989) 'Is Britain facing the twilight of parenthood?', in H. Joshi (ed.) *The Changing Population of Britain*, Oxford: Basil Blackwell, pp. 12–26.
Brown, A. and Kiernan, K. (1981) 'Cohabitation in Great Britain: Evidence from the General Household Survey', *Population Trends* 25: 4–10.
Coleman, D. (1988) 'Population', in A. H. Halsey (ed.) *British Social Trends Since*

1900: A Guide to the Changing Structure of Britain, Basingstoke and London: Macmillan, pp. 36–134.

Davis, K., Bernstam, M. S. and Ricardo-Campbell, R. (eds) (1987) *Below Replacement Fertility in Industrial Societies: Causes, Consequences, Policies*, Cambridge: Cambridge University Press.

Department of Health and Social Security (DHSS) (1980) *Inequality in Health* (The Black Report), London: HMSO.

Easterlin, R. A. (1980) *Birth and Fortune*, London: Grant-McIntyre.

Elliott, B. J. (1991) 'Demographic trends in domestic life, 1945–87', in D. Clark (ed.) *Marriage, Domestic Life and Social Change: Writings for Jacqueline Burgoyne (1944–88)*, London and New York: Routledge, pp. 85–110.

Ermisch, J. (1990) *Fewer Babies, Longer Lives: Policy Implications of Current Demographic Trends*, York: Joseph Rowntree Foundation.

Finch, J. and Summerfield, P. (1991) 'Social reconstruction and the emergence of companionate marriage', in D. Clark (ed.) *Marriage, Domestic Life and Social Change: Writings for Jacqueline Burgoyne (1944–88)*, London and New York: Routledge, pp. 7–32.

Goldblatt, P. (1990) 'Social class mortality differences', in C. G. N. Mascie-Taylor (ed.) *Biosocial Aspects of Social Class*, Oxford: Oxford University Press, pp. 24–58.

Hajnal, J. (1965) 'European marriage patterns in perspective', in D. V. Glass and D. E. C. Eversley (eds) *Population in History*, London: Edward Arnold, pp. 101–47.

Illsley, R. (1986) 'Occupational class, selection and the production of inequalities', *Quarterly Journal of Social Affairs* 2: 151–61.

Joshi, H. (1987) 'The cost of caring', in C. Glendinning and J. Millar (eds) *Women and Poverty in Britain*, Brighton: Harvester Press, pp. 112–36.

Kiernan, K. E. (1989) 'The family: formation and fission' in H. Joshi (ed.) *The Changing Population of Britain*, Oxford: Basil Blackwell, pp. 27–41.

Kiernan, K. E. and Eldridge, S. M. (1987) 'Inter and intra cohort variation in the timing of first marriage', *British Journal of Sociology* 38: 44–65.

Laslett, P. (1989) *A Fresh Map of Life: The Emergence of the Third Age*, London: Weidenfeld & Nicolson.

Lesthaeghe, R. (1983) 'A century of demographic change in Western Europe: An exploration of underlying dimensions', *Population and Development Review* 9: 411–36.

Lesthaeghe, R. and Surkyn, J. (1988) 'Cultural dynamics and economic theories of fertility change', *Population and Development Review* 14: 1–46.

Lewis, J. (1992) *Women in Britain Since 1945*, Oxford: Basil Blackwell.

Marmot, M. G. and McDowall, M. E. (1986) 'Mortality decline and widening social inequalities', *Lancet* ii: 274–6.

Millar, J. (1987) 'Lone mothers', in C. Glendinning and J. Millar (eds) *Women and Poverty in Britain*, Brighton: Harvester Press, pp. 159–77.

Ni Bhrolchain, M. (1983) *Birth Spacing and Women's Work: Some British Evidence*, CPS research paper no. 83–3, London: Centre for Population Studies, London School of Hygiene and Tropical Medicine.

—— (1987) 'Period parity progression ratios and birth intervals in England and Wales 1941–71', *Population Studies* 41: 103–26.

Office of Population Censuses and Surveys (OPCS) (1978) Occupational Mortality, *Decennial Supplement 1970–2*, London: HMSO.

Preston, S. (1987) 'Changing values and falling birth rates', in K. Davis, M. S. Bernstam and R. Ricardo-Campbell (eds) *Below-Replacement Fertility in*

Industrial Societies: Causes, Consequences, Policies, Cambridge: Cambridge University Press, pp. 176–95.

Preston, S. H., Haines, M. R. and Pamuk, E. R. (1981) *Effects of Industrialisation and Urbanisation on Mortality in Developed Countries*, Solicited Papers 2, Proceedings 19th International Conference Manilla, Liège: International Union for the Scientific Study of Population.

Registrar General (1938) *Decennial Supplement: England and Wales 1931* Part IIa, London: HMSO.

Smith, R. M. (1979) 'Some reflections on the evidence for the origins of the "European marriage pattern" in England', in C. Harris (ed.) *The Sociology of the Family*, Social Review Monograph 28: 74–112.

Snell, K. D. M. and Millar, J. (1987) 'Lone-parent families and the welfare state: past and present', *Continuity and Change* 2: 387–422.

Social Trends (1990) London: HMSO.

Social Trends (1991) London: HMSO.

Stern, J. (1983) 'Social mobility and the interpretation of social class differentials', *Journal of Social Policy* 12: 27–49.

Townsend, P., Davidson, N. and Whitehead, M. (1988a) *Inequalities in Health: The Black Report and the Health Divide*, Harmondsworth: Penguin.

Townsend, P., Phillimore, P. and Beattie, A. (1988b) *Health and Deprivation: Inequality and the North*, London: Croom Helm.

van de Kaa, D. J. (1987) 'Europe's second demographic transition', *Population Bulletin* 42: 1–57.

Victor, C. R. (1991) *Health and Health Care in Later Life*, Milton Keynes and Philadelphia: Open University Press.

Winter, J. M. (1986) 'The demographic consequences of the war', in H. L. Smith (ed.) *War and Social Change: British Society in the Second World War*, Manchester: Manchester University Press, pp. 151–78.

Woods, R. (1982) *Theoretical Population Geography*, London: Longmans.

——— (1992) *The Population of Britain in the Nineteenth Century*, Basingstoke and London: Macmillan.

Wrigley, E. A. and Schofield, R. S. (1981) *The Population History of England 1541–1871: A Reconstruction*, London: Edward Arnold.

Chapter 3

Political sociology 1945–92

John Curtice

This chapter looks at how far social change has been responsible for political change in Britain since 1945. In particular it takes issue with one particular thesis. This is that an increasing fragmentation of the social structure has been responsible for a decline in Britain's two-party system with deleterious consequences for the country's system of government. The chapter argues that in fact social change has not been a primary cause of political change in Britain since 1945. Indeed, the importance of political as opposed to social influences is no more clearly underlined than in the ability of certain key features of the country's constitutional arrangements to constrain the impact of those changes that have occurred.

Until recently, there was a considerable consensus amongst electoral and political sociologists that social change had brought about significant political change in post-war Britain. The precise form and focus of the argument varies from author to author but central to many of the arguments is the claim that social class has declined as an influence in social life and thus in political preferences and behaviour. It is said that voters have become less likely to vote according to their social class (Franklin 1985; Rose 1980), more volatile (Crewe 1985) and less deferential towards authority (Marsh 1977; Beer 1982). Moreover, that the Conservative and Labour parliamentary parties have become more similar in their social composition (Johnson 1973; Mellors 1978), while their formerly rigid voting discipline is fraying at the edges (Norton 1978, 1980). As a consequence, political parties have become less able to act as integrative mechanisms that channel and prioritise political demands. Indeed, the formal system of representative democracy is increasingly being bypassed by an ever-widening plethora of pressure groups (Jordan and Richardon 1987), while a less deferential and better educated citizenry are also more likely to engage in unconventional forms of political protest, leaving formal membership of political parties in decline (Marsh 1977). British government has become 'overloaded' with an excess of demands from sectional interest groups who owe no loyalty to any political party. This has resulted in a stagnation in policy-making and has made it impossible for governments to give a new or coherent direction to public policy (King 1976; Brittan 1977; Beer 1982). In short, it is argued that fragmentation of the social structure has resulted in the fragmentation of government.

This thesis (or rather collation of theses) involves then a number of different political arenas. In part it focuses upon mass politics and the behaviour of the mass electorate. But it also makes assertions about the social background and behaviour of the political elite. And in between these two levels of political activity it also considers the role of pressure groups and forms of political participation other than voting behaviour. We thus need to examine the impact of social change at three different levels of politics.

Our explication of the thesis began with the electorate, so it will be convenient to start there. Commonly, proponents of the thesis argue that there has been a fragmentation of the class structure reducing the cohesiveness and distinctiveness of both the middle and the working classes. They suggest that increased social mobility and material affluence have resulted in a narrowing of the differences in middle- and working-class life chances. The solidarity of the working class has been eroded by the decline of traditional, cohesive, working-class communities such as mining and steel towns. The spread of owner-occupation has given many in the working class a significant capital stake. Meanwhile, so far as the middle class is concerned, a division has opened up between, on the one hand, the traditional 'old' middle class of businessmen and the traditional professions and, on the other, the 'new' middle class in the public sector and in occupations that require technical expertise rather than entrepreneurial skill or workplace authority.

The accuracy or otherwise of these statements need not concern us here (but for a sceptical view, see Marshall *et al.* 1988). The question is whether or not there is any evidence that the association between class and voting behaviour has altered significantly during the post-war period. The argument which has been put forward is that the decline of class in social life has meant that it has declined in importance as a cue in voting behaviour, thereby opening 'the door to explosions in minor party voting such as were seen in 1974 and 1983' (Franklin 1985: 105). One major problem that faces us here is that the academic survey series known as the British Election Studies (Butler and Stokes 1969, 1974; Särlvik and Crewe 1983; Heath *et al.* 1985, 1991) was only inaugurated in 1963; this means that we can only analyse trends in the relationship between class and vote using a consistent measure of social class for the period from 1964 onwards. Indeed, most of the literature on the relationship between class and voting in Britain takes 1964 as the starting date for its empirical analysis for precisely this reason.

There are also two crucial conceptual distinctions that have to be borne in mind. The first is the difference between *absolute* class voting and *relative* class voting. By absolute class voting is meant the proportion of the electorate who vote for the party of 'their' class, that is the proportion of middle-class people who vote Conservative together with the proportion of working-class people who vote Labour. It is relatively easy to demonstrate – as is done in Table 3.1 – that this declined to a low point in the 1980s, when third-party support was at its highest. The difficulty is that we do not know which is cause and which is consequence. For under the definition of absolute class voting, any vote not cast for Conservative or Labour is regarded as a non-class vote. Thus any increase in third-party support must *logically* lead to a decline in absolute class voting.

In order to ascertain whether a decline in class voting is causally prior to, and thus a possible explanation of, the rise of third-party voting (and perhaps of greater electoral volatility), we have to look at relative class

Table 3.1 Absolute class voting

	Absolute class voting %	Two-party vote %
1964	64	88
1966	64	90
1970	60	90
Feb. 1974	56	77
Oct. 1974	57	77
1979	57	83
1983	52	72
1987	52	75
1992	56	78

Sources: Heath *et al.* (1991); British Election Study 1992. Absolute class voting is the total proportion of the electorate that is either middle-class and votes Conservative or is working-class and votes Labour. Two-party vote is the proportion of the total vote cast for Conservative and Labour.

voting. By this is meant the relative strength of the parties in the different social classes. Effectively we are interested in the proportion of the Conservative and Labour votes that come from the different classes. If these proportions have become more similar to each other, then there has been a decline in relative class voting.

The level of relative class voting has certainly varied from election to election.[1] We can see in Fig. 3.1 that it fell between 1964 and 1970 and fell again in 1979. But here we must take note of our second conceptual distinction – between 'trendless fluctuation' and 'secular decline'. The social changes that, it is argued, have resulted in a decline in class voting are usually thought to be gradual, continuous and long term. If they are responsible for a change in the level of class voting, then we should anticipate a gradual continuous decline in relative class voting – in short a 'secular decline'. However, what we see in Figure 3.1 is movement up

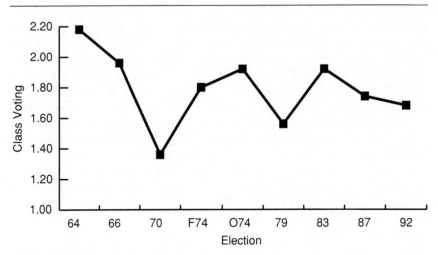

Figure 3.1 Relative class voting
Sources: Heath *et al.* (1991); British Election Study 1992

and down – or 'trendless fluctuation'.[2] True class voting appears to have been unusually strong in 1964 and much weaker in 1970; but since then it has fluctuated at a level in between those two extremes. But this fluctuation may well be accounted for by differences in the particular *political* circumstances of each election rather than long-term social change. We might note, for example, that relative class voting has been weaker at the end of periods of Labour government, which may reflect working-class disillusion with Labour's performance in office (Evans *et al.* 1991).

But might consideration of the pre-1964 period alter the picture? From the fragmentary evidence that we do have available, it would appear not. Heath *et al.* (1985) were able to piece together from different sources a set of figures for the relationship class/vote back to 1945 based on the manual/non-manual dichotomy. This did not reveal any evidence of secular decline in relative (or even absolute) voting prior to 1964; indeed it suggested that, if anything, the relationship between class and vote as measured by the British Election Survey of that year was unusually strong.[3] Further, another series in Durrant (1966) based on Gallup election polls also shows no evidence of secular decline in class voting.

There is, then, no evidence of a long-term secular decline in the relative strength of the Conservative and Labour Parties in each class – only of fluctuation. Further, such fluctuation is more easily explained by differences in the political circumstances of each election than by social change. And in the absence of any continuing evidence of a secular decline in relative class voting, the decline of class cannot be called upon to account for the rise of third-party voting.

The social change thesis also looks weak if we look at the evidence on volatility. One of the consequences of class dealignment, it is argued, is that voters are more prepared to switch their votes from one party to another. Class was a social bond that helped tie the voter to a party, even when the voter had little understanding of the party's policies or was not much enamoured of its performance in office. With the demise of social class as a cue to voting, the voter is less likely to remain loyal.

That the electorate was indeed more volatile appeared to be confirmed by the advent of large swings at by-elections in the 1960s and in general elections from February 1974 onwards. However, both the 1987 and the 1992 elections were notable for how little the result differed from their predecessors (Curtice and Steed 1992). But most importantly, when we look at the behaviour of individual voters rather than change in party fortunes, we do not find evidence of a consistent secular trend towards greater volatility. Thus 37 per cent of those eligible to vote in both the 1983 and 1987 elections failed to vote the same way both times – exactly the same proportion as switched between October 1974 and 1979 and just two percentage points higher than the figure for 1959–1964 (Heath *et al.* 1991).

But if the claim that there has been a change in the relationship between class and voting behaviour looks weak, perhaps social change might be an important explanation of political change in Britain in another way not originally considered by our thesis. For while the political significance of social class may not have changed, the sizes of the social classes certainly have. Those in white-collar employment now outnumber those in blue-collar employment. Moreover, the distribution of other social characteristics that have traditionally been associated with voting behaviour has also changed. Owner-occupation has become more popular; there has been a growth in higher education; and religious adherence has declined. And these social changes have been mirrored by changes in party fortunes. In particular, Labour's electoral support fell from 49 per cent in 1966 to as low as 28 per cent in 1983; it only recovered to 35 per cent by 1992. Might this drop be accounted for by a decline in the size of some of Labour's traditional social bases of support?

Even here, the answer appears to be no. Although changes in the size of social groups have been a net disadvantage to Labour, the impact on Labour's support has been small compared with the scale of its electoral decline. We can see this by comparing the *overall* national level of electoral support Labour actually received in 1987 with what it would have won in 1964 if its level of support *within* each social category had been the same as in 1987. The results are shown in Figure 3.2. We can see that changes in the size of the social classes could account for a 4.5 point drop in Labour support between 1964 and 1987. But if we take into account a wider range of social changes, this figure actually falls to just 4 points, not least because the decline of religious observance has operated to

Labour's advantage. This compares with an actual drop in Labour support between 1964 and 1987 of as much as 13 points, and still as much as 10 points after 1992.

Indeed, in further similar calculations Heath *et al.* demonstrate that political changes between 1964 and 1987 are better able to account for the changes in party fortunes in that period than is social change. For example, the Alliance fought all of the seats in 1987 while the Liberals fought only just over half of them in 1964. Heath *et al.* estimate that this is likely to have had just as much impact on the overall Labour vote as social change did during that period. Meanwhile, Labour's shift to the left in the 1980s may also have cost it about two percentage points – and its shift back to the right by 1992 a similar-sized benefit (Heath and Jowell forthcoming). In total, they estimate that long-term political changes could have accounted for a Labour decline of as much as 7.5 percentage points.

If social change appears not to have had the electoral impact upon mass voting behaviour which many have ascribed to it, what then of the political elite? How far has the social composition of the elite changed? A number of commentators have argued that the social composition of the two parliamentary parties has become more similar. In the Conservative Party those from aristocratic backgrounds have become less numerous. But the more dramatic change appears to have happened in the Labour Party. The party that was established to secure the election of working men to parliament has increasingly been dominated by men from the professional middle class (Johnson 1973). Indeed, for some commentators this narrow-

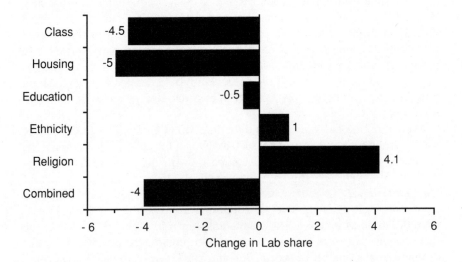

Figure 3.2 Estimated impact of social change on labour support 1964–87
Source: Adapted from Heath *et al.* (1991)

ing of the social distance between the two parliamentary parties was a further reason why class voting was in decline (Butler and Stokes 1974).

Table 3.2 summarises the trends in the social composition of the Parliamentary Labour Party (PLP) in the post-war period. It shows that the proportion coming from working-class occupations did indeed reach an all-time low after the 1992 election. However, the decline has not been a continuous one: in the 1970s and 1980s the proportion of workers in the PLP fluctuated. Further, the biggest change appears to have occurred not during the post-war period but in 1945. Ross (1955) calculates that whereas 41 per cent of the PLP were rank-and-file workers in 1945, the average in the 1918–35 period had been 72 per cent. The post-war gentrification of the PLP has been quite modest in comparison.

The educational background of Labour MPs tells a similar story. The proportion of those with a university education rose from 32 per cent in 1945 to 61 per cent in 1992. But again there has been no consistent trend since 1970 (the proportion was 56 per cent in both 1970 and 1987), and the most important change appears to have occurred in the immediate post-war period rather than thereafter. In the 1935 parliament just 19 per cent of the PLP were university educated while the figure had leapt to 41 per cent by

Table 3.2 Social composition of the Parliamentary Labour Party

	1951	% 1970	1979	1992
Professional	35	48	43	42
Business	9	10	7	8
Miscellaneous	19	16	14	28
Workers	37	26	36	22

Sources: Butler (1988); Criddle (1992). See also Burch and Moran (1985)

1950. Further, in some respects the post-war period has seen the Labour Party become less socially exclusive. Whereas in the 1945 parliament, 23 per cent of the PLP had been educated at public school, just 14 per cent had been in 1992.

The gentrification of the Labour Party in the post-war period has then been quite modest and by no means continuous. It has been particularly modest compared with what happened in 1945 itself. Before 1945 the PLP could accurately be characterised as a working-class party. But the middle-class hue has been important throughout the post-war period.

Moreover, although they may have narrowed, there are still some clear differences in the social origins of Conservative and Labour MPs. No more than 1 per cent of the Conservative Parliamentary Party has ever come from a working-class occupation. Meanwhile, although the percentage from business occupations declined in the late 1960s, more recently it has returned to its earlier level. Indeed, it is only in the proportion of those educated at public school (62 per cent) that the Conservative Party now clearly differs from its predecessors in 1945 (85 per cent). Further, although the proportions of those from professional occupations are similar in the two parliamentary parties, in the Conservative Party members of the traditional professions (especially law) predominate while in the Labour Party teachers and lecturers are most numerous. While both parties are predominantly middle class, they clearly come from different fractions of the middle class.

Again, evidence of a continuous trend is hard to come by if one looks at the social background of cabinet members. The first Labour cabinet of the last Labour Prime Minister, James Callaghan, in 1976 was clearly less working class than Attlee's first cabinet in 1945 – but it differed little from Harold Wilson's first Cabinet in 1964. Meanwhile there has been a small decline in the aristocratic component of Conservative cabinets – but again this had already happened by the early 1960s.

Table 3.3 Occupational background of Conservative MPs

	1951	% 1964	1979	1992
Professional	41	48	45	39
Business	37	26	34	38
Miscellaneous	22	25	20	22
Workers	–	1	1	1

Sources: Butler (1988); Criddle (1992); Burch and Moran (1985)

Our third arena is the pressure group. As the social structure fragments and political parties weaken, then pressure groups, it is argued, come to play a major role in the policy-making process. Some of these pressure groups represent economic interests, but others are promotional groups that advocate some cause such as nuclear disarmament or the plight of the homeless. This is in many respects a more difficult part of the thesis to evaluate. Although it is frequently asserted that pressure groups have increased in number or that promotional groups have become more active and prepared to engage in unconventional political activity, finding figures to confirm many of these claims is difficult. And there appear to be grounds for caution.

First, only a relatively small minority of people are members of a pressure group or engage in political activity outside an election period. Kavanagh (1987) reports that 6 per cent of people were group members in 1983, while a survey conducted in 1974 found that 17 per cent of people

Table 3.4 Social background of selected Labour and Conservative cabinets

	Aristocrat	Middle class	% Working class	Public school	Oxbridge
Labour					
1945	–	40	60	25	25
1964	4	61	35	35	48
1976	4	65	30	35	52
Conservative					
1951	31	68	–	88	56
1963	21	79	–	88	71
1970	22	78	–	83	83
1986	23	77	–	68	59

Source: Adapted from Butler (1988)

reported that they frequently or sometimes get involved in some group activity (Dalton 1988). We do not know how these figures have changed over time but it is clear that they are significantly lower than in the United States or even West Germany.

Second, much of the literature takes a selective view of those trends in group membership for which we do have data. Much is made of the undoubted rise in the membership of environmental groups (see, for example, Grant 1989). But, in contrast, both churches and traditional women's organisations have experienced a long-term decline in membership, as have, more recently, trade unions. Indeed, as Table 3.5 shows, the fall in the membership of these latter three groups since the early 1970s is two-thirds as big as the increase in the membership of environmental organisations.[4] Meanwhile there is only evidence of a modest increase in the membership of charitable organisations.

But although pressure group membership may not have increased as much as is sometimes claimed, party political membership has undoubtedly declined in the post-war period after having peaked in the early 1950s. Official party membership figures are notoriously unreliable. Until the

Table 3.5 Changes in group membership

	1971	1990	Change
Environmental organisations	0.8m	3.9m	+3.1m
Churches	9.6m*	9.1m	−0.5m
Women's organisations	1.4m	0.9m	−0.5m
Trade unions	11.1m	9.9m	−1.2m
Charitable organisations	1.9m	2.1m	+0.2m

Note: * Figure is for 1970
Source: Calculated from *Social Trends* (various)

1980s the Labour Party only allowed constituency parties to affiliate to the national party on the basis of a minimum membership of 1,000 people – and so the party's national membership effectively could not fall below 600,000. Even so, official Labour Party membership fell from a peak of 1,015,000 in 1952 to 666,000 in 1979. With the end of the minimum affiliation of 1,000, party membership was reported as being just 348,000 in 1980; 295,000 in 1983; and only 279,530 in 1992.

The Conservative Party, on the other hand, does not regularly publish membership figures at all. But there seems to be little doubt that membership has fallen considerably. The party reported an all-time high of 2,805,832 members in 1953, while an internal study estimated membership at just under 1.2 million in 1982/4 (Butler and Butler 1986).[5] By 1992 the membership was reported to be as low as 756,000. (Seyd *et al.* 1993) or according to another report perhaps not much more than 400,000 (Wynn Davies 1993). Further, survey data confirm the existence of decline. In 1964, 14 per cent of the electorate claimed membership of a political party compared with just 6 per cent in 1987.

But even if we accept that pressure groups have become a relatively more important source of political participation and have come to play a more important role in the British policy-making process, how far is this a consequence of social change? Two rather separate arguments have been put forward to support this view. The supposed increase in participation in interest group activity has been ascribed to an increase in the educational levels of citizens, giving them the political skills and knowledge required for more demanding forms of participation. Although those who are better educated are somewhat more knowledgeable about politics,[6] in Great Britain (unlike the United States) the association between education and political participation is a weak one. Further, claims that education results in a more sophisticated electorate less reliant on the political party as a cue are belied by the fact that there is a positive correlation between educational level and strength of voter's attachment to a party.[7]

The second argument looks at the changing nature of the state rather than at the changing nature of individuals. It is argued that the expansion of the state into a wider range of social and economic activities has required governments to consult more and more with those who might be affected. Indeed, as government casts its net more widely, the acquisition of the support of affected groups for proposed policies becomes yet more important as there are a limited number of battles that a government can fight at any one time. And indeed, some government experiences in the 1970s – such as the failure of the Industrial Relations Court introduced by Edward Heath's government or the British Medical Association's (BMA) opposition to the abolition of pay beds in NHS hospitals in 1975 – appeared to be evidence of the inability of governments to introduce radical new policy departures in the wake of opposition from vested interests.

It is often assumed in this argument that this expansion of the role of the state is a consequence of social change. An enhanced role for the state is seen as a necessary consequence of the development of advanced capitalism. But the experience of the last ten years would appear to challenge this assumption. The Conservative government headed by Mrs Thatcher between 1979 and 1990 was committed to rolling back the frontiers of the state. Although it failed to reduce government expenditure as a proportion of the gross national product until its later years, it succeeded in removing many nationalised industries from public control, as well as producing a fall in the proportion of households living in council houses from 31 per cent in 1981 to 21 per cent by 1992.

Furthermore, the period since 1979 has also challenged the claim that governments are unable to introduce new policies against the opposition of vested interests. The reform of the National Health Service has been proceeded with against the opposition of the BMA to some of its key proposals. The legal immunities of trade unions have been challenged successfully, and the opposition of one of the strongest unions in the 1970s – the National Union of Miners – to a reduction in the coal industry has been overcome. Although consultation with pressure groups remains pervasive, the government has at times been willing to curtail the consultation process (such as in the development of the NHS reform proposals) when it has believed that pressure groups would not agree with its major aims. The relationship between the state and pressure groups does not appear to be fixed or made immutable by the social structure of society. It is also influenced by political actions and choices.

Thus across all three areas of political activity that we have examined we must conclude that post-war British politics has not been driven by the motor of social change. The extent of the social change that has occurred has often been exaggerated. The change in the social composition of the two main parliamentary parties has been marginal. The decline in Labour's electoral base has been limited. And where social change has occurred, it has not always had the consequences claimed for it: upon closer scrutiny, the rise in electoral volatility appears non-existent and the rise in pressure group membership more limited than often maintained. Above all, social class remains an important cleavage at both elite and mass level.

Rather than the helpless plaything of sociological forces, post-war British politics has been vitally shaped by political choices and developments. The period since 1979 has shown that governments do not have to accede to the claims of pressure groups. The spread of Liberal candidatures, ideological shifts to the left and back, and their success or otherwise in office all appear to have played an important role in Labour's electoral fortunes.

But perhaps the most difficult problem with the thesis that we have been examining is that it understates the resistance that the British political system has demonstrated to the consequences of social, or indeed any other form of change. Many of the crucial features of the British Constitution have remained unchanged since 1945. The House of Commons is still dominated by two large parties who anticipate being able to form single-party governments with an overall majority in the House of Commons. For the most part, the executive remains pre-eminent over the legislature, with the consequence that consultations with ministers and civil servants remain the most important channel of pressure group influence. In other words, Britain still has an executive dominated two-party system.

But this is not because the system has not been challenged. Support for Britain's main third-party alternative rose from 2.5 percentage points in 1951 to 26 per cent in 1983. The Northern Irish party system separated itself from that in the rest of the United Kingdom in the early 1970s. Meanwhile, in Scotland, and to a lesser extent Wales, there has been a growth in support for nationalism. At the electoral level, the British party system has been as turbulent as any in post-war Western Europe.

Yet the two-party system of alternating majority governments has largely remained intact. It does so, of course, thanks to the electoral system which has insulated Westminster and Whitehall from much of the force of this electoral change. Even if social change had been responsible for a collapse in the strength of the two-party system at the popular level, we would have had to conclude that its impact on the way that Britain is governed had so far been muted. For the impact of social change upon politics is mediated by the political – and that includes constitutional – rules as well as the actions of politicians.

NOTES

1 The figure shows the size of the Conservative/Labour, salariat/working-class log odds ratio at each election since 1964. The odds ratio is simply the ratio of the proportion of each class that votes Conservative divided by the ratio of the proportion of the same two classes that votes Labour. The log odds ratio is simply the natural logarithm of this figure. The higher the log odds, the higher the level of relative class voting. For further details see Heath *et al.* (1991).

2 We should also note that even the apparent trend in absolute class voting reversed itself in 1992.

3 As measured by the log odds ratio, relative class voting was 1.9 in 1964 compared with 1.6 in 1945.

4 To those who might query whether women's organisations or churches are really politically active organisations, it might be pointed out that just over half of the membership of environmental organisations is accounted for by the National Trust (including the National Trust for Scotland), membership of which is much more a statement of leisure activities than of political proclivities.

5 Membership of minor parties did increase during the post-war period, but even at its peak in the mid-1980s membership of the two Alliance parties only reached approximately 160,000. The figure then fell dramatically with the collapse of the Liberal/SDP Alliance and had only recovered to around 100,000 by 1992.

6 Asked whether ten statements about British politics were true or false, those

respondents to the 1992 election study who had a degree on average got 7.7 correct whereas those with no educational qualifications got only 4.6 correct. Note however that 8 per cent of the electorate have a degree and that below that level the number of correct answers falls off rapidly. For example, amongst those with higher education below degree level the average number of correct answers was only 6.3.

7 For example, in the 1987 election study, 25 per cent of those with a degree or equivalent qualification were very strong identifiers with a political party, while only 17 per cent of those without an O level were. Only 5 per cent of those with a degree did not have a political identity at all, while the figure was 17 per cent of those without an O level.

REFERENCES

Beer, S. (1982) *Britain Against Itself*, London: Faber.

Brittan, S. (1977) *The Economic Consequences of Democracy*, London: Temple Smith.

Burch, M. and Moran, M. (1985) 'The changing British political elite 1945–83', *Parliamentary Affairs*, pp. 1–15.

Butler, D. (1988) 'Electors and elected', in A. Halsey (ed.) *British Social Trends Since 1900*, London: Macmillan.

Butler, D. and Butler, G. (1986) *British Political Facts 1900–1985*, London: Macmillan.

Butler, D. and Stokes, D. (1974) *Political Change in Britain*, London: Macmillan.

Crewe, I. (1985) 'Great Britain', in I. Crewe and D. Denver (eds) *Electoral Change in Western Democracies*, London: Croom Helm.

Criddle, B. (1992) 'MPs and candidates', in D. Butler and D. Kavanagh (eds) *The British General Election of 1992*, London: Macmillan.

Curtice, J. and Steed, M. (1992) 'The results analysed', in D. Butler and D. Kavanagh (eds) *The British General Election of 1992*, London: Macmillan.

Dalton, R. (1988) *Citizen Politics in Western Democracies*, Chatham, NJ: Chatham House.

Durrant, H. (1966) 'The Gallup polls 1945–64', in R. Rose (ed.) *Studies in British Politics*, London: Macmillan.

Evans, G., Heath, A. and Payne, C. (1991) 'Modelling trends in the class/party relationship, 1964–87', *Electoral Studies* X: 99–117.

Franklin, M. (1985) *The Decline of Class Voting in Britain*, Oxford: Clarendon.

Grant, W. (1989) *Pressure Groups, Politics and Democracy in Britain*, Hemel Hempstead: Philip Allan.

Heath, A. and Jowell, R. (forthcoming) 'Issues and images in the 1992 general election', in A. Heath, R. Jowell and J. Curtice (eds) *Can Labour Win?*

Heath, A., Jowell, R. and Curtice, J. (1985) *How Britain Votes*, Oxford: Pergamon.

Heath, A., Jowell, R., Curtice, J., Evans, G., Field, J., and Witherspoon, S. (1991) *Understanding Political Change*, Oxford: Pergamon.

Johnson, R. (1973) 'The British political elite', *European Journal of Sociology* XIV: 35–77.

Jordan, A. and Richardson, J. (1987) *Government and Pressure Groups in Britain*, Oxford: Clarendon.

Kavanagh, D. (1987) *British Politics: Continuities and Change*, Oxford: Oxford University Press.

King, A. (1976) 'The problem of overload', in A. King (ed.) *Why is Britain Becoming Harder to Govern?*, London: BBC.

Marsh, A. (1977) *Protest and Political Consciousness*, London: Sage.
Marshall, G., Newby, H., Rose, D. and Vogler, C. (1988) *Social Class in Modern Britain*, London: Hutchinson.
Mellors, C. (1978) *The British MP*, Farnborough: Saxon House.
Norton, P. (1978) *Conservative Dissidents*, London: Temple Smith.
——— (1980) *Dissension in the House of Commons 1974–1979*, Oxford: Clarendon.
Rose, R. (1980) *Class Does Not Equal Party*, Glasgow: University of Strathclyde Studies in Public Policy, no. 74.
Ross, J. (1955) *Electors and Elected*, London: Eyre & Spottiswoode.
Särlvik, B. and Crewe, I. (1983) *Decade of Dealignment*, Cambridge: Cambridge University Press.
Seyd, P., Whiteley, P. and Richardson, J. (1993) 'Who are the True Blues? The Conservative Party Members', Paper presented at PSA Annual Conference, University of Leicester.
Social Trends (various years), London: Central Statistical Office.
Wynn Davies, P. (1993) 'Tory membership hits all-time low', *The Independent*, 13 October.

Chapter 4

The family in post-war Britain

Chris Harris

The first thing to say about the family in post-war Britain is that socio-logists in general and the author of this paper in particular know very little about it. There are a number of reasons for this sociological ignorance. The first is that there is no such thing as *the* British family in the post-war (or any other) period in the empirical, descriptive sense. The population of these islands may be seen to belong to a vast number of overlapping and interconnected family groups, and this collection of families exhibits a bewildering variety of features whether one considers the *mentalités* of their interiors, the normative and empirical models of family life which the members of each group shared, the modes of articulation of families with the economy, the degree of openness and closure, and so on. Granted these variations are not random, but strongly associated with class, religion, occupation and settlement type. They are also associated with place. However, even if we hold these variables constant and confine ourselves to a consideration of a single family type specified in their terms, we are still confronted with a bewildering empirical variety.

This difficulty should not be misunderstood, however. To recognise empirical diversity is not to deny the existence of structural regularities that underlie it and cultural values that inform it. At the structural level, the system of family formation in these islands has been nuclear for at least five centuries. This tells us nothing about the distribution of household composition: it does indicate that at marriage the young couple is not under the jural, political, religious or economic authority of the natal groups of either partner and that whatever relationships may be empirically found to exist between the couple and such groups are the result of negotiation between formally autonomous parties and not the result of adherence to cultural prescriptions. At the cultural level, family behaviour has been informed by individualistic values, so that however strong the ties between family members may have been, their strength is the result of personal affection or loyalty to individuals arising out of family living rather than the result of affection or loyalty to a kin group. It is precisely the universal presence of these particular cultural and structural features which makes possible the diversity, which in turn makes empirical generalisation so difficult. Faced with this diversity, quite an enormous number of studies are required to begin to describe the variation in family life in any period, let alone to discern common features.

The second reason lies in the extremely underdeveloped state of British empirical sociology in 1945. Empirical social enquiry was at that time still firmly rooted in the study of social conditions, and given the social problems created by the depression and the dislocation of the war years, it was inevitable that the investigation of social conditions in connection with the problems of the post-war reconstruction should have been the prime concern of social enquiry.

It is often thought that sociologists in their capacity as students of the present have an enviable advantage over students of the past, since the object of the sociologist's study is readily available while the historian has access to the past only by means of a biased and fragmented collection of (often dubious) evidence. However, the wealth of evidence about the present is so overwhelming that there is no possibility of taking full advantage of its availability, and once selection takes place the sociologist is faced with a problem very similar to that of the historian. Sociological studies constitute signs that point towards the thing signified rather than accurately represent it, and the attempt to make sense of these evidences to construct a representation of the object of knowledge encounters all the difficulties that have to be overcome in historical work. There is, however, an additional difficulty experienced by the sociologist which is not encountered by the historian. The historian's construction and interpretation cannot affect the reality that it attempts to recapture. The work of the sociologist can affect the self-understanding of the very people whose lives are thereby described in a way that affects their future action. However, the social investigator is not a Martian and the evidence generated by social enquiry and its interpretation is influenced by the same social processes that have produced the reality which is its object. In this sense, the sociologist does not arrive with an answer of a kind unavailable to the historian but is rather part of the problem posed to all historians by their sources, a problem shared by anyone who attempts to use sociological work to reconstruct the reality to which they refer.

This chapter will therefore concentrate on a reconstruction of the image of the family which emerges from sociological work in the 1950s and 1960s. Unsurprisingly, the work was heavily influenced by its historical context both in terms of the type of investigation and the results produced. The war had resulted in a number of hasty marriages, which were followed by dissolution in the post-war period. It had also been associated with a loosening of the still strict sexual morality and this resulted in an increased number of illegitimate births. Families had been disrupted by evacuation, rehousing and mobilisation, leading to an increased awareness that individual pathology was rooted not only in social conditions but also in family circumstances. As a result, of eighty-two studies published between 1955 and 1970, 17 per cent were devoted either to family pathology or to family-related individual pathology. These studies constitute the largest single category and the proportion they form rises to 22 per cent if divorce is included.

The war had seen a massive increase in women's employment. In contrast to the period after the First World War, women did not return to the home when the war was over; the employment of married women remained high after the cessation of hostilities and rose thereafter. While a considerable proportion of this rise was accounted for by the rise in the proportion of women with adult children who were working, the employment of women whose children were young enough to require care also became more common. This both caused concern for the welfare of the children in such families and focused attention on the changing character of the marital relationship, predicated as it had traditionally been on a domestic division of labour in which the man was the sole wage-earner and the women concerned solely with domestic labour and childcare. As a result, the next largest category of studies (15 per cent) concerned married women working or 'modern' marital relations.

One of the most pressing post-war problems was housing. This problem had three origins: the inability of a substantial proportion of the population to rent or buy accommodation that conformed to standards demanded by the necessity to maintain public health in urban settlements; the deterioration of the housing stock generated in the period of rapid industrialisation a hundred years earlier; and the destruction of housing by enemy action. The housing shortage that resulted had obvious consequences for family formation and living and its solution, the building of new towns and peripheral housing estates, raised questions about family functioning under new and unprecedented conditions. In view of the importance of this problem, it is surprising that studies directed specifically towards family life and housing form only 7.5 per cent of the total; this is an indication of the lack of public awareness of the impact of the built environment on social functioning. This lack is highly characteristic of the period and the paucity of studies on this issue is an excellent example of the way in which social enquiry is skewed away from the reality to be investigated by attitudinal sets which researchers share with the society of which they are part.

If, however, one looks at the results of such studies, the picture changes markedly. Far more studies emphasise the importance of housing in their conclusions than are specifically directed towards the topic. It is not unreasonable to claim that if more notice had been taken of the results of such studies, some of the worst mistakes of housing policy in the 1960s and 1970s could have been avoided. It must also be said that the bibliographies here used to substantiate my argument entirely ignore the work of government agencies. Of particular relevance here is the work of John Madge and Vere Hole at the Building Research Station in the 1960s. Indeed the 1960s were, *par excellence*, the decade that saw the sharpest increase in the awareness of the social consequences of public policy, though as far as housing was concerned this was too late.

Of equal importance, numerically, to family studies concerned with housing were studies concerned with the effect of the family on educational performance. Both these topics link with a third category which, though still numerically small, has rightly acquired much greater prominence: studies of immigrant families that emphasise housing as a key factor in determining family and community organisation.

The last major category, which is of equal numerical importance to housing and education, comprises studies of intergenerational relations, chiefly of parents and married children and parents and adolescents. The interest in education reflects a wider concern with the transmission of property, occupation and aid between adult generations and the discovery that such transmissions were still of major importance. This may appear obvious to the contemporary reader but at the time it was necessary to counter a widespread sociological prejudice that this was no longer so in societies with nuclear systems of family formation, an individualistic culture and an occupational system based on achieved rather than inherited characteristics. The interest in intergenerational relations reflects the development of adolescence as a distinct developmental stage and social category on the American pattern and the emergence of what was later to be conceptualised as a 'youth culture'.

With one exception, whose discussion will be deferred until later, the categories Pathology, Women's Employment/Marital Relations, Intergenerational Relations, Housing and Education represent the only numerically significant foci of attention and between them account for nearly two-thirds of the studies reported. Other categories of study are, however, important in that they reflect major changes in the society and subsequent developments in the subdiscipline. It was at this period that systematic attention was first given to the effects of legal provision on family functioning, to the process of marriage, to social determinants of fertility and contraceptive use, to the effects of television, and to the family life of the elderly. It witnessed the discovery of the traditional working class and its correlative family forms, a conceptualisation called forth by the necessity to label what, it was claimed, was fast disappearing.

This last development reflects an enduring characteristic of British social enquiry, rooted as it was in the 'condition of England' question of the previous century: its concern with the lower strata of society on the one hand and with social pathology and social problems on the other. This has had the disadvantage of encouraging the assumption that the working class (who after all, on any definition, comprise over 70 per cent of the population) somehow shares common institutions and a common culture, and is the unique locus of problem individuals and groups. One of the most important contributions of the Institute of Community Studies has been to continue the tradition of lower strata enquiry while breaking away from the focus on the pathological. The whole series of studies that it has produced has been concerned with the family in particular places (hence 'community studies') which focus in anthropological fashion on the mode of life typical of a given population: on 'the normal' rather than the deviant.

Nothing could, however, be further from the truth than to suppose that the Bethnal Green studies (Marris 1958; Townsend 1957; Young and Willmott 1957) were not concerned with social policy. Indeed, it is alleged that on one occasion the Director of the Institute, Michael Young, when it was suggested to him that the first and most well known of the studies *Family and Kinship in East London* was about 'Mum', the dominant head of the three-generation Bethnal Green extended families, replied 'No it isn't; it's about planning'. The studies were not inspired primarily by the desire to chronicle a rapidly disappearing way of life. Their inspiration was rather an evolutionary one: to understand that way of life as having evolved over a period of time as an adaptation to economic and environmental circumstances. Whether or not it optimised family survival and functioning, it was sufficient to ensure it. To institute, through slum clearance and relocation to peripheral estates, a major change in the environment of a functioning social mechanism was to risk severe breakdown unless the environmental intervention was of a kind to ensure that the new environment was at least as likely to promote the viability of the family as the old.

This point can be put another way. In conditions of poor housing and low and uncertain wages the autonomy and viability of nuclear family households had been difficult to achieve. Such households were enabled to survive through transfers of help and support from the senior to the junior generations. Typically, this aid was repaid as, in the midlife of the children, it began to flow back again towards their now elderly parents. Each household was not therefore an isolated, autonomous, independent unit that planners could move around without affecting its internal functioning. It was rather a nodal point in a dense, locally based network characterised by long-term exchanges of aid and support. Slum clearance and relocation of 'families' (i.e. nuclear family households) disrupted an intricate system of reciprocal exchange which maintained the viability of households and sustained nuclear family functioning.

This thesis may be given a contemporary gloss: the dependency culture contemporaneously bemoaned by new right political theorists is not the result of the working class having been taught by socialist administrations not to depend on themselves but upon the state. It is, rather, the result of the destruction, in the post-war years, of those circumstances that enabled the members of the working class to depend upon each other. It will be cured not by the attempt to inculcate an enterprise culture but by creating the conditions under which individuals and families (whose resources are too meagre to be able to depend upon themselves) can once again begin to depend on each other, through mutual exchange and co-operation.

The Bethnal Green studies, however, do not stand alone as the sole origin of the astounding discovery that nuclear family households are part of a wider system of social relationships. This belated recognition of a banal but crucially important and still insufficiently understood social fact is due also to the increase in Britain, in the 1950s, of the influence of social anthropology on British family studies. The influence of anthropology was manifest in two ways. First, through an interest by anthropologists in the study of 'Western' kinship. A leading figure here was Professor (now Sir) Raymond Firth, whose kinship seminar at the LSE in the late 1950s spawned a number of studies, of which his own *Two Studies in Kinship* (1956) and the report of the research he directed into middle-class kinship (Firth *et al.* 1970) are best known. At the same time, Elizabeth Bott at the Tavistock Institute was attempting to understand the relationship between the internal organisation of the family and its external social environment by postulating a connection between the role relationship of the spouses and the degree of connectedness of their external social networks (Bott 1957). The second anthropological influence was reflected in the number of community studies undertaken in Britain in the 1950s and early 1960s. These typically provided information about family life in a way that showed its relation to other social institutions and groups and recorded the pervasive influence of kin ties in, at any rate, small settlements.

We can now name the other chief category into which the bibliographic items of the period fall. Seventeen per cent of these concerned relations between the elementary family and kin outside the household, 'extended' kinship networks, or dealt with the question of the extended family.

Some people viewed and still view the first Bethnal Green study as being significant chiefly for its discovery, in the heart of what was then the largest metropolis in the world, of a form of family that was at that time widely thought (at least by sociologists) to have been destroyed by the twin forces of urbanisation and industrialisation. This is an interpretation of the study foisted on it by the dominant American sociological consensus of the time, which still retained a strongly evolutionary view of society and history. The rediscovery of the local community, of the traditional working class, of the traditional working-class community in which ties of kinship were of prime importance, was not of course the result of the growing importance of such communities but of their demise. It is therefore part of a wider post-war *mentalité* which perceived there to be a sea change taking place in social life which involved loss as well as gain and which sensitised researchers to the presence of the past as well as the future in the present. This parallels a similar shift in sensibility during the early nineteenth century, when it was felt necessary to specify who we once were in order to define what we were in the process of becoming. It too was characterised by a similar sense of loss, and similar confusions as to the points in the past when disappearing features of the social scene originated.

The myth of a *pre-industrial* past, characterised by the formation of extended family groups, served to explain what was felt to be wrong with the family *now*, namely its isolation, its closure and its emotionally suffocating nature. The perception that the past is still with us gave place in an extraordinarily short space of time to the perception that we were firmly located in the future. The illusion, as I believe it was, that the closed, privatised, isolated nuclear family household was already typical of the British family, was due in large degree to the disappearance almost over-night in the mid-1960s of the empirically-based community study and its replacement by what I might call *Guardian* women's page sociology written by and for a mobile and increasingly privatised middle class.

What exactly has been going on in the British family as far as isolation, privatisation and closure is concerned is extremely difficult to establish for the two reasons cited at the beginning of this chapter – the dearth of empirical studies that tap this particular aspect of family life and the fact that the answer depends on which social category is under consideration and where its members live. It is sufficient to note that the evidence gathered from studies not directed to this issue and outside the period under consideration throws doubt on the proposition that British families in the post-war period were typically isolated in the sense of being out of contact with wider kin. This erroneous perception is due to a number of related causes. First is the very real growth, from a relatively low base, in the number of families that had lost contact with wider kin. Second, the families thus isolated occurred primarily in the most vocal strata and sectors of the population: those that supplied the opinion makers and leaders. Finally, growing concern began to be voiced by those in the social services *vis-à-vis* problems created by people in the more vulnerable strata who had lost kin support.

It is important in the latter case to distinguish two quite different phenomena: families lacking any significant kin contact and families affected by environmental changes that, while not preventing contact, disrupt the flow of support to family households. The problem of the care of the elderly is a case in point. Many infirm elderly persons living alone can without difficulty be maintained in their households if they have many kin who live close by and who can 'keep an eye' on them by 'popping in' on their way about their normal business. If these elderly persons are separated from their network members by only a few miles this blanket care becomes impossible, requiring either the institutionalisa-tion of the elderly person or the provision of costly domiciliary social services.

It must be recognised, however, that demographic as well as environmental factors played a part in creating the myth of family isolation. I refer not merely to the fact that, in the post-war period, as a result of earlier falls in family size, elderly people had fewer kin, and the proportion of the elderly with few siblings and no children was increasing. It was also the case that the falling age of marriage had resulted in a decrease in the degree of proximity of adult children to their elderly parents. Late marriage means that dependency in old age tends to occur early in the marriages of their children, before, that is, they have moved far away from their parents. Early marriage creates a situation in which the children's marriages may be of over twenty years' duration by the time the old person needs care, and twenty years is long enough for the children to have moved sufficiently far away from their parents to make care of them difficult.

The case of the care of the elderly is also an example of the popular misconstruction of social change as 'moral decline'. The very real problem posed by the isolated elderly was immediately interpreted as evidence of decline in family responsibility, of family disorganisation, rather than of social changes outside families' control. There was some attempt to correct this by comparing institutionalisation rates in the 1950s with those at the beginning of the century and to show that there was little difference between them. Another mode of attack which I myself adopted was to demonstrate that if family care (it would now be referred to as 'community care') of the severely disabled elderly were to have ceased, in Swansea in 1960, institutional provision would have had to be increased elevenfold. Nothing could have been further from the truth than the assumption that 'the family' had abandoned its responsibility for the elderly to the state, which remained very much a carer of the last resort.

This returns us to the centrality of the Bethnal Green studies and the community studies tradition. They illuminated the problem of 'social pathology' by showing the mechanisms operating to ensure normal social functioning and hence made it possible to locate the causes of the pathology in factors that disrupted these processes, rather than morally stigmatising their victims. A shorthand expression for normal support mechanisms was required in popular discourse and this became 'the extended family'. This was unfortunate since it introduced a confusion between family form and the articulation of the family household with its kin network. There is no reason whatever to suppose that extended family households were ever a major household type after the Industrial Revolution, even in the most traditional working-class communities. Whatever we were losing in the 1950s and 1960s, it was not the extended family household, nor were such households, in this period, archaic survivals. Such households were formed, at a particular stage of the family cycle, and were one particular form of kin aid to young couples: their incidence appears to have been related to both housing shortage and housing type. As such they were temporary, pragmatic deviations from the normatively prescribed system of nuclear family formation, not an alternative system. Such households were domestic groups, not productive groups, and that meant, given the traditional domestic division of labour, that the ties of filiation that linked the elementary families were between women, i.e. between mothers and daughters. However, it does not follow that when, with the maturation of the children, the members of the elementary family cease to form a common household, they cease to form a social group. However, the maintenance of the capacity to function as a group depends upon frequency of interaction. The separation of the members by geographical distance makes group interaction difficult and in its absence the group can disintegrate into a network, i.e. a set of dyadic interactions.

In my own study of the family in Swansea in the 1960s (Rosser and Harris 1965), we attempted to deal with the 'extended family' issue in the following way. What we claimed, in effect, was that in the past the elementary family remained a group, even after its children had married and formed households of their own. This was possible because of the geographical stability and the cultural and occupational homogeneity of its members. The key social change that had transformed this situation in the period under study was an increase in mobility – geographical, occupational and cultural – which led to the dispersal and diversification of the elementary family. This led to lower levels of interaction, a decline in group sentiments, and to the inability of members to act together. In other words the group tended to degenerate into an extended kin network. This, of course, did not isolate the elementary families that composed it, but posed difficulties in the exchange of, particularly, domestic services and lowered the effectiveness of kin support to family households.

This formulation, which we crudely expressed as the contrast between the stable and the mobile society, uses the issue of the extended family and wider kin support for households to relate the other key themes of the period: intergenerational relations, housing, education and marital relations. More needs to be said about the last two.

In this period the creation of equal opportunities in education (as in health care) was, it was thought, going to result in a transformation of society. We now know that this view was far too sanguine, and that educational and health outcomes are as much determined by economic inequality as the reverse. This current perspective should not blind us to the very real changes that the post-war educational reforms brought about and their consequences. Occupational mobility through educational success, was *initially* vastly increased. At the same time the progression and diversification of the opportunity structure through technological advance and changed patterns of consumption led to the erosion of the solidarity of groups, both familial and residential, which were based on forms of occupational community. Educational change has consequences for family functioning as well as family functioning having consequences for educational outcomes.

As far as marriage is concerned, the increasing number of married women taking paid employment has complex and diverse consequences, which differ according to the point in the process which the rise in female employment has reached. After the war the increase in the employment of married women with mature children meant a reduction in the availability of grandparental help with childcare at a point when the proportion of young mothers with children who were going out to work was beginning to rise, thus diminishing the flow of services from the older generation to the younger. By the end of the period the increase in the number of elderly was beginning to pose strain on middle-aged women who found themselves faced with providing services both to their married children and their own parents. Changing demographic and women's employment patterns, taken together, meant that the demand for domestic services by family members from the middle-aged was increasing, due in part to the higher participation rates of young women, while its supply was diminished by increased female employment in middle age.

The net result was to reduce the size of flows of intergenerational aid between women within the elementary family at a point when the adequacy of the support provided by wider kin was being reduced. Though my own study lacked the historical perspective necessary to grasp these points, it did raise the issue of women's increased labour force participation on extended family functioning.

The consequences of these changes for marital relationships and women's consciousness were profound. The Bethnal Green studies wrote of the great transformation of married life which had taken place in Bethnal Green, a claim which has since been derided by some feminist writers. However, in making this judgement the authors were only reflecting the consciousness of their informants: they reported that mothers continually told their daughters that they 'didn't know they were born' and contrasted the behaviour of the traditional Bethnal Green husband, 'mean with money and callous in sex' with the domesticated, pram-pushing, family-centred husband of the early 1950s. Young women were taught, in other words, to compare their own lot with their mother's and count their blessings. By the end of the 1960s, however, not only had the generation who remembered the bad old days gone, but their replacements, being themselves employed, were no longer able to offer the same help and support once provided by 'Mum': services their daughters were likely to require all the more due to the fact that they were more likely to be working when their children were young. The deficit of domestic labour, given the decline in effective network support which had taken place, could be remedied only from one source, the husband.

The period witnesses therefore a major shift in women's reference groups generated by the changes we have described. Women ceased to compare their own lot, favourably, with that of their mothers and began to compare it, unfavourably, with that of their husbands. This shift was a result partly of generational change but also, more interestingly, of a transformation of relationships within the post-nuclear elementary family, between mothers and daughters: a transformation of relationships which extended beyond the nuclear group.

The Bethnal Green studies and Bott's study both tended to assume that the erosion of wider kin ties and of the effectiveness of kin support to the nuclear family household would transform marital relationships, making them more 'joint' and less 'segregated'. The implication (to put it crudely) is that wives would rely on husbands to replace the services provided by 'Mum'. It was not put that crudely, of course, and the reason for this is that the studies of the period did not focus on domestic *tasks* but on social *relationships*. A specification of the tasks performed by kin outside the household would have immediately revealed that however joint the relationship, however companionable the marriage, however great the sharing, however blurred the boundary demarcating the traditional division of domestic labour, the husband would not be able to replace 'Mum', and that some replacement of 'Mum' was what was required in situations where wives with young children were engaged in full-time work.

This relates to two other themes characteristic of the period which were given emphasis towards its end: concern over rising divorce rates and the embourgeoisement of the working class. In the early part of the period the 'moral decline' school of social criticism was much in evidence before it was temporarily swept aside by a wave of radical critiques of the family associated with the coming of what the moral decline school labelled 'the permissive society'. Defenders of the family against the accusation that its members were abandoning their responsibilities claimed that the rising divorce rate reflected not lower but higher standards in marriage. To put it less moralistically, success in marriage was becoming more difficult.

One of the reasons for this, it can now be seen, was the shift of the basis of familial solidarity from ties of filiation between women to the marital relationship. Since ties of filiation are central to extended family groups and since the marital relation is central to nuclear groups, there is a structural sense in which the assumption that family change during the period was from the extended to the nuclear family is correct. But correlative to this change was the increasing interdependence of spouses, who looked to each other to supply a whole range of needs that went far beyond housework and childcare: a range which it was on the whole unlikely that they would be able to supply. This point could briefly be formulated by saying that the period was witnessing an increase in the isolation of the married couple as opposed to the nuclear family.

This increased isolation, and the increased fragility of marital relationships associated with it, is one aspect of the decline of local community and the growth of individualism and its correlate, the privatised nuclear family. In their study, which investigated the hypothesis that income mobility generated social and cultural mobility, Goldthorpe *et al.* (1969) claimed that the privatised nuclear family was characteristic of geographically and occupationally mobile affluent workers. Their response was to propose that the social classes were converging on a new pattern rather than one adopting the pattern of the other. The implication is that the post-war period was a time of fundamental change in the traditional conceptions and attitudes in which social and family life were rooted.

This is indeed the impression one receives from the sociological work of the period. However, this impression is misleading. Contemporary consciousness in modern, that is rapidly changing, societies is always characterised by the awareness of change and the attempt to grasp its character by building triadic models in which today is contrasted with both yesterday and tomorrow. The experience of the evanescent character of today required that it be contrasted with a stable and disappearing past: the mobile with the stable society. It does not follow that because those who live through a given period conceive it as a time of fundamental change, that this is necessarily the case. When the sociography of a given present is combined with the sociographies of that present's yesterday and tomorrow, it is possible that what will strike the historian most forcefully is change rather than continuity. I say 'historian' because such judgements cannot be expected from investigators who are living through and are part of changes they describe; the making of such judgements is a distinctively historical task.

REFERENCES

Bott, E. (1957) *Family and Social Networks*, London: Tavistock.

Firth, R. (1956) *Two Studies of Kinship*, LSE Monographs in Social Anthropology, London: London School of Economics.

Firth, R., Hubert, J. and Forge, D. (1970) *Families and their Relatives*, London: Routledge.

Goldthorpe, J. H., Lockwood, D., Bechhofer, F. and Platt, J. (1969) *The Affluent Worker in the Class Structure*, Cambridge: Cambridge University Press.

Marris, P. (1958) *Widows and their Families*, London: Routledge & Kegan Paul.

Rosser, C. (1983) *The Family and Social Change* (student edition), London: Routledge.

Rosser, C. and Harris, C. C. (1965) *The Family and Social Change*, London: Routledge.

Townsend, P. (1957) *The Family Life of Old People*, London: Routledge & Kegan Paul.

Young, M. and Willmott, P. (1957) *Family and Kinship in East London*, London: Routledge & Kegan Paul.

BIBLIOGRAPHY

Cerny, V., Dahl, N., Kamiko, T. and Aldous, J. (1974) 'International developments in family theory', *Journal of Marriage and the Family* 36: 1.

Current Sociology (1969) 27: 1–3.

Chapter 5

Women in Britain since 1945: companionate marriage and the double burden

Penny Summerfield

Women's lives appear to have been transformed since 1945. The square-shouldered and sculpted costumes, tapering to the knee, the neatly curled hair and hats of 1945 have been replaced by a multiplicity of less formal and more startling styles in the 1990s. Such superficial changes seem to signal deeper alterations of life-style, attitudes, experience and behaviour. Women's role in marriage and the family appears to be quite different, coinciding with a dramatic expansion of paid work for married women. And the language in which women and women's issues are publicly discussed has changed. In 1945 a discourse of difference dominated and the rhetoric of equality was subdued. By 1990 the position had been reversed.

This chapter explores these themes, drawing on the sociological research which has flourished since the war to discuss the implications of changing styles of marriage and the advent of the double burden of home and work for women, in the period since 1945.

MARRIAGE: INSTITUTION TO RELATIONSHIP?

Sociologists writing in the 1950s and 1960s argued that they were witnessing a change in the way marriage was popularly understood and practised. Formerly, they argued, marriage was seen as an institution in which roles and responsibilities were defined by convention and norms were maintained by community and kinship pressures. By the post-war period, so the argument went, marriage was being redefined as a relationship in which the partners negotiated their roles in accordance with personal preferences rather than externally imposed expectations. (See, for example, Young and Willmott 1957; Berger and Kellner 1964.) Official thinking on marriage followed the same path. The report of the government's Working Party on Marriage Guidance, *Marriage Matters* (1979) took this line, paving the way for the Marriage Guidance Council's indicative change of name to 'Relate' in 1990.

An important aspect of marriage as a relationship was the idea that it was 'companionate', implying a co-operative arrangement of some kind. The Royal Commission on Population observed in 1949 that there was now greater emphasis on 'the wife's role as companion to her husband as well as a producer of children' and that this had raised women's status in marriage (Royal Commission on Population 1949: para. 103). The idea that husband and wife formed a team or partnership became prevalent (see, for example, Beveridge 1948) and in the 1950s a growing volume of sociological studies claimed that the members of the marital team were becoming equals. Seventy-five per cent of the couples studied by Ferdynand Zweig in 1952 claimed 'absolute or "near" equality' in their marriages (Zweig 1952; see also Young and Willmott 1957; Willmott and Young 1960).

There were some exceptions to the new norm, such as the Yorkshire mining community 'Ashton', studied by Dennis, Henriques and Slaughter in the 1950s, where marital roles were sharply differentiated between men as breadwinners and women as home-makers. (Dennis *et al.* 1956). Patterns were also different in ethnic minority communities. Sheila Patterson found examples of the 'egalitarian' unit among young, working-class West Indian immigrants in London between 1955 and 1958. In such units 'both partners contribute financially, and share responsibility and authority for the children'. However, she thought that for economic reasons 'non-legal unions' which were highly inegalitarian, or 'maternal families' in which a mother brought up her children on her own, would remain more common among Afro-Caribbeans (Patterson 1965: 263, 290).

By the 1960s and 1970s companionate marriage was no longer regarded as an interesting new phenomenon, but was strongly normative. Geoffrey Gorer found that the couples he surveyed in 1969 identified 'comradeship, doing things together' as the most important thing for a happy marriage, whereas in his 1955 survey it was placed sixth (Gorer 1971; Gorer 1955: 138). The view was prevalent in the 1970s and 1980s that successful marriage demanded communication and sharing, and that their absence explained marital problems. In 1975 Mary Grant's problem page in *Woman's Own* magazine declared, 'Marriage is changing. These days it's more about needs and feelings than about the rules, rights and duties of being a husband and wife' (quoted by Richards and Elliott 1991: 37). In 1983 the Study Commission on the Family made a similar statement, concluding 'companionship and equality between women and men in families is considered crucial to a successful relationship' (Study Commission on the Family 1983: 3).

From the 1940s there were those who observed that the ideal of companionate marriage was not easy to attain. Many of the problems related to women's role within it. One area of difficulty concerned the relationship between women's domestic work and paid work outside the home. The other was the possibility that companionship in the context of the much-vaunted sexual revolution of the 1960s made marriage more unstable.

DOMESTIC WORK

In spite of widespread assumptions that companionate marriage involved 'equality', the language of difference was strong in the twenty years after the war. William Beveridge, architect of the post-war welfare state, is representative of many who accepted uncritically the idea of 'the house-wife'. But Beveridge thought that differentiation of function between men and women was the basis for the teamwork that took place in companionate marriage and was compatible with it so long as women were not over-whelmed by domestic drudgery. He believed this should not be so because of domestic improvements like piped water, electricity and modern kitchens, and the help given to the housewife by welfare state provisions such as subsidised food and housing, the National Health Service and family allowances. All the same, Beveridge believed that the volume of work done by the housewife had actually risen because of post-war con-sumerism. She had become 'an auxiliary labour force for the distribution of consumer goods'. In view of this, he advocated further collectivisation of tasks like washing, cooking and childcare which absorbed much of her time (Beveridge 1948: 264)

The post-war tide, however, was moving away from collective provision for domestic labour. As far as washing was concerned, the do-it-yourself laundrette and the domestic washing machine largely replaced municipal or commercial laundry services in the 1960s, as advertisers piled upon the individual woman the responsibility of achieving a gleaming white wash. The subsidised British Restaurants, created during the Second World War to provide community meals when bombing disrupted domestic cooking, were phased out afterwards. Nursery provision was dramatically reduced after the war, when Ministry of Health subsidies were removed from wartime nurseries, and local authorities had to decide whether to continue this form of comprehensive day-time care for babies and small children at their own expense. The few that did were in areas of labour shortage, where the Ministry of Labour encouraged steps to release women for paid work (Summerfield 1989). By 1965 there was nursery care for only 10 per cent of 3 and 4 year-olds, the same proportion as in 1938 (Blackstone 1971: 91) Women's response was to set up the Pre-School Playgroups Association in 1962. But this form of self-help was not the equivalent of full-time institutional care.

Beveridge wrote of the housewife as if she were classless. In fact, the housework burden for the middle-class wife was dramatically increased by the decline in domestic service. The Census shows that the number of women in residential domestic service declined from over two million in

1931 to 750,000 in 1951 and 200,000 in 1961. This meant that while some women found more remunerative and less subservient work outside service, the type of woman who had formerly employed servants now had to cope with that housework herself, possibly with some intermittent help from a 'daily' or, from the 1950s, an 'au pair' girl. Naomi Mitchison commented that it was in some ways easier for middle-class women to pursue careers in the 1930s, when there was still a plentiful supply of servants, than in the 1950s (Mitchison 1979).

The late 1940s and 1950s were characterised by attempts to impart the ideal of 'home-making as a career' to women of all social classes (Wilson 1980: 43). It was urged particularly strongly in educational literature. The Norwood Report (Norwood 1943), the blue-print for the secondary education arrangements provided under the 1944 Education Act, recommended that girls should be taught domestic science because they were all 'potential makers of homes'. John Newsom, Chief Education Officer for Hertfordshire, went further, advocating a secondary school curriculum for girls in which all subjects were linked by their applicability to the home. Only the exceptionally able minority of girls (who were in any case seen as abnormal) were to share the boys' curriculum (Newsom 1948). The Crowther Report of 1959, on the education of 15 to 18 year-olds, also emphasised domestic subjects for girls, as did Newsom's official Report of 1963 on the less able half of the secondary school population. Though Newsom and Crowther acknowledged that girls typically entered paid jobs when they left school, they dismissed such work as a mere stopgap before a young woman began her true 'career' as wife and mother.

Popular literature such as women's magazines carried the same kind of message. Wartime magazines addressed the wife and mother upon whose thrifty use of rationed goods national survival depended. This approach was maintained until the 1950s by the constraints of paper restrictions and food rationing (which did not end until 1953) and by the scarcity of luxury goods. However, as production of consumer goods increased in the 1950s, the emphasis on austerity housekeeping was replaced by the appeal to the affluent consumer. By the 1960s five out of six women saw at least one magazine per week which urged upon her the virtues of new discoveries such as the delicatessen and the avocado, advised her on furnishing and household gadgetry, and encouraged her to become a home decorator. Women readers were also expected to spend time and money on keeping themselves young and attractive, aided by the magazines' advice on dress, hairstyling and the use of beauty products. Spending on clothes, footwear and cosmetics rose 78 per cent between 1956 and 1965 (White 1970: 218, 182).

The magazines were not only marketing individual commodities, they were selling a new life-style. However, in spite of the increasing numbers of married women in paid work and the importance of their income to the new consumerism, the mass weeklies stood resolutely against women undertaking a dual role. The pronouncements at the end of a *Woman's Weekly* story of 1951 about the suffering caused to her family by a mother who had gone out to work are representative: 'Home-making is the most useful of all the talents. To make a man feel happy and comfortable and to make a child feel cherished. No women's work is more important than these' (White 1970: 142).

PAID WORK

During the 1960s such views were increasingly in tension with the pull of the labour market. In 1951 women formed 31 per cent of the total work-force, almost the same as the pre-war proportion of 30 per cent in 1931 (Routh 1965: Table 20). But between 1951 and the late 1980s the accelerating trend was towards the levelling out of numbers. In 1961 women formed 33 per cent of those in employment, 37 per cent in 1971, 40 per cent in 1981 and 45 per cent in 1987 (Joshi 1989). The increase was mainly one of married women. There were important demographic reasons for this. Firstly, between 1951 and 1961 the sex ratio balanced after a century in which women outnumbered men, so more women married. Secondly, there was a trend towards earlier marriage from 24.6 years for women in 1951 to 22.6 years in 1971, so women were married for more of their adult lives. And thirdly, patterns of family formation changed. In the 1950s and 1960s women had smaller numbers of children, born close together, in the early years of marriage (Elliott 1991). In the 1970s and 1980s families were still small, but more women deployed contraception (notably the Pill which became available during the 1960s) to space their children so that they could return to work between births (Ni Bhrolchain 1986). Taken together, these changes meant that a higher proportion of women married, and that more of them were available to enter the labour market because child-bearing occupied less of their lives. In 1955 of all women at work 48 per cent were married, compared to 64 per cent in 1985. In 1931 the figure was a mere 16 per cent. Richard Titmuss remarked on the significance of the fact that one-fifth of the married women under 50 at work had children of school age in 1958: 'it is probable that the lives of about four million families in Britain are now affected by the paid employment of the wife or mother outside the home' (Titmuss 1958: 102–3).

At face value it seems odd that this increasing involvement of women in the world of work coexisted with the sustained ideology that women were primarily home-makers. But this is less surprising when the terms on which women were working and their own views of their work are taken into account. Jane Elliott points out that there was little change in women's participation in *full-time* work between 1951 and 1981. In both years 30 per cent of all adult women worked full-time. This sector comprised mainly young women without children, and increasingly over time, older women whose children had grown up. But there was a huge increase in part-time work, from 5 per cent of adult women working part time in 1951 to 27 per cent in 1981. In that year women part-timers constituted 42 per cent of the female workforce. Elliott comments, 'All of the post-war increase in women's employment is accounted for by the increase in part-time jobs' (Elliott 1991: 101).

The post-war ideology of women's work did not proclaim women's equality with men in the workforce. On the contrary, even recruitment literature urging women to rejoin the workforce emphasised feminine difference. For example, the Government's Economic Survey of 1947 depicted women as temporary workers, helping in a crisis 'for whatever length of time they could spare', and doing *women's* work in factories, services and agriculture, rather than 'jobs usually done by men'. The appeal was not aimed at 'women with very young children' (Cmd 7046 1947). Wartime reservations about collective care for the young children of women workers, based on health and emotional grounds, were reinforced after the war by a growing literature on the psychological ill effects of 'maternal deprivation', led by John Bowlby's publications, notably *Maternal Care and Mental Health* (1952). Anxieties increasingly centred on the link between juvenile delinquency and the 'latch-key child' of the working mother, especially the Afro-Caribbean mother, who tended more than her white counterparts to take full-time work, given the low earnings of black men (Lewis 1991: 78). In the 1940s and 1950s official literature calling on women to come into the workforce skirted round such influential views by depicting women's paid work as essentially marginal, both to the economy and in women's lives.

There is evidence that women themselves saw paid work, especially part-time work, in the same way, and accepted the double burden as a specifically feminine phenomenon. A study of Peek Frean's biscuit factory in Bermondsey, South London in the 1950s found that the women working part time there wanted 'an opportunity to earn money to raise the standards of living of the family as a whole' (Smith 1961: 20). The researchers concluded that 'this new role was in every sense subsidiary to the traditional one of wife and mother' (Jephcott *et al.* 1962: 106). Later surveys, such as those undertaken by Viola Klein (1965) and Audrey Hunt (1968), and local studies such as a survey of women's work on Tyneside in 1978, confirmed these findings. Women wanted to work for economic reasons primarily to do with attaining a desirable standard of living for their families, but this work had to fit around family demands on their time. Tyneside women expressed gratitude to employers who made this possible (North Tyneside CDP 1978: 39) On their side, employers reaped benefits from part-time employment. Studies undertaken from the 1950s to the 1980s established that part-timers in non-manual and professional as well as manual work were on average more productive than full-timers and less prone to absenteeism, as well as costing less in terms of bonuses and benefits (including sickness and maternity leave and holiday pay) (Smith 1961; Hagger 1973; Chessum 1989). There were sound economic reasons for women's part-time work to become an entrenched employment practice.

Coinciding with this institutionalisation, attitudes to married women going out to work gradually changed. In the 1940s official sources such as the Reports of the Royal Commission on Equal Pay (1946) and the Government Social Survey on Women and Industry (1948) took the view that no woman would (or should) want to work if her husband earned enough. Indeed, in the 1940s there were still defenders of the marriage bar. Under it women had been forced to retire on marriage from numerous jobs, including teaching and the Civil Service, from which the bar was dropped in 1944 and 1946 respectively. Its passing was mourned by at least some male opponents (Wilson 1980: 46). In the 1950s Myrdal and Klein debated the issue of women combining home and work, notably the effects on children of mothers working, versus the economic need to enlarge the labour supply. Their defence of women's right to participate in the labour force was cautious. It should not go beyond the 'bi-modal' pattern already established, under which a woman worked before the birth of her first child, and rejoined the labour force when her children were older (Myrdal and Klein 1956).

Klein's work on married women workers in the 1960s noted the increasing numbers in professional work such as teaching and nursing. Simultaneously there was growing concern from other quarters to recruit talent from wherever it might be found in order to promote economic growth (Women's Group on Public Welfare 1962; Seear et al. 1964). The Robbins Report on Higher Education in 1963 reflected these concerns, though its main emphasis was on the unequal distribution of places in higher education for girls compared with boys, as well as for the children of manual workers compared with those of business and professional fathers. Robbins recommended an expansion that would enable more girls of all social classes as well as more lower-class boys to take degrees. The proportion of women university students rose from 25 per cent in 1963 to 40 per cent in 1981 (Acker and Warren-Piper 1984: 28).

In the 1960s the literature on girls' education did not analyse the structural barriers to women's participation in advanced education, particularly in the fields of science and technology. It coexisted with pieces of research that accepted that there should be different outcomes for girls and boys, even where the education provided was apparently the same (Dale 1969, 1971, 1974; DES 1975). However, the concentration of girls on arts and social science subjects and the tendency for both sexes but particularly girls to avoid science and technology became a cause of anxiety in the context of the 'skills shortage' of the 1980s. Educational research began to look at the ways in which social interaction at home and at school exaggerated differences between boys' and girls' abilities, and how this might be changed (DES 1980; Kelly 1981; Harding 1983).

Such thinking was stimulated by the mounting demands from women in the 1970s that their opportunities in education and employment should cease to be determined by their functions as wives, mothers and home-makers. Increasing dissatisfaction was expressed with educational provision that emphasised difference, and attention was drawn to inequality in provision (Byrne 1978; Deem 1980; Weiner 1985). Myrdal and Klein's defence of the bi-modal working pattern, on the grounds that it would not upset sexual divisions in the family and society, was submerged beneath demands that sexual divisions *should* be challenged. Second-wave feminism, emerging from the civil rights activism, the labour movement and the student movement of the late 1960s, demanded women's right to continuity of employment through their childbearing years, for equal pay and opportunities at work, and for an end to discrimination in education (Stacey and Price 1981; Coote and Campbell 1982).

The Equal Pay Act of 1970 and the Sex Discrimination legislation of 1975 gave a boost to a rhetoric of egalitarianism, encouraging consideration of issues such as the way language made women invisible or inferior. No longer could employers specify sex in recruitment advertisements (with a few exceptions such as the prison service), and the debate began on whether titles such as chairman and postman should be replaced by gender-neutral terms. Research undertaken in this climate was highly critical of the extent to which sexual divisions had in fact been allo-cated. Women in both manual and non-manual work appeared to be in subordinate positions to men, indeed to occupy a secondary sector of the labour market in which – along with black people, the disabled and the elderly – they were treated as more dispensable and less skilled than white men (Barron and Norris 1976).

The trend seemed to be in the opposite direction from greater equality and improved opportunities. Work by Catherine Hakim in 1978 showed that women formed a smaller proportion of workers classified as skilled in 1971 than in 1951; that in spite of a century of educational development, less than 10 per cent of higher professionals were women. The main areas of expansion for women were in clerical and shop work (Hakim 1978).

However, the dual labour market seemed to operate in these areas too. Research on clerical work in the 1970s and 1980s showed that women were concentrated in lower-status, poorly paid office jobs, with little chance of promotion. Seventy per cent of office staff and 99 per cent of typists and secretaries were women in 1979–80, but only 14 per cent were office managers (Griffin 1985: 113; Mackie and Pattullo 1977: 74–6) Office work was nevertheless seen by teachers and parents as 'a good job for a girl' – as long as she was white. Griffin found that Asian and Afro-Caribbean girls formed a smaller proportion in clerical and related occupations than their white contemporaries and she and others documented the institutionalised racism they faced (Griffin 1985: 113). Rex and Tomlinson commented in 1979 that 'whereas the white woman typically becomes a secretary or a shopworker, the immigrant woman works in a factory, or in a hospital, and rather less frequently in service industries' (Rex and Tomlinson 1979: 107). Brown noted that this was a relatively static situation. The distribution of Asian and Afro-Caribbean women in the employment structure was much the same in 1982 as it had been twenty years earlier (Brown 1984). Asian women have been concentrated in the most exploitative sector of all: home-working (Phizacklea 1988).

Even a profession like teaching could be said to operate a dual labour market. More women than men were primary headteachers before 1961. But after equal pay was introduced in that year, local authorities tended to appoint men rather than women: by 1987, 80 per cent of primary headships were held by men. At secondary school level, comprehensivisation and co-education worked against women's opportunities. In 1987, 84 per cent of secondary heads were men, compared with just 64 per cent in 1922 (Acker 1989: 10; Summerfield 1987: 2).

Research in the 1980s found that women were working for the same reasons and making the same kinds of compromises as they had been at Peek Freans in the 1950s (Pollert 1981; Cavendish 1982; Dex 1988). Even women in the professions and in relatively well-paid managerial jobs were putting their families first and sacrificing their careers for those of their husbands. In spite of the egalitarian tone of the post-1970s era, married women's rising labour force participation coincided with persistent gender divisions at work and at home.

In the 1980s there was vigorous debate about the causes of these persistent inequalities. Was it the capitalist economic system or the institution of patriarchy under which male power was institutionalised throughout society and above all in marriage? Feminist research emphasised the exploitative nature of marriage as a labour contract enforced by various forms of coercion, including violence (Dobash and Dobash 1979; Delphy 1984). By implication, it cast doubt on the possibility of achieving equality through companionate forms.

MARITAL INSTABILITY AND THE 'SEXUAL REVOLUTION'

Immediately after the war the divorce rate rose sharply to 3.7 divorces per 1,000 married people. It dropped to 2 per 1,000 in the 1950s, but then returned to the 1946-50 level by 1968, and proceeded to climb steeply through the 1970s, stabilising at around 12 per 1,000 in the 1980s (Elliott 1991: 91). While the specific pattern followed by the rise can be accounted for by the timing of legislation, the overall increase still requires explanation.

In 1956 the Royal Commission on Marriage and Divorce pointed to many causes but was most concerned about the 'greater demands' imposed by the new style of companionate marriage. The Commission thought that husbands found 'the changed position of women' difficult to accept; that wives did not fully appreciate their obligations and responsibilities; and that the contemporary emphasis on sexual satisfaction weakened restraints on extramarital sex (Royal Commission on Marriage and Divorce 1956: para. 45). Some members of the Commission would have liked to abolish divorce in order to preserve 'the concept of marriage as a life-long union of one man with one woman' (RCMD 1956: para. 54). Titmuss thought that the companionate ideal created higher expectations, so it was not surprising that more marriages were failing. However, he noted that a majority of those who divorced did remarry (Titmuss 1958: 100). Indeed, the proportion of remarriages in the total number of marriages rose from 20 to 36 per cent between 1950 and 1987, following the same trend as divorce (Elliott 1991: 95).

Subsequent research revealed that women in particular had high expectations of marriage. In 1955 Gorer found that wives most valued understanding and thoughtfulness in their husbands and regarded selfishness, especially in domestic matters, as their greatest failing. Husbands, on the other hand, wanted wives who were good household managers and who did not nag them, suggesting a fundamental incompatibility (Gorer 1955: 128–9). Writing about marriage in the 1960s and 1970s, Richards and Elliott concluded: 'There is abundant evidence that women, especially, are likely to seek closeness and shared understanding and their high expectations are not always met' (Richards and Elliott 1991: 47). And Mansfield and Collard noted that women in the 1980s had especially strong expectations about the satisfactions to be derived from marriage and were often disappointed (Mansfield and Collard 1988). The number of divorce petitions filed by wives rose from 45 per cent in 1946–50, to 73 per cent in 1977 (Elliott 1991: 92). There is no single reason for this, but one factor is the expansion of married women's work between 1946 and 1977, which provided a margin of economic independence sufficient to give women the confidence to dissolve a marriage that was not living up to their expectations (Martin and Roberts 1984). It looks as though the companionate ideal, coupled with women's work opportunities, increased the instability of individual marriages, while not weakening the institution of marriage as such.

The same could be said of another practice which apparently threatened conventional marriage. Cohabitation, the non-legal union that Patterson observed in Afro-Caribbean communities in the 1950s, became increasingly common. But rather than constituting an alternative to marriage in the 1960s and 1970s, it was in the main 'a prelude to marriage'. Cohabitation signalled a commitment to a sexually monogamous relationship and church weddings remained important even for those who had been living together (Richards and Elliott 1991: 48).

The significance of the growing acceptability of cohabitation for women was that loss of virginity before marriage was no longer as taboo as it had been. Advice to women in magazines relaxed considerably between the 1950s and the 1970s. Whereas a young woman was advised to take a chaperone with her if she was spending a night at her fiancé's all-male family home in 1955, by 1975 such a woman was encouraged to go on holiday with her boyfriend so long as she 'took precautions' (Richards and Elliott 1991: 40–1). And a rising number of women reported pre-marital sexual experience: 39 per cent of women born 1914–24; 43 per cent born 1924–34; and 75 per cent marrying 1971–5 (Chesser 1956; Dunnell 1976). All the same, there is evidence of a persistent double standard in the 1960s and 1970s. Geoffrey Gorer found that more people disapproved of pre-marital sex for women than for men in 1969: 27 per cent of men and 49 per cent of women thought men should not have sex before marriage, whereas 43 per cent of men and 68 per cent of women thought women should not do so (Gorer 1971). The gradual disappearance of taboos on pre-marital sex coincided with greater acceptance of the unmarried mother, renamed the single parent in the 1970s. The proportion of mothers bringing up children on their own rose from 2 to 4 per cent between 1961 and 1987 (Central Statistical Office 1989).

The evidence about women's marital aspirations suggests that women after the war were seeking the 'New Man' who was understanding and considerate and did his domestic bit. Research on masculinity revealed changes between the 1950s and the 1980s, particularly in the social acceptability of men taking an active role in parenting (Bell *et al.* 1983). But in practice, even in the case of dual earner families, the parts played by men and women in running the home and in childrearing remained very different. Martin and Roberts in 1984 showed that men 'are somewhat more likely to take an active role in housework and child care if their wife has a paid job' but 54 per cent of women who worked full time and 77 per cent of those working part time did all or most of the housework (Martin and Roberts 1984: 114). Neither high levels of male unemployment nor dual earning were leading to a breakdown of the sexual division of labour at home.

CONCLUSION

What can one conclude about the extent to which women's lives changed between 1945 and the 1990s? Although the subordinate position of women in the labour market persisted, the increased proportion of married women in paid work meant that more wives had their own earnings, however modest, in the 1990s than in 1945. Complete dependence on a husband's allowance became relatively rare. At the same time, women's roles as consumers, not just of goods but of new life-styles, grew in importance and the double burden of home and work became institutionalised. Coinciding with this, women's expectations that marriage should involve sharing and companionship rose while their tolerance of marriages that did not meet this ideal fell. Yet the high incidence of remarriage and relatively low proportion of lone mothers do not signify a widespread rejection of marriage by women. Feminist research of the 1980s emphasised that the changes that took place did not bring women greater equality, even though the language in which women's issues were discussed shifted towards egalitarianism. A research question for the 1990s is whether the precarious compatibility of companionate marriage and women's double burden can continue into the twenty-first century.

SUGGESTED FURTHER READING

The best overview of the history of women in the period is Jane Lewis's recent book, *Women in Britain since 1945* (1991). Readers should also consult Pat Thane's article 'Towards equal opportunities? Women in Britain since 1945' (1991), Elizabeth Wilson's *Only Halfway to Paradise* (1980) and David Clark's invaluable collection *Marriage, Domestic Life and Social Change* (1991).

REFERENCES

Acker, S. (ed.) (1989) *Teachers, Gender and Careers*, London: Falmer Press.
Acker, S. and Warren-Piper, D. (1984) *Is Higher Education Fair to Women?*, Guildford: SRHE.
Barron, R. D. and Norris, G. M. (1976) 'Sexual divisions and the dual labour market', in D. L. Barker and S. Allen (eds) *Dependence and Exploitation in Work and Marriage*, London: Longman.
Bell, C., McKee, L. and Priestley, K. (1983) *Fathers, Childbirth and Work*, Manchester: EOC.
Berger, P. and Kellner, H. (1964) 'Marriage and the construction of reality', *Diogenes* 46: 1-24.
Beveridge, W. (1948) *Voluntary Action*, London: Allen & Unwin.
Blackstone, T. (1971) *A Fair Start: The Provision of Pre-School Education*, London: Allen Lane.
Bowlby, J. (1952) *Maternal Care and Mental Health*, Geneva: World Health Organisation.
Brown, C. (1984) *Black and White Britain*, London: Heinemann.
Byrne, E. (1978) *Women and Education*, London: Tavistock.
Cavendish, R. (1982) *Women on the Line*, London: Routledge & Kegan Paul.
Central Advisory Council for Education (1959) *15 to 18* (Crowther Report), London: HMSO.
Central Advisory Council for Education (1963) *Half Our Future* (Newsom Report), London: HMSO.
Central Statistical Office (1989) *Social Trends*, London: HMSO.

Chesser, E. (1956) *The Sexual, Marital and Family Relationships of the English Woman*, London: Hutchinson.

Chessum, L. (1989) *The Part-time Nobody: Part-time Women Teachers in West Yorkshire*, Bradford: WYCROW.

Clark, D. (ed.) (1991) *Marriage, Domestic Life and Social Change: Writings for Jacqueline Burgoyne 1944–88*, London: Routledge.

Committee on Higher Education (1963) *Higher Education* (Robbins Report), Cmnd 2154, London: HMSO.

Coote, A. and Campbell, B. (1982) *Sweet Freedom, the Struggle for Women's Liberation*, London: Picador.

Dale, R. R. (1969; 1971; 1974) *Mixed or Single Sex School?*, London: Routledge and Kegan Paul (3 vols).

Deem, R. (ed.) (1980) *Schooling for Women's Work*, London: Routledge & Kegan Paul.

Delphy, C. (1984) *Close to Home*, London: Hutchinson.

Dennis, N., Henriques, F. and Slaughter, C. (1956) *Coal is our Life*, London: Tavistock.

Department of Education and Science (DES) (1975) 'Curricular differences between the sexes' *Education Survey* 21, London: HMSO.

—— (1980) 'Girls and Science', *Matters for Discussion* 13, London: HMSO.

Dex, S. (1988) *Women's Attitudes Towards Work*, London: Macmillan.

Dobash, R. E. and Dobash, R. (1979) *Violence Against Wives: a Case Against the Patriarchy*, London: Open Books.

Dunnell, K. (1976) *Family Formation*, London: HMSO.

Elliott, J. (1991) 'Demographic trends in domestic life 1945–87' in D. Clark (ed.) *Marriage, Domestic Life and Social Change*, London: Routledge.

Finch, J. and Morgan, D. (1991) 'Marriage in the 1980s: a new sense of realism?' in D. Clark (ed.) *Marriage, Domestic Life and Social Change*, London: Routledge.

Gorer, G. (1955) *Exploring English Character*, London: Cresset Press.

—— (1971) *Sex and Marriage in England Today*, London: Nelson.

Government Social Survey (1948) *Women and Industry*, London: Central Office of Information.

Griffin, C. (1985) *Typical Girls*, London: Routledge & Kegan Paul.

Hagger, A. (1973) 'Recruiting school mums', *Industrial and Commercial Training*.

Hakim, C. (1978) 'Sexual divisions within the labour force', *Department of Employment Gazette*, London: HMSO.

Harding, J. (1983) *Switched off: the Science Education of Girls*, London: Longman.

Hunt, A. (1968) *A Survey of Women's Employment*, London: Government Social Survey.

Jephcott, P., Seear, N. and Smith, J. (1962) *Married Women Working*, London: Allen & Unwin.

Joshi, H. (1989) 'The changing form of women's economic dependency' in H. Joshi (ed.) *The Changing Population of Britain*, Oxford: Blackwell.

Kelly, A. (ed.) (1981) *The Missing Half: Girls and Science Education*, Manchester: Manchester University Press.

Klein, V. (1965) *Britain's Married Women Workers*, London: Routledge & Kegan Paul.

Lewis, J. (1991) *Women in Britain since 1945*, Oxford: Blackwell.

Mackie, L. and Pattullo, P. (1977) *Women at Work*, London: Tavistock.

Mansfield, P. and Collard, J. (1988) *The Beginning of the Rest of Your Life? A Portrait of Newly-wed Marriage*, London: Macmillan.

Martin, J. and Roberts, C. (1984) *Women and Employment: a Lifetime Perspective*, London: HMSO.

Mitchison, N. (1979) *You May Well Ask: A Memoir 1920–1940*, London: Victor Gollancz.

Myrdal, A. and Klein, V. (1956) *Women's Two Roles: Home and Work*, London: Routledge & Kegan Paul.

Newsom, J. (1948) *The Education of Girls*, London: Faber.

Ni Bhrolchain, M. (1986) 'Women's paid work and the timing of births: longitudinal evidence', *European Journal of Population* 2: 43–7.

North Tyneside CDP (1978) *North Shields: Women's Work*, Newcastle-upon-Tyne: Newcastle-upon-Tyne Polytechnic.

Norwood, C. (1943) *Curriculum and Examination in Secondary Schools: Report of the Committee of the Second School Examinations Council*, London: Board of Education.

Parliamentary Papers (1947) *Economic Survey for 1947*, Cmd 7046, London: HMSO.

Patterson, S. (1965) *Dark Strangers: a Study of West Indians in London*, London: Penguin.

Phizacklea, A. (1988) 'Gender, racism and occupational segregation' in S. Walby (ed.) *Gender Segregation and Work*, Milton Keynes: Open University Press.

Pollert, A. (1981) *Girls, Wives, Factory Lives*, London: Macmillan.

Rex, J. and Tomlinson, S. (1979) *Colonial Immigrants in a British City*, London: Routledge & Kegan Paul.

Richards, M. P. M. and Elliott, B. J. (1991) 'Sex and Marriage in the 1960s and 1970s' in D. Clark (ed.) *Marriage, Domestic Life and Social Change*, London: Routledge.

Routh, G. (1965) *Occupational and Pay in Great Britain 1906–60*, Cambridge: Cambridge University Press.

Royal Commission on Equal Pay (1946) *Report* Cmd 6937, London: HMSO.

Royal Commission on Marriage and Divorce (RCMD) (1956) *Report* Cmd 9678, London: HMSO.

Royal Commission on Population (RCP) (1949) *Report* Cmd 7695, London: HMSO.

Seear, N., Roberts, V. and Brock, J. (1964) *A Career for Women in Industry?*, London: Oliver and Boyd.

Smith, J. H. (1961) 'Managers and married women workers', *British Journal of Sociology* 12: 12-22.

Stacey, M. and Price, M. (1981) *Women, Power and Politics*, London: Tavistock.

Study Commission on the Family (1983) *Families in the Future: Final Report of the Study Commission*, London: Study Commission on the Family.

Summerfield, P. (ed.) (1987) *Women, Education and the Professions*, Leicester: History of Education Society Occasional Publication 8.

—————— (1989) *Women Workers in the Second World War*, London: Routledge.

Thane, P. (1991) 'Towards equal opportunities? Women in Britain since 1945' in T. Gourvish and A. O'Day (eds) *Britain Since 1945* London: Macmillan 1991, pp. 183-208.

Titmuss, R. M. (1958) *Essays on the Welfare State*, London: Unwin.

Weiner, G. (ed.) (1985) *Just a Bunch of Girls: Feminist Approaches to Schooling*, Milton Keynes: Open University Press.

White, C. L. (1970) *Women's Magazines 1693-1968*, London: Michael Joseph.

Willmott, P. and Young, M. (1960) *Family and Class in a London Suburb*, London: Routledge & Kegan Paul.

Wilson, E. (1980) *Only Halfway to Paradise: Women in Postwar Britain: 1945–1968*, London: Tavistock.

Winship, J. (1987) *Inside Women's Magazines*, London: Pandora.

Women's Group on Public Welfare (1962) *The Education and Training of Girls*, London: National Council of Social Service.

Working Party on Marriage Guidance (1979) *Marriage Matters*, London: HMSO.

Young, M. and Willmott, P. (1957) *Family and Kinship in East London*, London: Routledge and Kegan Paul (reprinted Penguin 1962).

Zweig, F. (1952) *Women's Life and Labour*, London: Victor Gollancz.

Chapter 6

Old age and gerontology

Anthea Tinker

The focus of this book is the exploration of key themes in post-war social experience from interdisciplinary perspectives. This interdisciplinary approach is particularly appropriate when considering the position of old people in post-war British society because this is the approach adopted in gerontology, the study of ageing. Gerontology is the scientific study of all aspects of the ageing processes, biological, medical, psychological and social.

The development of gerontology as an academic discipline is in its infancy in the United Kingdom in contrast with the United States of America, where the scale of publications and research is more extensive than anywhere else in the world (Warnes 1989). Two strands of gerontology are developing (Tinker 1990). One focuses on the processes of ageing and here the main fields of specialism are biology and the social sciences. The other is geriatric medicine with its concern for the diagnosis and treatment of physical and mental disorders in elderly people. As I have noted elsewhere, it is obviously important to bring together the psychological, social and cultural studies with biomedical knowledge and clinical application to enable an understanding of the processes and problems of ageing (Tinker 1989). In the main, this chapter draws on the contributions of the social sciences.

THE IMPORTANCE OF AN HISTORICAL APPROACH

Before looking at how the main social science disciplines have illuminated the understanding of the position of old people in post-war Britain, it is worth noting the growing interest in an historical approach. Although a great deal of evidence on elderly people has been amassed from the snapshot approach of surveys, attention has been increasingly turning to the importance of understanding this group in an historical context. Looking back at the lives of people gives meaning to their current position and helps understand why they may act as they do. It is particularly relevant when considering a group of elderly people, most of whom have lived through two world wars and a depression.

A biographical approach when interviewing elderly people is one adopted by some researchers and advocated by even more. One of the first to advocate such an approach was Johnson, who suggested that social gerontologists had relied too much on surveys and similar empirical work (Johnson 1976). Commenting on Johnson's criticisms, Gearing and Dant agree that it is necessary to unravel the complex biographical strands (such as family, upbringing, marriage, work, parenthood, retirement, widowhood and so on) in a person's life to 'better understand the way the individual experiences "old age", and his/her present needs, satisfactions and problems' (Gearing and Dant 1990: 145). A biographical, or life history, approach can be therapeutic for the old person; it may help assess their needs and is a useful research tool to aid an understanding of their lives.

The study of cohorts, a group of individuals born at a similar time who experience the same historical events at about the same time in the life cycle, is generally considered to be a fruitful way of understanding the lives of elderly people. A cohort is often related to a time span of between five and ten years. As Victor points out, 'the central thesis of the cohort explanation of the age related differences in behaviour is that it is these shared experiences which influence the norms, values and attitudes of cohort members' (Victor 1987). She goes on to state that there have been few empirical studies of the effect of events upon the subsequent development of a cohort. However, her own work shows the tendency for older people to evaluate their standards of living in terms of the conditions they experienced as young adults rather than their current standards (Victor 1985).

The work of Abrams is relevant in the context of cohorts and it brings out clearly one of the most important issues that arises – that it is dangerous and misleading to regard elderly people as a homogeneous group (Abrams 1989). He shows striking differences between younger (aged 65–74) elderly people and older ones (aged over 75). Their shared life events will have been different and this may lead to different attitudes and expectations. He shows, for example, from various surveys that the younger group were much less involved in religious activities and beliefs, much less antagonistic to non-white and non-Anglo-Saxon minority groups, to left-wing extremists and unmarried mothers. They were more interested in party politics, less right-wing, less confident in their own political attachments, and less likely to express confidence in the activities and achievements of the Church, the police and Parliament (Abrams 1989: 172–3). The younger group were also much less satisfied with their circumstances than five years previously. Commenting on these findings, Abrams suggests that,

Their early experience may have been less effective in conditioning them to 'adjust through acceptance' and to find satisfaction in their current circumstances. . . . Clearly more of the younger elderly of 1981 than their predecessors had accepted the 'liberation' attitudes adopted by intellectuals during the 1930s and which became commonplace during the third quarter of the century.

(Abrams 1989: 173)

It is interesting that attempts are now being made to formulate other distinctions based on age. The Third Age, for example, has been defined by the Carnegie Inquiry as people aged 50–74. Some, however, have suggested definitions based more on activity patterns. Laslett, one of the first to identify this age, describes the ages thus: 'First comes an era of dependence, socialization, immaturity and education; second comes an era of independence, maturity and responsibility, of earning and of saving; third an era of personal fulfilment, and fourth an era of final dependence' (Laslett 1989: 4). The Carnegie Inquiry, which was set up in 1991, also suggested activity patterns when they described their investigation as being into the issues affecting the life, work and livelihood of those who have finished their main career, bringing up their children, or both, but still have many years of healthy and active life ahead of them.

However, even the current tendency to divide older people into different groups has its limitations. Not only may there be differences between various age groups, but more important, there are wide differences in the health, income and other circumstances of people of the same age.

THE INFLUENCE OF DEMOGRAPHY

One of the most important starting points for understanding elderly people in post-war British society is demography. The rapid growth in the number and proportion of elderly people has affected the provision of services but less, it will be argued later, the influence of elderly people themselves. In many ways it seems that the public have only recently become aware of the growth in numbers and seem to think that the increase will be as dramatic in the future. In effect they are only catching up on the historical position rather late in the day; hence many of the headlines about 'a granny crisis'. The key changes affecting the population of elderly people that have taken place since the end of the Second World War are now outlined using figures from the 1951 Census.

The first major change is in the overall increase in the United Kingdom in numbers of elderly people (defined here as over the age of 65). In 1951 there were 5.5 million elderly people out of a total population of 50.3 million. That represents a percentage of 10.9 per cent. In 1989 the number of elderly people was 9.0 million out of a population of 57.2 million. The percentage had risen to 15.7 per cent. Looking back even further, the percentage of elderly people in 1901 was only 4.7 per cent. Looking further ahead another twenty years, it is projected that numbers of elderly people will then increase by about three-quarters of a million (2011 to 9.7 million) and the percentage will rise by about only just over half a per cent (to 16.2 per cent) (Central Statistical Office (CSO) 1982 and 1991). It can therefore be seen that the biggest change took place between 1901 and 1951. The change in the period we are considering was also substantial but not as great as before. The major effect of this increase in numbers and proportions of elderly people has been a growth in the services, such as pensions, which almost all elderly people now receive.

The second major change has been in the increase in the numbers and percentages of very elderly people. Whereas the number of people over the age of 80 was only 0.7 million in 1951, representing 12.7 per cent of all the over 65s, numbers had increased to 2.1 million in 1989, representing 23 per cent. A further rise to 2.7 million (28 per cent) is projected by 2011. The numbers of people over the age of 80 went up fourfold between 1951 and 1989. The increase in centenarians is even more striking. In 1951 there were only 271 but this number had risen to 2,410 in 1981.

Much of the increase in numbers has been due to rises in the number of births in the early years of the century. However, people are also living longer. Whereas the expectation of life in 1951 was 66.2 for a man and 71.2 for a woman, it had risen to 71.5 for a man in 1985 and 77.4 for a woman (CSO 1982 and 1989). While many of these very old people, however one defines them, will be in good health, some will need a great deal of help with personal and domestic tasks and with health services. Very little is known about other effects on society of this rise in numbers of very elderly people. Has it, for example, altered the image of older people? To assess that, one would need a detailed comparison that included many other intangible factors, such as the change in appearance of old people. Improvements in health and dental care, mass production of clothes, and the widespread use of cosmetics have all contributed to a more attractive image. On the other hand, the increasingly early retirement of this group from paid employment may have led to a decline in their status.

An illustration of the importance of demography to understanding post-war society is to consider briefly the position of older women. Not only are there many more elderly women than men, but one in three women aged 75 and over are widows in Britain (Gibson 1990). Even more significant is the availability of care for them. As Gibson has pointed out,

the mother of 1900 would probably have had some three to four children who would have reached adulthood, and within her progeny there was likely have been at least one daughter. Few doubted the importance of the daughter in caring for her aged or dependent parents

(Gibson 1990: 86–7)

Not only has family size declined in this country, but it cannot be assumed that all couples have children. It is estimated that in 1996–2001 over half of women aged 85 will have only one or no living children (Gibson 1990: 88).

THE DEVELOPMENT OF THE WELFARE STATE IN THE CONTEXT OF SOCIAL POLICY

Historians, but not perhaps all politicians and members of the public, will note that the welfare state was not something which suddenly emerged at the end of the Second World War. The foundations had been laid during the war, particularly by the vision of Beveridge and his 1942 report *Social Insurance and Allied Services* (Beveridge 1942). While the report is mainly remembered as laying down a blueprint for health and social services, the broader aims of full employment were an integral part of the plan. As Thane has noted,

> More than any other wartime blueprint for post-war social reconstruction the Beveridge Report caught the popular imagination and came to symbolise the widespread hopes for a different, more just, world. These hopes were embodied in the term which, although not quite new, came into wide currency after the publication of the report: the 'welfare state'.
>
> (Thane 1982: 253)

It should be noted, incidentally, that Beveridge preferred the term 'social service state'. To quote Thane again:

> the term welfare state expressed for very many people something greater than a simple description of the activities of government in respect of one area of its activities. It expressed the desire for a more socially just, more materially equal, more truly democratic society, in short, everything that pre-war society had not been.
>
> (Thane 1982: 253)

One of the most striking subsequent developments was the widespread adoption of comprehensive services. No longer were the major services, in particular health, provided for different categories of people depending on how much they could pay and from what source. Where a universal service was provided, everyone was entitled to use it. For a generation of people used to highly selective services this was a major change. We know little from research, however, about the effect on people's usage of services. More is known about income support services, where first national assistance and then Social Security systems have been found to be less used by elderly people. Lack of claimants from those entitled to benefits has been shown to be related to the stigma felt by elderly people who had experienced, or heard of, workhouse regimes. The fierce independence of many elderly people who grew up in an era where there were few universal benefits can still be seen in surveys that show not only the reluctance of this group to claim benefits but also their intense pride in ensuring 'a decent funeral'.

It will be interesting to see the effect on different generations of people of a return to more selective social policies to which both the Conservative and Labour Parties seem committed. Are they more acceptable to elderly people who may be more used to them than are younger generations? Although elderly people are likely to gain more than other age groups from some of the selective services, such as home improvement grants, this is principally because they have lower incomes. But for the Conservatives it is not just a move towards more selective policies but an attempt to change the climate of opinion. The Secretary of State for Social Services in 1987 declared:

> Slowly the idea gained ground that the only action that could affect events was Government action; individuals or even groups were power-less to help themselves or adequately support one another. The job therefore has been to change this depressing climate of dependence and revitalise the belief which has been such a powerful force through-out British history; that individuals can take action to change their lives; can do things to control what happens to them.
>
> (Moore 1987)

In the field of social policy it is easy to forget the effect of adequate pensions. Although there is still room for great improvement in the level of pensions for many elderly people, the right to a pension has made them more independent. The development of many new services in the public sector in post-war Britain, such as home helps, meals, physiotherapy, aids and adaptations, have enabled many more elderly people to live indepen-dent lives. Nor should the great advances in housing be forgotten. The building of small houses, bungalows and flats following government advice and subsidy, particularly following the 1969 Circular, *Housing for Old People* (Ministry of Housing and Local Government 1969), was a great improvement for people who moved from clearance areas and from poor housing. Sheltered housing, self-contained accommodation grouped with a warden and communal facilities, developed during the post-war period so that now about 5 per cent of elderly people live in this kind of semi-supported environment.

In order to explain some post-war changes in social policy, it is useful to examine the concept of social need. Social need has been defined as *normative, felt, expressed* and *comparative* (Bradshaw 1972). *Normative* is what the expert or professional defines as need in any given situation. An expert, for example, may lay down a minimum standard of nutrition and if an individual or group falls short of this, they are identified as being in normative need. *Felt* need is equated with want. When assessing need for a service, people are asked whether they feel they need it. *Expressed* need is felt need turned into action. Under this definition, need is seen as those people who demand a service such as by registering on a waiting list. In *comparative* need, a measure of need is found by studying the characteristics of those in receipt of a service. If people with similar characteristics are not in receipt of a service, then they are in need. Looking at these definitions, perceptions of need have changed in all categories. For example, in the case of normative need, professionals now have standards different to those they held in the immediate post-war years; for example, it is now expected that most people will have access to a television. For felt and expressed need, the experience that elderly people have been through is known to affect the way they see their needs. Old people who have suffered the shortages and hardships of world wars perceive their needs very differently from those who have not, as Abrams has demonstrated (Abrams 1989). Research on relative and absolute poverty also shows how perceptions change according to the period under discussion (e.g. Townsend 1979).

ECONOMIC FACTORS

The constraints of this chapter do not allow an extensive examination of the effect of economic factors. But it is relevant to note the growing interest of economists in the circumstances of elderly people, particularly since the 1970s. This has been partly because governments have been concerned about escalating costs. From the government's point of view, interest has focused on the cost of pensions for a growing number and proportion of older people and on costing alternative kinds of care. Before turning to these topics, the debate about dependency should be noted because it is bound up with the economic status of old people.

In discussions about dependency, the need to consider longer-run historical trends has been noted (P. Johnson 1989). Johnson believes that implicit in much of the writing on the social construction of dependency is

the belief that elderly people were in many ways more independent in a pre-welfare state. Townsend, for example, has written that 'such "structured" dependency is a consequence of twentieth-century thought and action'. Historians such as Richard Smith and David Thomson, however, have shown how enduring and old fashioned are many twentieth-century patterns of thought and action – such as retirement from the workforce in old age, and the provision of financial and other services for elderly people by the community rather than by kin.

(Johnson 1989: 63)

Johnson concludes that it is highly contestable whether structured dependency has increased in twentieth-century Britain. He maintains that in terms of both their ownership of assets and income they are less dependent on the vagaries of either the labour market or the goodwill of kin (ibid: 71).

Another related aspect of the effect of economics on old people is illustrated by changing attitudes to them and to the labour market. Valued and sought-after by employers during the Second World War and immediately afterwards during labour shortages, they then tended to be ignored. In the late 1980s and early 1990s, with shortages of labour caused by a lack of young people, the services of elderly people are once more in demand, although this was balanced by the recession of the early 1990s.

Concern about the cost of pensions has grown in recent years. In Great Britain expenditure on retirement pensions rose from £5,662 millions in 1976–7 to an estimated out-turn in 1988–9 of £19,237 millions (CSO 1991: 87). However, the gross national product increased much more sharply during this period. At least part of this is accounted for by the rise in the number of pensioners, and pressure will grow in the first quarter of the next century for the same reason. Of all social security benefits, retirement pensions are by far the largest, accounting for 40 per cent of total expenditure.

Concern about costings of forms of housing and care stem largely from the knowledge that all forms of institutional care are high and likely to rise even more. Hence the attempts to cost places for elderly people in alternatives. The conclusions from research about the high cost of all kinds of institutional care have fitted in well from the elderly person's point of view with their general dislike of this form of care. It is fortunate that the work of economists reaches similar conclusions to findings of research on elderly people, who almost always wish to stay in their own homes. Some research shows that the older they become, the more pronounced becomes this desire (Salvage 1986). Recent work on innovatory schemes to enable elderly people to remain at home with help from professionals, neighbours and family through intensive domiciliary care and alarms means that a fair degree of independence is possible, even for very frail elderly people (Tinker 1984; Challis and Davies 1986).

Other important economic factors relate to the uneven spread of services. As elderly people have migrated to seaside and other areas often referred to as 'Costa Geriatrica', services have not always kept pace.

It is important not to consider economic matters solely in terms of services and of elderly people being a 'burden' on society. For a growing proportion who received both a state and an employment-related pension, standards of living have increased. The growing proportion of elderly people who are now home-owners also means that they have access to wealth as never before. None of this is, of course, to underestimate problems of poverty, especially among the very old and among women.

POLITICAL INSIGHTS

The Royal Commission on Population, which was set up in 1944, forecast the growth in numbers of elderly people in the population and said:

> the strength of the pensioners as a potential pressure group, already very considerable, may be expected to grow. Considerable political courage may therefore be needed to resist pressure for higher rates of benefits. It is most important that Ministers, Members of Parliament, and public opinion at large should appreciate these implications.
>
> (quoted in Abrams and O'Brien 1981)

This potential political strength has not been realised. Among possible explanations are differences between elderly people, dislike of being labelled old, and an awareness of lack of power. It could also be argued that there are few issues over which there would be agreement amongst the elderly, with pensions being the obvious exception. It is also interesting that elderly people have been almost totally ignored by the political parties.

In contrast to the comparatively weak position of elderly people in the UK is that of the United States with, for example, the grey panther movement and the American Association of Retired Persons. In the United States elderly people are becoming increasingly involved in lobbying and advocacy and Oriel has speculated about the effect that this growing citizen participation will have on programmes (Oriel 1981). The growing number and self-awareness of Third Agers may also have an effect.

SOCIOLOGICAL PERSPECTIVES

The interest of sociologists in elderly people is longstanding. In particular, work carried out on families in the post-war period has contributed greatly to a knowledge of how elderly people fit into modern society and their role in it. Studies in the 1950s, for example, by Townsend and colleagues, showed the strong links between family members, the way nuclear families form part of a wider pattern of social relationships, and the extent of care given by younger families to their elderly relatives. These sociological studies have since been validated by numerous social surveys which have shown how family care surpasses all kinds of state help (e.g. Hunt 1978). Sociologists also helped to develop theories of reciprocity, which showed that relationships between family members were rarely one-sided.

Changes in the family in post-war Britain are having profound effects on the lives of elderly people. Halsey, discussing social trends since the Second World War, notes major changes in the family (Halsey 1987). These include:

- more women, especially married women, in employment;
- less childbirth, but more illegitimate childbirth;

- more divorce and remarriage and more one-person households;
- more men economically inactive whether as unemployed, retired or drawn into the domestic economy;
- a population with higher formal qualifications.

All these changes will affect both the current and future lives of old people. Halsey discusses the hypothesis that there is a widening gap between different parts of the population. He says:

> A hundred years ago discussion of Disraeli's two nations' was the stock-in-trade of political arithmeticians. In the 1980s most social observers in Britain agreed that the Marxist polarisation thesis of the 1840s, with its prophecy of mass pauperisation, of exploited labour and the accumulation of surplus value into fewer and fewer capitalists hands, had been tested and found wanting in the natural laboratory of Victorian history. By and large the social trends ran in the opposite direction and, however slowly and haltingly, continued to do so through the first three quarters of the twentieth century. But now the question is raised as to whether a new version of the two nations has appeared in the last decade in the form of a widening division between a prosperous majority in secure and increasingly well remunerated employment by contrast with a depressed minority of the unemployed, the sick, the old, and the unsuccessful ethnic minorities.
>
> (Halsey 1987: 17)

He concludes that on the evidence of the distribution of wealth and income, social divisions and spatial polarisation there is evidence of a

> more unequal society as between a majority in secure attachment to a still prosperous country and a minority in marginal economic and social conditions, the former moving into the suburban locations of the newer economy of a 'green and pleasant land', the latter tending to be trapped into the old provincial industrial cities and their displaced fragments of peripheral council housing estates.
>
> (Halsey 1987: 14)

THE CONTRIBUTION OF PSYCHOLOGY

Psychologists have added a great deal in recent years to enable us to understand the role, expectations and images of elderly people. It is often these perspectives which illuminate our understanding of groups more than do hard statistical data. An understanding of changes in behaviour, learning, memory, personality, adjustment and achievements of older people have made a major contribution to the growth of knowledge about this group. Findings have suggested that: (a) there is a peak for most kinds of scientific achievement in the early thirties; (b) that in philosophy, music, arts and literature there is a more variable pattern; and (c) that achievements in leadership tend to occur in later life – often peaking in the fifties or even later. This is a powerful discovery when considering the role of older people in society (Cunningham and Brookbank 1988).

It is also being realised that images can have a powerful effect on how elderly people are seen. For example, it has been argued that the image presented by research during the period 1945–65 was

> of a growing sector of the population, able to remain active in the community after withdrawal from full-time paid labour, but only with the assistance of that community. Moreover the need for assistance increased with age. The need to channel economic and social resources to the elderly population thus helped to present its image as a 'burden' on the community.
>
> (Harper and Thane 1989: 46)

CONCLUSIONS

In this chapter it has been shown that it is necessary to bring together the contribution of many different disciplines when trying to understand the lives of old people in post-war Britain. No one discipline will give a complete picture but illumination from those described here can give a rich tapestry that history alone cannot provide.

REFERENCES

Abrams, M. and O'Brien, J. (1981) *Political Attitudes and Ageing in Britain*: London: Age Concern.

Abrams, M. (1989) ' "Third Age" lives in the next generation: changing attitudes and expectations', in A. M. Warnes (ed.) *Human Ageing and Later Life*, Sevenoaks: Edward Arnold.

Beveridge, Sir W. (1942) *Social Insurance and Allied Services*: London, HMSO.

Bond, J. and Coleman, P. (1990) (eds) *Ageing in Society: an Introduction to Social Gerontology*, London: Sage.

Bradshaw, J. and Bryant, R. (1972) *Welfare Rights and Social Action: the York Experiment*, London: Child Poverty Action Group.

Bury, M. and Macnicol, J. (1990) (eds) *Aspects of Ageing*, Egham: Royal Holloway and Bedford New College.

Butler, A. (1985) (ed.), *Ageing: Recent Advances and Creative Responses*, London: Croom Helm.

Central Statistical Office (1982) *Social Trends* 12, London: HMSO.

—— (1989) *Social Trends* 19, London: HMSO.

—— (1991) *Social Trends* 21, London: HMSO.

Challis, D. and Davies, B. (1986) *Case Management in Community Care*, Aldershot: Gower.

Cunningham, W. and Brookbank, J. (1988) *Gerontology: the Psychology, Biology and Sociology of Ageing*, New York: Harper and Row.

Gearing, B. and Dant, T. (1990) 'Doing biographical research', in S. Peace (ed.) *Researching Social Gerontology*, London: Sage, pp. 143–59.

Gibson, C. (1990) 'Widowhood: patterns, problems and choices' in M. Bury and J. Macnicol (eds) *Aspects of Ageing*, Egham: Royal Holloway and Bedford New College, pp. 82–103.

Halsey, A. (1987) 'Social trends since the World War II', *Social Trends* 17, Central Statistical Office, London: HMSO, pp. 11–19.

Harper, S. and Thane, P. (1989) 'The consolidation of "Old Age" as a phase of life, 1945–65', in M. Jefferys (ed.) *Growing Old in the Twentieth Century*, London: Routledge, pp. 43–61.

Hobman, D. (1981) (ed.) *The Impact of Ageing*, London: Croom Helm.

Hunt, A. (1978) *The Elderly at Home*, London: HMSO.

Jefferys, M. (1989) (ed.), *Growing Old in the Twentieth Century*, London: Routledge.

Johnson, M. (1976) 'That was your life: a biographical approach to later life'; in J. Munichs and W. van den Heuval (eds) *Dependency and Interdependency in Old Age*, The Hague: Nijhoff.

—— (1990) 'Dependency and interdependency', in J. Bond and P. Coleman (eds) *Ageing in Society: An Introduction to Social Gerontology*, London: Sage, pp. 209–28.

Johnson, P. (1989) 'The structured dependency of the elderly: a critical note', in M. Jefferys (ed.) *Growing Old in the Twentieth Century*, London: Routledge, pp. 62–72.

Laslett, P. (1989) *A Fresh Map of Life: Emergence of the Third Age*: London: Weidenfeld & Nicolson.

Ministry of Housing and Local Government (1969) *Housing for Old People*, Circular 82/69, London: HMSO.

Moore, J. (1987) Speech of the Secretary of State for Social Services on the future of the welfare state, 26 September.

Munichs, J. and van den Heuval, W. (1976) *Dependency and Interdependency in Old Age*, The Hague: Nijhoff.

Oriel, W. (1981) 'Ageing as a political force', in D. Hobman (ed.) *The Impact of Ageing*, London: Croom Helm, pp. 33–52.

Peace, S. (1990) (ed.), *Researching Social Gerontology*, London: Sage.

Salvage, A. (1986) *Attitudes of the Over 75s to Health and Social Services*, Cardiff, Final Report, Research Team for the Care of the Elderly.

Thane, P. (1982) *The Foundation of the Welfare State*, Harlow: Longman.

Tinker, A. (1984) *Staying at Home: Helping Elderly People*, London: HMSO.

—— (1990) 'Why the Sudden Interest in Ageing?'. Inaugural lecture, London, Kings College.

Townsend, P. (1979) *Poverty in the United Kingdom*, Harmondsworth: Penguin.

Victor, C. (1985) 'Welfare benefits and the elderly' in A. Butler (ed.) *Ageing: Recent Advances and Creative Responses*, London: Croom Helm, pp. 160–77.

—— (1987) *Old Age in Modern Society*, London: Croom Helm.

Warnes, A. M. (1989) (ed.) *Human Ageing and Later Life*, Sevenoaks: Edward Arnold.

Chapter 7

Employment and industrial structure

Christopher M. Law

The opportunity to work and the kind of job one has are the most important determinants of the life-style of a person and their family. Employment provides not only income but also status in society, self-esteem, the possibility of personal achievement, and the opportunity for social contact. An individual's prospect for employment is shaped by personal factors such as education, training, skills, determination, contacts and perhaps luck. However, the wider economic environment is also very important. If there are not enough jobs in the economy for all those who want to work, then some will be unemployed. If some of these jobs are only part time and/ or seasonal, then some people may be forced to accept less work and thus less income than they would like. They may, in fact, be forced to take more than one job in order to achieve an adequate income on which to live. The shape of the economy will also determine the type of opportunities that are available for work, including whether a person works for himself or herself, or for a firm; which industries are important; and the mix of occupations within these industries. Finally, where one lives is important, since all these factors just mentioned vary from place to place. The opportunities for work may be very different for a young person in Guildford than for one in Middlesbrough.

This chapter will examine these opportunities for employment in terms of the wider economic setting. Economies are dynamic and the structure of employment in Britain has changed significantly since the end of the Second World War. Current trends are likely to continue into the future as well as new trends appearing. This chapter provides a broad perspective on these changes.

THE GROWTH OF EMPLOYMENT

The number of jobs in a country like Britain is a function of the demand arising from the economy. If economic activity expands, then we should expect the number of jobs to grow, and vice versa if the economy contracts. However, the relationship between economic growth and employment is not a simple one, since rising productivity means that fewer workers are required to produce the same results. These efficiency gains vary between industries as we shall see later.

Since the last war the number of jobs in the United Kingdom has increased from about 22 million to 26 million in 1990. This reflects steady, if relatively slow, economic growth compared with many other advanced countries in this period. There has also been a growth of population with consequent demands for more goods and services.

The growth of employment has not been a continuous process and in this respect it mirrors the cyclical pattern of economic expansion. Several years of increase may be followed by contraction, as during a recession firms either lay off workers or allow the workforce to decline through natural wastage. In the 1970s, employment grew to reach 25.4 million in 1979, but during the deep recession of the early 1980s it fell to 23.6 million in 1983. Subsequently it expanded again to reach 26.9 million in 1990 but then decreased to 24.9 million in 1993. Obviously it is going to be much easier to find a job during a period of growth than in a recession when firms are shedding rather than taking on workers.

Governments would clearly like to have continuous economic growth and therefore continuous employment expansion, but world economic trends, balance of payment difficulties, and the need to balance budgets may cause them to change monetary policies such as altering interest rates and raising taxes, which curtail growth and reduce employment opportunities.

MALE AND FEMALE JOBS

The composition of employment between men and women has changed significantly in the post-war period. After the war, over two-thirds of the labour force was male and less than a third was female. In practice, the number of men employed has remained between 14 and 15 million while the number of women employed has increased from about 8 million in 1950 to about 11 million in 1990.

On the supply side, many more women want to work than in the past. In the early post-war period there was still a strong social convention that stressed that the primary role of a married woman was to stay at home and look after her family. Today it is more accepted that women can work and have a career if they wish; indeed, feminist ideology emphasises the virtue of women being economically independent. Also, with rising aspirations for material goods and pleasure, many women want to work to increase the family's income.

On the demand side, the distinction between men and women's work has been greatly reduced. This is partly because many heavy manual jobs either have been transformed through mechanisation, or the industries in which they are found have declined in importance. At the same time, many jobs requiring no manual strength have been created. These include clerical jobs and many part-time jobs (see p. 89).

As social attitudes and family patterns continue to change, it is likely that these trends in employment will do likewise, with women forming half the labour force by the end of the century.

UNEMPLOYMENT

There is a difference between the number employed and the size of the labour force, which is represented by the unemployed, whether recorded or concealed. In an ideal world, labour supply and demand would be equal and everyone who wished would have the opportunity to work. In practice there will always be some people unemployed either because they are changing jobs or because, if they are young people, they have not found one yet. A further group of people with disabilities have a high propensity to unemployment. For many years after the last war, one of the principal objectives of government economic policy was to keep unemployment low, but this was replaced in the 1970s and 1980s by the objective of reducing inflation (see Figure 7.1).

The most obvious measure of unemployment is the monthly figure published by the Department of Employment. However, the way these statistics have been collected and recorded has been changed many times so that it is not strictly valid to compare them over different periods. In practice, the government's figure largely excludes those people who are not eligible for unemployment benefit, so that it has never been a comprehensive account of those who are looking for work. Married women have generally been excluded from benefit and in recent years many other groups have been removed, including those on work training schemes. For what these figures are worth, they show that unemployment was at a record low in 1955 when 264,000 were recorded as out of work, equal to 1.1 per cent of the working population. During recessions we should expect unemployment to rise but fall back in the subsequent recovery. In the early 1980s the level of unemployment rose to 3 million by 1985, equal to 13.5 per cent of the labour force. By the 1990s, after several further changes in the definition of the unemployed, the level after falling had begun rising again as recession began to bite. Since the early 1980s not only has the rate of unemployment increased, but the number of long-term unemployed has also greatly risen.

The Census of Population also records the number of people out of work and this figure is more reliable since it is not linked to administrative procedures for distributing benefit. However, this statistic is only available every ten years when the census is held.

Another way of indicating the level of unemployment is through the use

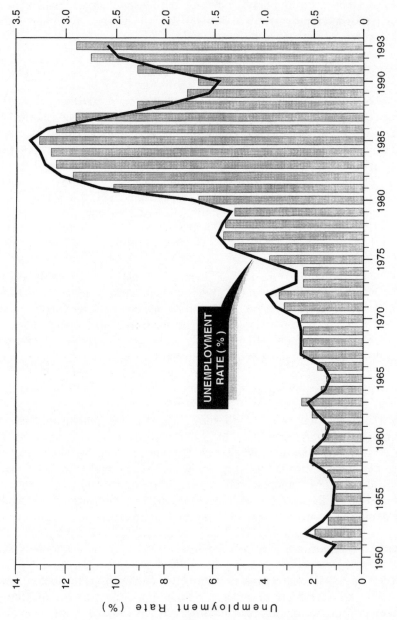

Figure 7.1 Unemployment rate (%) 1950–93

of activity or participation rates. These figures show the proportion of people working; when low, they would suggest 'hidden unemployment'. Male activity rates have fallen as more men have either become students in their youth and delayed entry into work, or have taken retirement earlier than would have been the case in the past. For women, there has been a significant increase in activity rates, which explains the growth of women workers discussed in the last section. This increase in activity rates has mainly affected married and older women who are returning to work after their children have passed infancy.

FULL-TIME AND PART-TIME WORK

Many people wish and expect to work full time. Only in this way will they be able to earn sufficient income to have the life-style they desire. However, others may welcome part-time work. Married women can combine domestic duties with earning money. Students can supplement their grants while studying. People in their sixties can ease the transition from full-time work to complete retirement. There are many other reasons why part-time work may be preferred, even if only for a short period of a person's life.

There has always been some part-time work, particularly in catering, retailing and tourism. In other sectors many employers, partly for bureaucratic reasons, preferred full-time units and felt, probably falsely, that part-timers were less committed and less knowledgeable about the job. However, in recent years these attitudes have changed. Firms pay less national insurance for part-timers, have fewer obligations for sickness and pensions, and are less likely to have to give increments. There are thus significant financial advantages in substituting part-timers for full-timers. In addition, many firms have an uneven flow of work and therefore it is sensible to employ workers only when they are needed. In retailing, most of the business in on Friday and Saturday, so that sales staff can be employed mainly for this period. Most part-time jobs are in the service sector rather than in manufacturing. Occasionally employers are forced to take on part-timers because they cannot find enough full-time workers.

For both supply and demand reasons then, the amount of part-time work has increased considerably in recent years. By 1989, nearly 25 per cent of the workforce was employed part time, but of these 80 per cent were women. A significant part of the growth of female employment discussed earlier has been through part-time work, and 45 per cent of all female jobs are part time. In fact, much of this increase in female employment has been of married women returning to work on a part-time basis after their children have grown up, on a scale not seen before. In contrast, only 9 per cent of male jobs were part time, but interestingly there was a 100 per cent increase during the 1980s.

SELF-EMPLOYED AND EMPLOYEES

Another aspect of employment is the division between the self-employed and employees. The self-employed work for themselves and usually run small businesses, anything from farming, building repairs and guest houses to shops. Employees work for other people, often in large organisations such as major manufacturing companies or public authorities.

Many people value the opportunity to work for themselves. It means being your own boss, not being pushed around by others, and able to achieve your own objectives. But it can be precarious with no higher body to fall back upon when things get difficult. For much of the twentieth century, it appeared that 'one-man' or family businesses were being squeezed out by the large organisations which gained economies of scale. It was impossible to think of one man making cars or running an oil refinery. Even in the service sector, the family-run corner shop has been pushed out by the large supermarket chain. But technological change has not all been one way and the recent fall in price of many electronic devices, such as computers, has brought these machines within reach of the small firm. In addition, the political ideology of the 1980s in Britain stressed the importance of enterprise and the role of the entrepreneur.

The statistics for the self-employed show that in the 1960s and 1970s there were about 1.75 to 2 million in this category or about 7 to 8 per cent of the workforce. During the 1980s the number increased to 3 million or 12.3 per cent of the workforce, equivalent to one out of every eight persons. Naturally the government saw this as a vindication of their policies, but critics interpreted these figures differently. For many companies, like milk delivery firms, there was a financial advantage in terms of tax and benefit obligations in turning employees into self-employed. On this basis it is too early to conclude from the evidence that there has been a genuine explosion of the self-employed.

THE INDUSTRIAL STRUCTURE

A job can be classified in at least two important ways, by industry and occupation. In an industrial classification a shorthand typist working in the steel works would be classified to the steel industry, whilst in an occupational system they would be classified as a clerical worker. In this section we concentrate on the industrial classification.

It is convenient to begin by examining the broad structure of industry before looking at the detail. Activities are often divided between primary, concerned with producing materials including food; secondary, in which materials are processed or manufactured; and tertiary, concerned with the provision of services. In the post-war period there has been an absolute and relative decline of the primary and secondary sectors and a growth of the

Table 7.1 The industrial structure of the United Kingdom

	1951	1971	1991
Employment (000s)			
Agriculture, Forestry and Fishing	1,225	680	556
Industry*	9,466	9,071	5,401
Construction	1,429	1,728	1,647
Services	10,560	12,636	17,820
Total	22,680	24,115	25,424
Share (%)			
Agriculture, Forestry and Fishing	5.4	2.8	2.2
Industry*	41.7	37.7	21.2
Construction	6.3	7.1	6.5
Services	46.6	52.4	70.1
Total	100.0	100.0	100.0

Note:
* Industry includes Mining and Quarrying and Public Utilities
Sources: 1951 and 1971 Census of Population; 1991 Census of Employment plus estimates for self employed, HM Forces and work related government training programmes.

tertiary sector (Table 7.1). These shifts reflect several factors. First, there have been much greater opportunities for mechanisation and automation and consequential reduction of labour in the primary and secondary sectors than in the tertiary sector. Many services are very labour intensive and it is difficult to conceive of replacing, say, a receptionist or a teacher with a machine. Within the manufacturing sector some jobs have been lost as the result of 'flexibility', with workers being trained to be multi-skilled. Second, there has been a shift of expenditure towards the services which may reflect higher living standards and expectations. With more money, people may choose to spend an increasing amount on services, for instance, eating out at a restaurant. At the same time the government has been spending more on services, particularly in areas like health, where there has been an increase in employment. Third, in recent years some activities have been transferred from one sector to another, creating a statistical illusion that there has been a shift. In the past many manufacturing firms had their own transport and catering sections, but now these have been contracted out to separate firms and the work appears within the service sector. These shifts in industrial structure mean that fewer people work on the farm, down the mine, or in the factory, and are more likely to be found within an office. Because of the shift away from mining and manufacturing the present time is often described as post-industrial, or alternatively there is said to have been a 'tertiarisation' of the economy.

Within these broad headings it is possible to see that there are

Table 7.2 Employment in industry in the United Kingdom (000s)

	1951	1971	1991
Coal mining	766	340	80
Other mining	77	53	68
Public utilities	364	370	270
Coal and petroleum products	40	59	15
Chemicals	411	513	315
Metal manufacture	571	551	166
Mechanical engineering	909	1,085	684
Electrical engineering	559	858	504
Instruments	88	132	90
Office equipment	35	52	72
Motor vehicles/aircraft	590	751	
Railway engineering	152	47	453 ⎫
Shipbuilding	299	190	⎬
Other metal goods	531	590	280
Textiles	1,024	581	181
Clothing and leather	828	561	257
Food, drink and tobacco	765	755	543
Non-metallic mineral manu.	343	310	174
Wood and furniture	331	307	214
Paper and printing	521	619	465
Other manufacture	266	333	279
Total	9,466	9,071	5,111

Source: 1951 and 1971 Census of population; 1991 Census of Employment, employees only

considerable differences between the performance of industries. In terms of employment some have been in long-term decline, and these include agriculture, coal mining, shipbuilding, railway engineering, textiles, clothing, railways and ports (Tables 7.2 and 7.3). Some industries within this group have seen output rise but because of increasing productivity, employment has fallen. Others have seen both output and employment fall. The latter include industries such as textiles and clothing, where, because of labour costs, production has shifted to developing countries where labour is cheap. Other industries have declined in Britain because our competitors like Germany and Japan are more efficient. Many industries such as mechanical engineering grew in output and employment in the early post-war period, but have subsequently experienced some decline; partly from increasing productivity and partly from overseas competition. All the advanced countries have been losing some manufacturing to developing countries in what is called the 'new international division of labour'. Previously these countries were mainly concerned with sending primary products to Western countries. Within manufacturing, attention is often directed at the newer industries where growth

Table 7.3 Service employment in the United Kingdom (000s)

	1951	1971	1991
Wholesaling	3,040	{ 807	952
Retailing		{2,284	2,365
Transport	1,398	1,164	1,345
Finance/business	*	1,455	2,652
Education	530	1,403	1,794
Medical	647	1,016	1,561
Central government+	1,126	840	1,869}
Local government	610	772	
Hotels and catering	890	700	1,221
Other services	*	*	1,937
Total	10,560	12,638	15,695

Notes:
* No comparable figures available
+ includes Defence
Sources: 1951 and 1971 Census of Population; 1991 Census of Employment, employees only.

might be expected. These include the high-technological industries such as chemicals and electronics, which involve a great deal of research and development. New products are constantly being developed and these will provide jobs in the future. In contrast, older industries supply markets where there is little growth and they also experience productivity improvements so that employment is falling. Over time we can see that the industrial structure as revealed by employment patterns is constantly changing, with older industries becoming relatively less important and new industries growing to take their place.

Within the service sector outside transport there has been a widespread growth of employment, but the rates of increase have varied over the period. Most public services grew rapidly until the mid-1970s. Since then their performance has varied with some showing declines in recent years. The Conservative government under Mrs Thatcher attempted (unsuccessfully) to reduce the size of the public sector. Local government was hit hard in the late 1980s, but the health service was protected. Some parts of the public sector, such as defence, have been clearly affected by world events, and are suffering large job losses in the 1990s. In recent years finance and business services have been the fastest-growing industries, but the 1990–2 recession has stopped this, at least temporarily. Other activities that have experienced employment growth in recent years are related to the tourism and leisure industries and include hotels and restaurants. These general trends, which favour the service sector for employment growth, are likely to continue in the 1990s and beyond.

THE OCCUPATIONAL AND SOCIO-ECONOMIC STRUCTURE

There are various ways of classifying a person's job other than by industry. One distinction is between blue collar and white collar or manual and non-manual. Another way is according to the skill level, and yet another way is according to responsibility. Whichever way is used, it is always difficult to agree as to how all jobs should be classified, and how to compare them over time. However, there is general agreement on the broad changes.

Firstly, the number of manual jobs is decreasing, since either the industries where these were important are declining, or where the industries remain important, the jobs are being mechanised. More and more jobs are becoming non-manual and white collar. Secondly, the range of skills required by industry is increasing and the share of the highly skilled workers is rising. However, because of mechanisation and automation, some manual workers are being deskilled. This has led to the suggestion that there is an increasing polarisation of the labour force between the highly skilled and the low or unskilled. Because of the gap between these two groups it becomes impossible for many people to move upwards within their place of work or firm. In other words, it is becoming less easy for the tea boy to move up through the organisation to become managing director in most firms.

If we take these ideas and those of the early sections of this chapter, we can see how employment opportunities divide the population, perhaps into many different classes or perhaps into only two. The dual labour market hypothesis suggests that the population can be divided into two groups. At the bottom is a group of people who are either unemployed or who have a high propensity to be unemployed at some time. They have low skills and thus, when working, low incomes. They are more likely to be employed part time and/or have few rights for benefits with regard to sickness, holidays or pensions. The second group contains more skilled workers, usually working full time for large organisations with good rights to benefits. Whilst this model is probably too simple, it does point to certain trends in society and why perhaps an underclass is developing, both here in Britain and in the United States.

These ideas can be extended by consideration of households. With more married women working, there has been a great increase in dual income households and, as a consequence, average household income has increased. This is one reason, along with others such as the general increase in the standard of living, why more households have been able to buy their own home. However, the increase in dual income households may result in greater inequality if the dual labour market hypothesis is accepted. There will be a great difference between the household with two high-skilled and high-income earners with secure jobs than the one with two workers but with low incomes, insecurity and perhaps part-time characteristics.

GEOGRAPHICAL PATTERNS

The spatial pattern of employment changes in post-war Britain can be classified in two ways. First, on a north–south dichotomy with employment north of the Severn–Humber line either declining or growing more slowly than in the south. Second, in terms of an urban–rural shift with jobs declining in cities, particularly the inner city, and growing in less urbanised areas, and at an increasing distance from cities as the post-war period has progressed.

For much of the twentieth century the key factor in explaining the spatial patterns of employment change and unemployment was the industrial structure of areas. In the north and west of the country, industries such as coal mining, shipbuilding and textiles were declining, but few new industries were developing. In contrast, in London, and to a lesser extent in Birmingham and the Midlands, the new engineering industries including vehicles and chemicals were developing. There are several reasons for this pattern of new industries, many of which involve the role of London as the administrative and commercial capital of the country. Some of the former growth industries, such as vehicles, have now gone into decline, causing problems for areas like the West Midlands. The growth of service industries has also been concentrated on London, again reflecting the commercial role of the city. Increasingly, major companies have come to have their head office either in London or nearby, and this has resulted in ancillary business services clustering in this area as well. London also performs a role as a world financial capital, with resulting job increases in the area. Since 1934, governments have been attempting to shift employment northwards away from the south east and the Midlands through regional policy, but although hundreds of thousands of jobs have been moved, the division between the north and the south has not been eradicated. Perhaps this was because the policy was focused on manufacturing industry and ignored the service sector where most employment growth was taking place. For a brief period between 1967 and 1976 the Selective Employment Tax discriminated in favour of manufacturing employment in the assisted areas and against all other employment elsewhere. In fact, this policy only re-emphasised the old difference between an industrial north and service-based south, but this time with the added dimension that northern branch factories were controlled by head offices in the south.

The urban–rural shift is a product of several factors. During the early post-war period, public utilities were improved in the more rural parts of the country, reducing the longstanding differences in the standards of

Table 7.4 Regional shares of employment (%)

	1951	1971	1991
South East	30.9	32.0	32.6
(including London	18.9	15.2	14.7 ⎫
(ROSE*	12.0	17.4	17.9 ⎭
East Anglia	2.5	2.8	3.6
South West	6.2	6.6	7.8
West Midlands	9.4	9.7	9.2
East Midlands	6.9	7.2	6.9
Yorkshire and Humberside	8.3	7.8	8.4
North West	13.3	12.2	10.7
North	5.8	5.6	5.0
Wales	4.6	4.4	4.3
Scotland	9.7	8.9	9.1
Northern Ireland	2.5	2.3	2.4
Total	100.0	100.0	100.0

Notes
* ROSE = Rest of South East England
Because of regional boundary changes, figures may not be comparable between 1971 and 1989. This particularly affects Yorkshire and Humberside and the East Midlands.
Sources: 1951 and 1971 Census of Population (and Law, 1980); 1991 Census of Employment, employees only

provision in these areas compared to the towns. From the 1960s onwards, motorways and upgraded trunk roads improved the accessibility of many areas previously considered remote. At the same time television, not to mention mains sewers, enabled people to live in these areas without feeling cut off from civilisation. Meanwhile, many people were finding that the quality of life in large cities was poor in contrast to the perceived high-quality environment of rural areas. These factors all helped to shift jobs to small towns as manufacturing and commercial firms decentralised from large cities. In the case of London, the major source of employment movement, it was like a ripple effect. In the 1920s, firms were moving 20 miles from the city, in the 1950s 30 miles, in the 1960s 50 miles, and by the 1980s 100 miles.

At the same time as this process was occurring, deindustrialisation was affecting the inner cities. Some closures were in industries that were declining, while other firms wished to concentrate production on sites with newer factories, more space for parking, and better access to motorways. The closure of docks, railway goods yards and gas works also played a part in the loss of jobs and the increase in derelict land. Inner-city decline affected all the major cities including London, but the impact was greater elsewhere as there were fewer new activities developing.

Table 7.4 summarises these trends in terms of the share of employment by region. In the case of London there has been a major decrease in manufacturing jobs, but this has largely been compensated for by an increase in service jobs. In the area outside London within a radius of 100 miles, sometimes referred to as the 'Greater South East' and including parts of East Anglia and south west England, there has been a major growth of employment in both manufacturing and services, initially caused by firms decentralising from London, but now having a momentum of its own. In the Midlands the prosperity of the first twenty-five years after the war has given way to some decline as engineering industries have suffered from worldwide competition. In the rest of Britain, old industries have declined and the new industries introduced through regional policy have not been sufficient to compensate for the loss of jobs, with consequent high levels of unemployment. Exceptions to this generalisation include attractive rural areas, such as north Yorkshire, which have received in-migrants, and north east Scotland, which has benefited from North Sea oil. However, some major cities such as Glasgow and Liverpool have experienced severe economic problems. One consequence of the in-migration of firms to northern Britain is that female activity rates have risen.

The opportunities for work thus vary considerably across Britain. A young person growing up in the area around London will have opportunities to work in high-tech firms and in the administrative offices of large service firms. They will find that while at school or attending higher education there are opportunities to work part time during term time and full time during the vacation. Likewise, married women will find more opportunities for part-time work, and for all people there will be more opportunities to establish a small business. In contrast, the young person in Teesside or Sunderland will find that the prospects of unemployment are high, and that when opportunities are available they are likely to be in the branch plants of manufacturing firms, which require low-skilled workers and offer low pay. For all, the opportunities for part-time work will be much less than in the south, as will the chances of success in establishing a new firm.

CONCLUSION

The post-war period has witnessed a dramatic change in the structure of employment. The coming of the post-industrial society has seen the demise or reduction of many of the old staple industries and their replacement either by light industries or work in the service sector. These changes are epitomised when old smokestack factories are pulled down and replaced by a business park including offices.

The pattern of work has been changing. A key word today is flexibility, which means that there is no monolithic pattern but rather a great variety or work practices. There is more part-time work, more seasonal or occasional work, more shift work, more multi-skilling on the factory floor, and less stereotyping of jobs between men and women.

There have been changes in the opportunities to work. Overall the number of jobs has not grown sufficiently, so that unemployment has risen. However, the opportunities for women appear to have grown since most of the increase in jobs is accounted for by them. Not unexpectedly, it is the unskilled who have suffered and wherever they are concentrated, as in the inner city and on peripheral council estates, unemployment is high. Superimposed on this is the north–south division, so that when similar areas are compared, conditions are always worse in the north.

REFERENCES

Champion, A. G. and Townsend, A. (1990) *Contemporary Britain: A Geographical Perspective*, London: Edward Arnold.

Dicken, P. and Lloyd, P. E. (1981) *Modern Western Society*, London: Harper & Row.

Law, C. M. (1980) *British Regional Development since World War I*, Newton Abbot: David & Charles.

Chapter 8

Non-manual labour

Rosemary Crompton[1]

INTRODUCTION

The expansion of non-manual employment has been one of the most important changes in the British occupational structure since the war. Census data show that in 1951, 36 per cent of the occupied population were classified as employers or non-manual workers, and 64 per cent as manual workers. By 1981, 52 per cent were classified as employers or non-manual workers, and only 48 per cent as manual workers. Recession and 'shake-out' have served further to speed these processes, as employment in manufacturing (where manual employment is concentrated) has declined, and employment in the service sector has risen.[2] The expansion of non-manual work has also been closely associated with the other major change in the structure of the labour force in Britain, the increasing employment of women (31 per cent of the labour force in 1951, 39 per cent by 1981). The proportion of women in non-manual employment has remained fairly stable since the Second World War and in 1981 women were 43 per cent of non-manual workers, 24 per cent of employers and proprietors, and 29 per cent of manual workers (all figures from Price and Bain 1988).

The growth of non-manual employment has had significant implications for many aspects of post-war British society. In this chapter the major topic that will be addressed is the import of these changes in the employment structure for a number of debates relating to social class. Two major areas will be discussed: first, the erosion of the historico-sociological convention whereby the manual/non-manual distinction was regarded as a significant *class* boundary, and second, the impact of the employment of women. In the concluding discussion, the possible consequences for social attitudes of the development of non-manual employment and the consumerist service economy will also be briefly discussed. First, however, the rather different uses and definitions of the class concept within sociology and history will be described.

'SOCIAL CLASS' IN SOCIOLOGY AND HISTORY

In sociology – and indeed, in social policy and the social sciences more generally – the occupational hierarchy has long been employed as a convenient medium through which to operationalise the 'class structure'. In Britain, 'commonsense' occupational class schemes such as those of the Registrar General, or the ABCDE categorisations of psephologists and market researchers, divide up the occupational hierarchy into aggregates comprising jobs that are held to be broadly similar in respect of their levels of social standing and material rewards. These 'social class' differences have long been associated with a range of other social indicators ranging from levels of infant mortality to 'class'-associated variations in voting behaviour (Reid 1981). However, there have also been developed within sociology 'theoretical' class schemes. These have drawn upon the theories of Marx and Weber as well as contemporary sociologists such as Dahrendorf, Lockwood, Bendix, Lipset and so on in the formulation of their 'class' categories. Thus the employment aggregates identified by neo-Marxists such as Wright (1985), and radical Weberians such as Goldthorpe *et al.* (1987), are held to represent 'classes' in a theoretical sense. These theoretically informed empirical approaches are, like 'commonsense' class schemes, focused upon the structure of employment. As Goldthorpe has stated: 'class analysis begins with a structure of positions, associated with a specific historical form of the social division of labour' (Goldthorpe 1983: 467).

However, this 'structure of positions' approach has been widely criticised, in particular by the Marxist social historian E. P. Thompson. He emphasised that class is a *historical* phenomenon: 'I do not see class as a "structure", nor even as a "category" . . . the finest-meshed sociological net cannot give us a pure specimen of class . . . class is a relationship, not a thing' (Thompson 1968: 9, 11). Thus Thompson argues that a class 'structure' cannot be identified independently of the relationships and actions that constitute 'classes' as they emerge as historical phenomena.

Approaches similar to Thompson's are also to be found within sociology: for example, in empirical accounts of the structuring of class relationships within localities (Bagguley *et al.* 1989), or of particular occupations such as Newby's study of agricultural workers (Newby 1977). Such studies, like Thompson's, are directly focused upon *processes* of class structuring, rather than on the identification of a 'class structure' at the macro level.

There are, therefore, a range of different theoretical and methodological approaches to the study of 'social class', which are not always acknowledged. The investigation of class structures on the one hand, and processes of structuring on the other, *are* closely related topics. However, the methodological assumptions underlying these different approaches are not the same. It might be suggested, therefore, that evidence relating to one might not always be conclusive in relation to the other. An example of this possible source of confusion will be discussed below in relation to the debates concerning the 'proletarianisation' of non-manual employment.[3] It will also be suggested that debates as to the location of women in the class structure have become similarly confused with debates relating to the impact of women's employment on class processes.

Another problem associated with employment and occupation-based approaches to the class structure is that 'class' effects cannot be kept separate from other factors structuring employment. In particular, the 'specific historical form of the social division of labour' associated with the 'structure of positions' (Goldthorpe 1983) is also *gendered*. The hierarchical ordering of commonsense class schemes reflects this in that female-dominated occupations have tended to be ranked lower than those that are male dominated. These differences are reflected in everyday speech; male 'breadwinner' jobs are better rewarded than female 'pin-money' jobs. The employment structure also reflects the division of labour between men and women in the domestic sphere. 'Class structures' derived from the structure of employment, therefore, will tend to reflect the pattern of gender relations that prevailed at the time of their initial construction. These implicit assumptions, however, have not usually been explicitly acknowledged. Nevertheless, the fact that employment structures *are* gendered has led to a number of difficulties for class analysis in sociology, particularly those approaches focusing primarily on the aggregation of jobs within the class structure rather than on the processes of class structuring.

OCCUPATIONS AND THE 'CLASS STRUCTURE'

In 1972, Parkin claimed that 'the fact that we do speak of a class system suggests that we can distinguish some significant "break" in the reward hierarchy. In Western capitalist societies, this line of cleavage falls between the manual and non-manual occupational categories' (Parkin 1972: 24–5). Twenty years ago, Parkin's statement would have been regarded as uncontentious. Non-manual employment, of course, encompasses the upper ranges of the occupational structure – professionals, managers, and so on – occupations which in commonsense (and sociological) terms would unambiguously be distinguished from a 'working class'. Even at the lower levels of the non-manual hierarchy, however, employees historically have had consistently different attitudes and behaviour as compared with manual workers. They have been less likely to join trade unions or engage in industrial action, have tended to vote Conservative rather than Labour, and as researchers of childrearing and educational achievement have demonstrated, have tended to interact differently with their children and have different aspirations for them (Newsom and Newsom 1963; Douglas 1964). In 1958, these themes were brought together in David Lockwood's classic historical/sociological study of a lower-level, non-manual occupation: the clerk (*The Blackcoated Worker*).

Lockwood argued that the market, work and status situation (that is, material rewards and promotion prospects, position in the social division of labour, and social standing) of the male clerk placed him in a different class situation, as measured by 'life chances', to that of the manual worker. Thus the clerks' reluctance to join trade unions, for example, was not a consequence of their 'false consciousness' of their true class situation, as Marxists had argued (for example, Klingender 1935), but because their objective class situation was, in fact, different. Clerks had better terms and conditions of employment than manual workers and, most importantly, the opportunity to be upwardly mobile in occupational terms.

Lockwood's insights concerning the links between occupation and social class were further developed in collaborative empirical work carried out in the late 1960s, namely the *Affluent Worker* study.[4] This research was primarily a study of manual workers, but a sample of fifty-four men in clerical grades drawn from two of the establishments studied was also included, mainly in order to demonstrate the persisting *class* differences between manual and even low-level non-manual employees. In contrast to the manual workers, non-manual workers were held to have a 'bureaucratic' orientation to work, the primary meaning of work being 'service to an organisation in return for a steadily increasing income and social status and for long-term security – that is, in return for a career' (Goldthorpe *et al.* 1969: 39).

Although the clerk and the manual worker shared a common situation as propertyless employees, therefore, clerks were nevertheless regarded as occupying a different *class* situation from that of manual workers. As we have seen, the proportion of non-manual workers has expanded considerably since the 1960s. During the 1960s and 1970s many liberals argued that these occupational developments in Western industrial societies signified a transition to 'post-industrialism' (Bell 1974). That is, to a form of society where, contrary to Marx's predictions concerning the 'immiseration' of the proletariat and the division of capitalist society into 'two great hostile camps', *actual* developments within the occupational structure of advanced societies had resulted in a growth in the 'middle classes'. Thus 'deproletarianisation', rather than 'proletarianisation', was in process.

Such changes were of considerable concern to the trade union movement in the 1960s. As Bain argued: 'If the trade union movement is to maintain its relative position in the power structure of this country and to continue to play an effective role in the industrial relations system, it will have to recruit these workers' – and in 1964, the density of white-collar union membership was only 29 per cent as compared to 51 per cent amongst manual workers (Bain 1970: 1, 27). Questions relating to trade unionism, however, were as we have seen only a part of the larger debate relating to class and the occupational structure – put crudely, did the apparent expansion of higher-level occupations signify a gradual transition to a 'middle-class' society?

Such predictions, however, were apparently challenged by the outbreak of radicalism and protest at the end of the 1960s, particularly amongst the educationally privileged who would be subsequently recruited to the upper levels of the burgeoning non-manual sector. It was argued that a 'new class' was in the process of development within non-manual employment (Gouldner 1979). Such non-manual workers, in contrast to occupational groups such as the clerks described by Lockwood, were described as a potential source of criticism of, and challenge to, the prevailing social order. However, an alternative, and rather different source of inspiration for critiques of the thesis of 'deproletarianisation through occupational change' came from the revival of academic interest in the labour process following the publication of Braverman's *Labour and Monopoly Capital* in 1974.

As is well known, Braverman argued that, far from the expansion of non-manual employment reflecting a process of 'deproletarianisation', much of non-manual work had itself been 'proletarianised'. The application of Taylorism in the office, and the development of automation through mechanisation and computerisation, had effectively deskilled the lower-level clerical worker. Such processes were extending into management and other middle-class employees. 'The proletarian form', he argued, 'begins to assert itself' in respect of 'the mass employments of draughtsmen and technicians, engineers and accountants, nurses and teachers, and the multi-plying ranks of supervisors, foremen and petty managers' (Braverman 1974: 407–8). Service occupations and the retail trade – which encompass a number of groups, such as shop assistants, who had conventionally been classified as non-manual workers – were but a part of the 'giant mass of workers who are relatively homogeneous as to lack of developed skill, low pay, and interchangeability of person and function' (Braverman 1974: 359). In short, far from the expansion of non-manual employment reflect-ing a process of occupational upgrading, these jobs had become routine and deskilled, proletarian rather than middle class.

Following Braverman, a number of empirical studies explored the labour processes associated with non-manual occupations (Wood 1982, 1989; Crompton and Jones 1984; Carter 1985). Much of this research concen-trated on the nature of non-manual work tasks and their location in relation to structures of power and authority within the organisation. Many of these jobs were indeed found to be relatively 'deskilled', their incumbents subject to close control and far from positions of authority. The study of non-manual labour *processes*, therefore, apparently supported Braverman's thesis. However, these findings are apparently contradicted by the evidence of large-scale sample surveys of the occupational/employment *structure*, using 'theoretical' class schemes (Wright and Martin 1987; Rose *et al.* 1987; Goldthorpe 1990). For example Wright, whose Marxist class scheme had been much influenced by Braverman's analysis, found that the proportion of managers, supervisors and experts within the US occupational structure had increased considerably between 1960 and 1980 (these findings did not rest upon the analysis of standard occupational categories – which would, of course, have arrived at the same conclusions – but upon Wright's Marxist class scheme).

At the level of the employment structure as a whole, therefore, it would seem that a measure of occupational 'upgrading' has indeed occurred. This argument is supported by the fact that over the last twenty years, administrative, technical and professional occupations have been expanding at a more rapid rate than lower-level clerical occupations. Nevertheless, few would argue nowadays, as did Parkin and other sociologists in the 1960s and 1970s, that the major 'class' cleavage within the structure of employment is that between manual and non-manual employees. As the proportion of the occupied population in non-manual employment has increased, so has the heterogeneity of this grouping. Fragmented, routinised, non-manual work associated with jobs in data processing, retail services and so on has many characteristics – lack of autonomy, low pay, restricted promotion prospects, etc. – which have conventionally been associated with manual employment. This effective blurring of the manual/non-manual boundary, however, has been overshadowed by even more significant changes associated with non-manual employment, which have also influenced debates relating to social class – notably the increased employment of women, and the growth of 'consumer capitalism'.

WOMEN, CLASS AND NON-MANUAL EMPLOYMENT

The location of women within the class structure is an issue that has been the subject of much contention (Allen 1982; Goldthorpe 1983, 1984; Stanworth 1984; Crompton and Mann 1986; Crompton 1989b). In Britain, much of the debate on gender and class within the sociological mainstream has tended to concentrate on how women may be fitted into the occupational class structure (such schemes having normally been constructed in relation to male employment); whether the individual or the household should be the unit of class analysis; whether a wife should take her class position from her own or her husband's occupation; and so on. Many of these issues have been generated as a consequence of the practical difficulties caused by the fact that the persistence of occupational segregation – men are concentrated into 'men's' jobs and women into 'women's' – makes it difficult to accommodate individual women within existing employment-based schemes. The debates relating to 'class analysis', therefore, have often been determined by the problems of employment-aggregate, class-structural approaches (given the persistence of occupational segregation). They have tended to overlook the wider question: namely, the significance of the penetration of the occupational order by women for both the structure of employment and society in general. There is, of course, a body of feminist literature that discusses these questions (Walby 1986; Bradley 1989), but it may be suggested that 'malestream' class analysis in sociology has had a tendency to marginalise such contributions.

The problems which the increase in women's paid employment has generated for employment-aggregate, class-structural approaches is further exacerbated by the fact that women's employment is concentrated in lower-level, non-manual work – which, as we have seen, has always been regarded as a crucial theoretical category in class terms. Nearly half of all non-manual workers are women, and in some of the largest non-manual occupational categories, such as clerical and retail sales, women constitute the clear majority (78 per cent in both cases).

Women, therefore, are in the lower-level jobs, in clerical rather than administrative and managerial work; they are nurses rather than doctors, primary school teachers rather than university lecturers. It is a relatively straightforward matter to give a broad-brush account of gender segregation within non-manual work. The expansion of the welfare state after the Second World War generated a range of 'caring' jobs in education, health and the social services that were and are considered particularly suitable for women, as they reflected the kinds of tasks associated with females within the domestic division of labour. Consumerism and the growth of the service economy have also extended the number and range of such tasks in the 'public' sphere of waged labour. The increase in women's employment has been an expansion of employment for married women, and in Britain, over 40 per cent of women work part time; most of these women are married. Studies such as the *Women and Employment* survey (Martin and Roberts 1984) have described the characteristic combination of domestic and employment career of British women: full-time work after the end of full-time education and up to the birth of the first child; followed by part-time work, or a break in employment, between births; followed by an increasing return to full-time work as children reach school age and beyond. In 'human capital' terms, both interrupted employment patterns and the generally lower level of work-related qualifications obtained by women make it more likely they will be located in lower-level jobs. Even in professional occupations, women tend to be in those which are poorly paid, such as teaching, nursing, speech therapy and so on (Crompton and Sanderson 1990). The situation is changing (women are spending less of their economically active lives out of the labour force, levels of qualification are improving rapidly, and the growth of part-time work seems to have reached a plateau and may even be in decline), but the influence of the factors that have contributed to the particular location of women within the non-manual sector are likely to persist for at least the next decade.

Much lower-level work in the personal services and retail industries is routine and deskilled, even though it may be classified officially as 'non-manual'.[5] However, within the non-manual sector, the most interesting sub-category, in relation to the debates being reviewed in this chapter, is that of office work. The general category of office work cuts across industrial sectors and defies precise classification, although some sectors such as finance, public administration and so on will be almost wholly composed of office workers. The largest single occupation within the category is 'clerical'. From a situation in the nineteenth century in which women were formally excluded from clerical jobs in prestigious concerns such as banks, insurance companies and the civil service, women now dominate in all branches of clerical employment (Anderson 1988).[6]

Within the clerical category, women have always been practically 100 per cent of typists, shorthand writers, secretaries and office machine operators (Crompton 1988). In recent decades, therefore, the feminisation of clerical work has been of low-level, non-specific office jobs: jobs that were once predominantly the preserve of men on a bureaucratic career track, such as in banking. Lockwood (1958) had described bank clerks as the 'aristocrats' of the clerical world, and in these upper reaches, women were at first taken on to carry out only routine machine work and other specific low-level, female tasks. However, throughout the 1950s and 1960s formal discriminatory practices such as the marriage bar, separate pay rates and 'women only' grades were gradually removed and women appeared on the counters and in front offices, in a situation of formal equality with their male colleagues. Women in such clerical jobs, however, did not get promoted. Their lack of qualifications and broken employment patterns (as described above) tended to make them ineligible for promotion within bureaucratic career structures, and in any case, male exclusionary practices persisted even though formal barriers had been brought down (Crompton and Jones 1984). Indeed, it was apparent that there was a deliberate strategy of bringing in short-term female employees to protect male career paths as low-level clerical work became increasingly routinised. For example, at the 1969 Institute of Bankers Cambridge seminar, G. V. Bradley said that

> experience has shown that it is possible to maintain an even flow of male recruits while controlling fluctuations in numerical requirements by varying the rate of female recruitment . . . if initial recruitment has

been sufficiently selective possibly 75 per cent of entrants (i.e., men) should become managers'.[7]

The strategy appears to have been successful, as research carried out in the late 1970s and early 1980s demonstrated that no women had reached managerial levels in the clearing banks studied (Llewellyn 1981; Crompton and Jones 1984; Heritage 1983).

Thus, despite the routinisation and deskilling of many non-manual work tasks, the career prospects of many – probably the majority – of *men* in occupations such as clerical work were maintained. The 'class' or 'life-chance' differential between *male* non-manual and manual workers, therefore, might be argued to have persisted despite technological downgrading. In 1973, Giddens described women as

> in a sense the 'underclass' of the white-collar sector. They tend to monopolise occupations which not only have a low economic return, but which are lacking in subsidiary economic benefits, have limited security of tenure, and offer little in the way of chances of promotion.
>
> (Giddens 1981: 288)

Similarly, in 1986 Mann described female clerical and sales workers as a quasi-class fraction 'inhabiting a buffer zone between manual and non-manual male workers' (Mann 1986: 47).

If employment-aggregate segregation *were* complete – that is, if all men worked in 'men only' jobs and all women worked in 'women only' jobs – then the problems which have beset occupational class analysis might be resolved by the construction of separate scales for men and women. A version of this strategy is employed by Mann and Giddens, in their identification of female clerical workers as an 'underclass', or a 'quasi-class fraction'. However, employment-aggregate segregation by gender is by no means complete, and considerable changes appear to be taking place in significant areas of non-manual work – that is, in professional and managerial occupations.

In Britain, all of the professions have an increasing proportion of women qualifying for them, and the increases are most marked, and most recent, in the finance professions and law (Crompton and Sanderson 1986, 1990). Between 1971 and 1981, whereas the percentage increase of men in professional and managerial occupations was 16 per cent, that of women was 45 per cent. The banks, which have been used as a recurring example throughout this discussion, have at last begun to promote the entry of women into management. In 1983, Barclays Bank was reported to the Equal Opportunities Commission for practices similar to those advocated by Mr Bradley (Crompton and Sanderson 1986, 1990). Women with lower-level qualifications (O levels or CSEs), as recruits to the low-level, unpro-motable labour pool, stood more chance of being offered a job than women with higher level qualifications ('A' levels), and vice versa for men. Barclays have changed their recruitment practices – as have the other major clearing banks – from uniportal to multi-tier entry. Although women still predominate amongst the lower grades at entry, in 1985/6, they were also 54 per cent of those recruited to the Accelerated Training Programme (ATP), from which the managers of the future will be recruited (Crompton 1989a). In a major clearing bank, a quarter of those who have reached Appointed Officer (i.e. managerial) grades below the age of 30 are now women.[8]

It is not possible to be certain of the extent to which these changes in the clearing banks have been brought about by pressure from groups such as the EOC, or whether they would have occurred in any case as a consequence of factors such as increasing qualification levels, labour force participation, and so on amongst women. Another recent consideration has been the current shortage of young people, the bank's traditional source of recruits, who are entering the labour force. This has come to be known as the demographic 'time-bomb' (see Department of Employment 1988).[9] It is of course important to continue to explore the question of causal primacy, but whatever the precise reasons, there can be little doubt that the proportion of women in the upper levels of the non-manual occupational hierarchy will increase in the future.

CONCLUDING REMARKS

This chapter has focused on the issues of class and gender in relation to non-manual employment. A number of conclusions might be suggested concerning the possibilities for further developments relating to the inter-relationships between gender, non-manual labour and processes of class structuring.

It should be recognised that within the social sciences, employment-aggregate approaches to the empirical investigation of 'social class' have in practice reflected the prevailing gender, as well as class-based, division of labour. There *have* been changes in class relations and structures, but there have also been changes in gender relations, and these are reflected in the occupational structure. The difficulties that the increasing and permanent presence of women in the non-manual labour force presents for earlier assumptions about the 'class situation' of important groups of non-manual workers, such as clerks, should be recognised by sociological class theorists. The gender of the occupant has significant consequences for the 'life-chances' associated with particular positions in the social and technical division of labour. Thus attempts to develop a unitary class scheme that may be applied unproblematically to the structure of occupational positions are not likely to be successful.

Nevertheless, the employment aggregation approach to class analysis should not be abandoned. Important issues relating to social policy – such as trends in the distribution of material inequalities, and current debates concerning the emergence of an 'underclass' – cannot be pursued without recourse to some measure of occupational inequality. However, as we have seen, economic and technological developments, as well as changes in the gender division of labour, have presented a series of difficulties for the employment-aggregate approach to class analysis, and it should be recognised that such measures can only ever be approximate. It is important, therefore, also to continue to investigate the processes of class structuring through a flexible approach that recognises the fluidity of occupational structuring and the part that gender relations play in this process.

At the macro level, the growth of non-manual occupations, particularly higher-level occupations such as managerial and professional jobs, has been linked to the development of a 'service class' (Goldthorpe *et al.* 1987; Lash and Urry 1987). However, it might be suggested that the extent of differentiation within the non-manual category is such that the identification of a single 'class' is potentially misleading.[10] As the non-manual labour force has expanded, so has the extent and range of occupational variation within it. Many lower-level, non-manual jobs, including clerical and some lower managerial occupations, are of a deskilled and routine nature. At the upper ranges of the hierarchy, there have been both an increase in professional and managerial occupations as well as further occupational fragmentation within these groupings.

A further argument for ceasing to treat 'non-manual workers' as a unitary group is that the boundaries between non-manual occupations are becoming more sharply drawn – that is, the long-range bureaucratic mobility that once characterised many non-manual occupations is in relative decline. The expansion of credentialed occupations (often state-regulated and sponsored), such as teaching and social work, will exclude individuals lacking relevant qualifications. Perhaps of more significance, however, is the introduction of multi-tier entry in organisations such as the clearing banks and other financial institutions. As a consequence, those recruited as clerks will be more likely to stay as clerks, and potential managers will be identified at the point of entry into the organisation. Such changes in recruitment practices will have the effect of consolidating the boundary between those in lower-level clerical and those in managerial occupations in the organisations concerned.

In fact, census data demonstrates that in relation to the employed population as a whole, the size of the junior non-manual occupational category (SEG classification) is static, and is probably in decline.[11] It is overwhelmingly female. This group may be technically 'proletarian' in respect of both the nature of its work and level of material reward, but it is unlikely to develop as a 'class' in the sense of a widespread self-consciousness of individuals within the category of the commonalities of their material situation, associated with co-ordinated efforts directed at improving it. Many of the women in this category will work part time (in the smaller establishments, often for other family members), and will have discontinuous employment careers. Thus it is likely that household, rather than occupation, will continue to have the major impact on such women's political attitudes and behaviours, as has been demonstrated in recent empirical investigations (Marshall *et al*. 1989). The lower-level, non-manual category will increasingly be internally stratified by age, rather than gender, as older women move into the supervisory positions once occupied by younger men on long-range mobility tracks, or older men who had been less successful in career terms.

Although women will continue to dominate lower-level, non-manual employment, an increasing minority will be found in higher-level professional and managerial occupations. The extent and intensity of involvement of such women in their 'employment careers' (in contrast to their 'domestic careers') will be greater than that of women in lower-level jobs. Men and women are represented disproportionately in professional and managerial occupations. In the professions, women are over-represented in occupations concerned with health, education and welfare, and are thus more likely to be state employees than are professional men (and thus to have been adversely affected by the policies of the present Conservative government). An increasing number of women are moving into managerial occupations, but at present they are concentrated in the younger age categories. The greater involvement of professional and managerial women in their employment is likely to be reflected in their attitudes and behaviour. For example, Savage's re-analysis of the British General Election Survey revealed a differential of 43 percentage points between young managerial women and young professional women in the extent of their voting Conservative: young professional women seeming to have a particular antipathy to the Tories (Savage 1991).

The upper levels of the non-manual workforce are stratified not only by gender, but also by occupation and sector of employment – that is, whether public or private. Despite the Conservative government's attempts to privatise state services, survey data nevertheless indicate that 66 per cent of professionals and 28 per cent of managers are either nationalised industry or public sector employees. Higher-level *state* employees, particularly professionals, have been shown to be much less likely to support Conservative policies than those are in the private sector (Savage 1991; Edgell and Duke 1991). These kinds of differences will be cross-cut by variations in occupational regulation, or the manner in which the exchange of expert services is controlled. In particular, there is a considerable difference between 'professionalism' and 'organisational incorporation' as modes of regulation (Crompton 1992). Occupational socialisation

might be expected to foster a degree of universalism amongst professionals, whereas in contrast the objective of organisational incorporation
is to foster a primary loyalty to the institution. A number of other factors
should also lead us to anticipate considerable fragmentation within the
upper levels of the non-manual category. For example, variations in
geographical mobility have long been argued to have an important effect
(Watson 1964; Savage *et al.* 1988). The geographically immobile amongst
the middle classes, it is suggested, manifest a primary involvement with
their locality, rather than their class or occupation.

Thus in recent years, it has increasingly been suggested that as a
consequence of change and fragmentation within the occupational order
– of which the growth of non-manual employment is but one manifestation
– the concept of 'class' is becoming increasingly irrelevant. Other issues,
such as consumption, are, it is argued, assuming considerably more significance in the shaping of people's attitudes and behaviour (Pahl 1989;
Holton and Turner 1989). Such arguments, however, rest upon a misap-
prehension of the varying definitions and applications of the 'class' concept
within sociology. In particular, employment aggregates are assumed to
constitute 'classes' in a theoretical sense. It is true that 'occupation' may
not be a primary source of social identity for the majority of employees in
the late twentieth century. However, it may be argued that this has in fact
never been the case, even in the earlier stages of industrialism. As has been
empirically established within industrial sociology, particular occupations
have always shown considerable variation in the extent to which they may
be a source of *personal* identity as far as their incumbents are concerned
(Brown and Brannen 1970; Gallie 1978). Nevertheless, the jobs that people
do still remain the most important determinants of their life-chances in a
material sense, their positions in relation to authority, and so on. Thus as
has been argued in this chapter, 'classes' as occupational aggregates still
remain of considerable significance for the investigation of a number of
key issues in social science.

Nevertheless, there is a sense in which the growth of non-manual
employment associated with the development of the service economy,
particularly the provision of consumer services, might be anticipated to
have had an impact on 'class' attitudes. With the growing dependence of
national economies, and employment levels, on the provision of consumer
services rather than on manufacturing industry, the kinds of qualities
required of the workforce taken as a whole have undergone a subtle shift.
Social skills, it may be argued, have become more important relative to
technical skills. Thus even at the lower levels of service employment,
employees are increasingly expected to aquire non-confrontational social
skills. The dominant ethos of management training, too, has changed over
the last decade. 'Human Resource Management' is now a significant element, and the massive popularity of books such as Peters and Waterman (*In*

Search of Excellence 1982) demonstrates the emphasis on teamwork and co-operation which has come to predominate. Even though the underlying structure of class inequality may still persist in modern societies, therefore, it may be suggested that the increasing frequency of personal service-based employment relationships might be expected to result in a decline in the frequency of overtly antagonistic employment situations, and that this might have a corresponding effect on employees' attitudes.

NOTES

1 This chapter was delivered to the editors in January 1992. The author's subsequent book (*Class and Stratification: an Introduction to Current Debates*, 1993) substantially develops the issues raised here.
2 The loss of jobs from manufacturing was particularly marked during the early 1980s. See '1984 Census of Employment and revised employment estimates', *Employment Gazette*, January 1987, pp. 31–7.
3 This brief summary has not described the whole range of different approaches to the 'class' concept. See Crompton (1993) for a more extensive discussion.
4 See Goldthorpe *et al.* 1968a, 1968b, 1969.
5 Indeed, it has become, increasingly, conventional to place retail workers in a separate category (Martin and Roberts 1984).
6 Nevertheless, interesting patterns of gender segregation still persist within the clerical category. See Crompton 1988.
7 Example taken from 'Women in banking – a review' by M. Povall (1982), published by the Permanent Secretariat, Commission of the European Communities.
8 Percentage calculated from raw data supplied to the author by a major clearing bank. The bank prefers to remain anonymous.
9 One of the effects of the recession that began in 1990 might be that these fears of a labour shortage will prove to be short-lived.
10 Those authors who have recently employed the service class concept (Goldthorpe; Lash and Urry) have recognised the extent of differentiation within it. Nevertheless, the association of the class concept with interests and attitudes suggests that members of the same 'class' should be more like each other than they are like other 'classes', and the extent of variation *within* the putative 'service class' suggests that this may not be the case.
11 Changes in the conventions relating to occupational labelling make it difficult to gauge the actual extent of decline within the 'clerical' or 'junior non-manual' grouping. A range of case study evidence (Ashburner 1987; Crompton 1990; Crompton and Jones 1984) suggests that the 'managerial' label may be applied at a rather lower level within the occupational hierarchy than was once the case, and as a consequence, the category includes a number of rather routine employees.

REFERENCES

Allen, S. (1982) 'Gender inequality and class formation' in A. Giddens and G. Mackenzie (eds) *Social Class and the Division of Labour*, Cambridge: Cambridge University Press.

Anderson, G. (ed.) (1988) *The White Blouse Revolution*, Manchester: Manchester University Press.

Ashburner, L. (1987) 'The effects of new technology on employment structures in the Service Sector', unpublished PhD thesis, University of Aston.

Bagguley, P., Mark-Lawson, M., Shapiro, D., Urry, J., Walby, S. and Warde, A. (1989) *Restructuring Place, Class and Gender: Social and Spatial Change in a British Locality*, London: Sage.

Bain, G. S. (1970) *The Growth of White-Collar Unionism*, Oxford: Clarendon.

Bell, D. (1974) *The Coming of Post-Industrial Society*, London: Heinemann.

Bradley, H. (1989) *Men's Work, Women's Work: A Sociological History of the Sexual Division of Labour in Employment*, Cambridge: Polity.

Braverman, H. (1974) *Labour and Monopoly Capital*, New York: Monthly Review Press.

Brown, R. and Brannen, P. (1970) 'Shipbuilders' (I & II) *Sociology* 4, (1 & 2): 71–84, 197–211.

Carter, B. (1985) *Capitalism, Class Conflict and the New Middle Class*, London: Routledge & Kegan Paul.

Crompton, R. (1976) 'Approaches to the study of white-collar unionism', *Sociology* 10 (3) September: 407–26.

——— (1988) 'The feminisation of clerical work since the Second World War' in G. Anderson (ed.) *The White Blouse Revolution*, Manchester, Manchester University Press.

——— (1989a) 'Women in banking: continuity and change since the Second World War', *Work, Employment & Society* 3 (2): 141–56.

——— (1989b) 'Class theory and gender', *British Journal of Sociology* 40 (4): 565–87.

——— (1990) 'Goldthorpe and Marxist theories of historical development', in J. Clark, C. Modgil and S. Modgil (eds) *John H. Goldthorpe: Consensus and Controversy*, London: Falmer Press.

——— (1992) 'Patterns of social consciousness amongst the middle classes', in R. Burrows and C. Marsh (eds) *Consumption and Class: Divisions and Change*, Basingstoke: Macmillan.

——— (1993) *Class and Stratification: an Introduction to Current Debates*, Cambridge: Polity.

Crompton, R. and Jones, G. (1984) *White Collar Proletariat: Deskilling and Gender in the Clerical Labour Process*, London: Macmillan.

Crompton, R. and Mann, M. (eds) (1986) *Gender and Stratification*, Cambridge: Polity Press.

Crompton, R. and Sanderson, K. (1986) 'Credentials and careers: some implications of the increase in professional qualifications amongst women', *Sociology* 20 (1) February: 25–42.

——— (1990) *Gendered Jobs and Social Change*, London: Unwin Hyman.

Department of Employment (1988) *Employment for the 1990s*, White Paper, London: HMSO.

Douglas, J. W. B. (1964) *The Home and the School*, London: Panther.

Edgell, S. and Duke, V. (1991) *A Measure of Thatcherism*, London: Harper Collins, Academic.

Gallie, D. (1978) *In Search of the New Working Class: Automation and Social Integration in the Capitalist Enterprise*, Cambridge: Cambridge University Press.

Giddens, A. (1973) *The Class Structure of the Advanced Societies*, London: Hutchinson (2nd edition 1981).

Goldthorpe, J. H. (1983) 'Women and class analysis: in defence of the conventional view', *Sociology* 17 (4): 465–88.

—— (1984) 'Women and class analysis: a reply to the replies', *Sociology* 18 (4): 491–9.

—— (1990) 'Employment, class and mobility: a critique of liberal and Marxist theories of long-term change' in H. Haferkamp and N. Smelser (eds) *Theories of Long-Term Social Change*, London: University of California Press.

Goldthorpe, J. H., Llewellyn, C. and Payne, C. (1987) *Social Mobility and Class Structure in Modern Britain* (2nd edition), Oxford: Clarendon Press.

Goldthorpe, J. H., Lockwood, D., Bechhofer, F. and Platt, J. (1968a) *The Affluent Worker: Industrial Attitudes and Behaviour*, Cambridge: Cambridge University Press.

Goldthorpe, J. H., Lockwood, D., Bechhofer, F. and Platt, J. (1968b) *The Affluent Worker: Political Attitudes and Behaviour*, Cambridge: Cambridge University Press.

Goldthorpe, J. H, Lockwood, D., Bechhofer, F. and Platt, J. (1969) *The Affluent Worker in the Class Structure*, Cambridge: Cambridge University Press.

Gouldner, A. W. (1979) *The Future of Intellectuals and the Rise of the New Class*, London.

Heritage, J. (1983) 'Feminisation and unionisation: a case study from banking' in E. Gamarnikow (ed.) *Gender, Class and Work*, London: Heinemann.

Holton, R. J. and Turner, B. (1989) *Max Weber on Economy and Society*, London: Routledge & Kegan Paul.

Klingender, F. D. (1935) *The Condition of Clerical Labour in Britain*, London: Martin Lawrence.

Lash, S. and Urry, J. (1987) *The End of Organized Capitalism*, Cambridge: Polity.

Llewellyn, C. (1981) 'Occupational mobility and the use of the comparative method' in H. Roberts (ed.) *Doing Feminist Research*, London: Routledge.

Lockwood, D. (1958) *The Blackcoated Worker*, London: George Allen & Unwin.

Mann, M. (1986) 'A crisis in stratification theory' in R. Crompton and M. Mann (eds) *Gender and Stratification*, Cambridge: Polity Press.

Marshall, G., Newby, H., Rose, M. and Vogler, C. (1989) *Social Class in Modern Britain*, London: Unwin Hyman.

Martin, J. and Roberts C. (1984) *Women and Employment: a Lifetime Perspective*, London: HMSO.

Newby, H. (1977) *The Deferential Worker*, London: Allen Lane.

Newsom, J. and Newsom, E. (1963) *Patterns of Infant Care in an Urban Community*, Harmondsworth: Penguin.

Pahl, R. E. (1989) 'Is the emperor naked? Some questions on the adequacy of sociological theory in urban and regional research', *International Journal of Urban and Regional Research* 13 (4): 711–20.

Parkin, F. (1972) *Class Inequality and Political Order*, London: Paladin.

Peters, T. J. and Waterman, R. H. (1982) *In Search of Excellence*, New York: Harper & Row.

Price, R. and Bain, G. S. (1988) 'The labour force', in A. H. Halsey (ed.) *British Social Trends since 1900*, Basingstoke: Macmillan.

Reid, I. (1981) *Social Class Differences in Britain*, London: Grant McIntyre.

Rose, D., Marshall, G., Newby, H. and Vogler, C. (1987) 'Goodbye to Supervisors?', *Work Employment and Society* 1 (1): 7–24.

Savage, M. (1991) 'Making sense of middle-class politics: a secondary analysis of the 1987 British general election survey' *Sociological Review* 39 (1): 26–54.

Savage, M., Dickens, P. and Fielding, T. (1988) 'Some social and political implications of the contemporary fragmentation of the "service class" in Britain', *International Journal of Urban and Regional Research*.

Stanworth, M. (1984) 'Women and class analysis: a reply to John Goldthorpe', *Sociology* 18 (2): 159–70.

Thompson, E. P. (1968) *The Making of the English Working Class*, Harmondsworth: Penguin.

Walby, S. (1986) *Patriarchy at Work*, Cambridge: Polity.

Watson, W. (1964) 'Social mobility and social class in industrial communities', in M. Gluckmann and E. Devons (eds) *Closed System and Open Minds*, Edinburgh: Oliver & Boyd.

Wood, S. (ed.) (1982) *The Degradation of Work? Skill, De-skilling and the Labour Process*, London: Hutchinson.

—— (1989) *The Transformation of Work?*, London: Unwin Hymen.

Wright, E. O. (1985) *Classes*, London: Verso.

Wright, E. O. and Martin, B. (1987) 'The transformation of the American class structure, 1960–1980', *American Journal of Sociology* 93 (1): 1–29.

Chapter 9

Poverty in post-war Britain

Joan C. Brown

The Beveridge Report in 1942 spoke of the need to conquer the five giant evils – want, disease, squalor, ignorance and idleness – each an aspect of poverty and often mutually reinforcing. The years 1944 to 1948 saw a range of important legislation and the adoption of major policy goals intended to overcome these evils. But the debate at the time was concerned not only with what should be done, but how it should be done.

First, there was a desire to endow people with rights. In social security this meant that the major emphasis was to be on benefit rights purchased through contributions to a new National Insurance scheme, and the minimal use of means testing. This concern for rights was in part a reaction to the bitter memories of the operation of the Household Means Test in the 1930s. But there were other pre-war patterns of discrimination against poor people. So there were also to be rights to the best available medical care, regardless of means, through a new National Health Service; and a right to be educated according to ability, regardless of parental income, through the 1944 Education Act.

Second, there would be an emphasis on opportunities rather than coercion. During the high unemployment of the 1920s and 1930s, coercion formed a significant part of the policies towards the unemployed. In the 1920s, there was much bitterness about the imposition of the actively-seeking-work rules. These operated from the assumption that unemployed people were malingerers, unless they could show proof to the contrary to a Local Employment Committee, through evidence of exhaustive job-hunting. Failure to satisfy the committee meant the loss of benefit (Deacon 1977). The rules were abolished in 1930 – buried in what Beveridge called a 'dishonoured grave' – but not deep enough, as it turned out.

In the 1930s, coercion was exercised through compulsory training under threat of loss of benefit. Beveridge intended to maintain this to counter any ill effects from another proposal – an insurance benefit for unemployment without any time limit on it. But the indefinite benefit was rejected by government, and parliament was against using training as a form of coercion. In future, there was to be a policy of full employment. The opportunity to work would be available for all. Training allowances would be offered to open doors to new skills, but through the Ministry of Labour, not through social security. Some coercive powers were retained, but as fall-back provisions, not as a key weapon.

A third goal was adequacy. This implied social security benefits set at least at subsistence level, in contrast to the poor level of insurance benefits in the 1930s. In social security this was pursued in a much more faltering way than the other goals, but the rates set under the 1946 National Insurance Act were intended to be roughly at subsistence level and to be – according to James Griffiths, Labour Minister of National Insurance – 'the beginning of the establishment of a National Minimum Standard' (House of Commons 1946: 1742). And there were new provisions for a five-yearly review of rates. Alongside this, there was a house-building programme aimed at ensuring decent standard housing, at affordable rents for lower-income families, and the end of the squalor of slums.

Fourth, the whole edifice was to be built on solidarity and not – as too often in the past – on the strong securing their own advantage and leaving the weak to go to the wall. The wartime years had shown the value of solidarity. In future, in Beveridge's words, the plan was that 'men stand together with their fellows' (Beveridge 1942: 13). Risks would be pooled through National Insurance, the costs of health and education be met from the common pool of taxation, and the community would share with the family the cost of children through Family Allowances.

Finally, there was a unifying theme – the need to offer dignity to the poor. This is well illustrated by the debate on the last of the main measures, the National Assistance Bill, on 24 November 1947, when Bessie Braddock reminded the House:

> Let us remember the queues outside the Poor Relief offices, the destitute people, badly clothed, badly shod, lining up with their prams. . . . These are the things we are repealing . . .
>
> They used to make soup every day and take it down to the central area of the city in a van and distribute it, and a piece of bread, to those who were hungry and waiting for it at a cost of a farthing a bowl. I have always remembered since then the terrible tragedy and horror on the faces of those in the queue when the soup was finished and there was no more to be sold.
>
> (House of Commons 1947: 1632–6)

In the same debate Arthur Woodburn, Secretary of State for Scotland, commented:

> I think that the greatest injury done to the poor in the past was not the fact that they were deprived of food or nourishment, but that they were

deprived of their self respect. The destruction of the dignity of the man was the greatest crime against the poor in days gone by.

(House of Commons 1947: 1653)

AN APPARENT SUCCESS

Rowntree's study of York in 1936 found 17.7 per cent of the population in poverty (Rowntree 1941). In 1950 he did a follow-up study. Using a still austere poverty line, he found only 1.66 per cent were in poverty. At a time of full employment, when family allowances were newly in payment and widows' benefits had been improved, many of the 1930s problems of poverty seemed to have disappeared. But among the minority who were poor, 68 per cent were pensioners and 21 per cent were poor because of sickness (Rowntree and Lavers 1951).

The benefit figures gave a similar message. Of the 1.3 million claimants on National Assistance at the end of 1950, nearly 62 per cent were pensioners and 17 per cent were sick or disabled non-pensioners. Some 10 per cent were lone mothers and a mere 5 per cent unemployed. When dependants were added, the numbers on National Assistance rose to 1.9 million. The most worrying statistic showed that 76 per cent of claimants were receiving supplementation of an inadequate National Insurance benefit (National Assistance Board 1951: 6), and were being means tested for the purpose.

But the persistence of means testing did not signify that the need for dignity had been forgotten. In 1954 the National Assistance Board pointed out that the 1948 Act required them to 'exercise their functions in such a manner as shall best promote the welfare of the persons affected' (National Assistance Board 1955: 12). In its 1955 report the Board said of its duties:

> For all alike the first and supremely important consideration is that the Board's officer should put an adequate cash allowance in payment promptly; and in so doing, he promotes the welfare of the applicant if he carries out the necessary investigation with courtesy and tact. To the minority . . . whose needs are not only financial the Board's officer can be of help mainly in recognising the nature of their special needs and advising them of what steps to take, or putting them in touch with some other body which can give the help they need.

(National Assistance Board 1956: 19)

The examples given included securing home helps or chiropody services for the elderly, school meals and welfare foods for the children of widows, someone to visit a lonely elderly person to read to them, or help from a probation officer for a family with domestic problems (National Assistance Board 1956: 28–31).

The picture given of National Assistance was not just a piece of public relations. It was confirmed by Townsend when he interviewed elderly people in Bethnal Green in 1954–5. He found that 'by and large the evidence was that National Assistance officials were sympathetic. Their "fairness" was generally acknowledged' (Townsend 1957: 184). Nevertheless, problems were beginning to emerge.

First, the Townsend study showed that elderly people dependent on National Assistance had a poor standard of living, pared down to the essentials. 'We used to have eggs for supper, or a kipper, but not now. We have perhaps a bit of toast. We always have something hot. We had to cut down on everything, I can tell you' (Townsend 1957: 178). This was not the hunger of the 1920s and 1930s, but there was a struggle to eke out a very limited income.

Second, it was becoming evident that a large number of elderly people had incomes below the National Assistance level and had not claimed supplementation. Here was clear poverty. For many, the reluctance to apply was tied to memories of the 1930s. They expected the same treatment from the Board as had been meeted out by Poor Relief (Townsend 1957: 184–5).

Third, there was a group on Assistance made poor by the Board's rules. These were unemployed and sick claimants subject to the wage stop. This was a hangover from the 1930s and required that the Board paid no more than the claimant had earned or would be likely to earn in the future, even if the allowance for the family would be below subsistence level. The object was to avoid undermining the financial incentive to work.

POVERTY REDISCOVERED – THE EARLY 1960S

For most of the 1950s, unemployment was low and the wage stop affected fewer than 3,000 people – including the sick – at any one time (Brown 1983: 35). But as unemployment rose, so did the numbers being wage-stopped. By 1965, there were 16,000 wage-stopped unemployed families with 56,000 children. These children, the Board wrote, were in families 'with a weekly income below the level of their needs as measured by the normal scale rates' (Ministry of Social Security 1967: 173). The problem, said the Board, lay with low wages and the fact that it had no power to help the working poor. In 1948, the problem of low wages had received little attention and this was coming home to roost.

In 1964/5, a new study by Abel-Smith and Townsend, *The Poor and the Poorest*, highlighted still more the weaknesses in anti-poverty policy (Abel-Smith and Townsend 1965). It showed that income poverty had not, as once thought, been ended by the post-war reforms. The measure used was the level of living offered by National Assistance rates. Taking into account that a certain amount of income could be disregarded, and that additional allowances were in payment for special needs, the study drew three lines: resources below the basic National Assistance scales; resources up to 20 per cent above the basic rates; and those 21–40 per cent above.

Based on these, plus actual rent, it was calculated for 1960 that 7.5 million people were living on low to very low income, or 14.2 per cent of the population. The problems identified were low wages, inadequate National Insurance benefits combined with low take-up of National Assistance, and poverty that arose because the family was not entitled to the full National Assistance allowance. Taking those below the basic rate on their own, 2 million people, 3.8 per cent of the population, were in households with exceptionally low incomes. The figures also showed that over 2 million children were living in low-income households (Abel-Smith and Townsend 1965: 66–7). A comparison with 1953 suggested that the numbers who were poor had greatly increased.

Around the same period, another problem was emerging which has been well described by Banting (Banting 1979: 14–65). The early 1950s had seen the completion of a massive slum clearance and council housing programme, producing some 300,000 houses at affordable rents, easing the acute housing shortage inherited from the war, and doing much to break the link between poverty and bad housing. But the Conservative government, which was responsible for much of this, was also keen to arrest the parallel decline of the private rented sector. While this decline was linked to slum clearances – which mainly involved private property – the government believed that rent controls, left over from the war, were having an adverse effect. In 1957, it initiated immediate decontrol over housing above a specified value and 'creeping decontrol' of the remainder. As a house was vacated, its rent would be fully decontrolled.

However, in London in particular, the Act coincided with a period of increased pressure on housing. Rents were rising, evictions increased and so did the numbers of homeless people. But it was the issue of Rachmanism which brought the matter to a head. It was the activities of the slum landlord Perec Rachman which led to the coining of this phrase. It described the practice of bullying, harassing and the sometimes violent treatment of tenants to drive them out of a property, which could then be sold or relet in multi-occupation for greatly increased rents.

1965–79 – MIXED VIEWS ABOUT POVERTY

The Rent Act of 1965, introducing rent tribunals to set fair rents, took the heat out Rachmanism – though it did not end the problem of homelessness. And while governments were never willing to accept as a poverty line either the National Assistance rates or the Supplementary Benefit rates which replaced them in 1966, it could not be denied that an increasing level of dependence on Supplementary Benefit (SB) was a sign that there were social problems that needed to be addressed. At the end of 1950, there had been 1.3 million National Assistance claimants – 1.9 million counting dependants. By the end of 1970, there were 2.7 million claimants on SB – some 4.2 million counting dependants. With minor fluctuations, this figure held steady during the 1970s (Department of Health and Social Security 1982).

That the numbers did not grow in this period, in spite of a substantial increase in the number of potential claimants – more elderly people, more lone parents, more unemployed people – can, to a considerable extent, be ascribed to a renewed pursuit of the rights and adequacy goals. New pension legislation, new benefits for disabled people, better provisions for uprating long-term benefits, increased access to National Insurance rights through the use of credits and, after 1975, Home Responsibilities Protection, all served to strengthen rights to pensions and other long-term benefits, and often to upgrade their rates. Several new and useful non-means-tested benefits were introduced. At the same time, the growth of occupational pensions – also subject to legislation which improved contributors' rights – bolstered the income of many elderly people, and assisted disabled people through ill health pensions.

The drive for new and improved rights could also be seen in the Equal Pay and Sex Discrimination Acts, employment protection legislation, redundancy pay, better maternity pay, the extension to twelve months of National Insurance rights for the unemployed, and the introduction of the Earnings Related Supplement for the short-term unemployed and the sick. For families, the introduction of Child Benefit and One Parent Benefit served the same purpose.

In housing too, the pursuit of adequacy continued, though the approach taken – the system building of high-rise estates – proved later to have been a serious error, with consequences for the 1980s. Homelessness persisted, but the 1977 Homeless Persons Act sought to end the separation of families and offered rights to some of the homeless population.

But the 1970s were not only a decade of increased emphasis on rights. They were also years that saw a much greater use of means-tested benefits. One aspect was the greater need to use Supplementary Benefit (SB). The relative stability of the end-of-year figures disguised higher usage – by 4 to 5 million claimants – during the year (Department of Health and Social Security 1982). But a more significant change was the introduction of new means-tested benefits: Family Income Supplement and housing benefits.

The first was restricted to the working poor with children, and was adopted as a cheaper way of tackling low-pay poverty than an increase in Family Allowance. The second built on and extended various schemes that gave rent rebates to poor council house tenants. The new schemes covered private tenancies, and rates as well as rents. These benefits were for low-income people not eligible for SB, and notably the elderly. They were a useful addition to the help available, but these and other means-tested benefits were to operate against much harsher public attitudes to the poor than in earlier years.

Central to this was the view taken of the unemployed – whose numbers reached 1.4 million in 1978 (Department of Employment 1978). For them, the public policy goals of solidarity and opportunities rather than coercion held on – though with difficulty – but dignity took a battering, and for the long-term unemployed, so did adequacy.

By the mid-1970s it was being claimed that improved benefits were reducing the incentive to hunt for work, so there was pressure – resisted at the time – to reduce benefits for the short-term unemployed. For the long-term unemployed, the abolition of the wage stop in 1975 eased one problem, but it was replaced by another. In 1973, a higher long-term rate of SB had been introduced, but the unemployed were excluded from this, so as to maintain the gap between benefits and low wages. The Supplementary Benefits Commission was concerned about evidence of the hardship being suffered by unemployed families with children, but it believed that the public would not tolerate higher rates for the unemployed (Supplementary Benefits Commission 1977: 4).

The year 1976 brought further evidence of public attitudes to the poor and to the unemployed. The EC undertook a public opinion survey on poverty. It found that 43 per cent of UK respondents – the highest percentage in Europe – believed poverty was caused by laziness and lack of willpower (Commission of the European Communities 1977: 72). In the same year there was an outburst of what Golding and Middleton called 'scroungerphobia'. The claim was that the social security population was riddled with welfare cheats, living high at the taxpayer's expense, although they were quite capable of working (Golding and Middleton 1978: 195–7).

Against this background, the increased use of means testing in the 1970s was almost bound to raise difficulties – and not only for the unemployed. The fear of being regarded as scroungers, added to the dislike of means testing and all it involved in loss of privacy and dignity, deterred many from claiming. The Family Income Supplement never reached much more than half of those entitled. Housing benefits also had take-up problems, and as many as 35 per cent of the eligible elderly were not claiming Supplementary Benefit (Department of Health and Social Security 1982).

At the same time, the pressure of both long- and short-term claimants on Supplementary Benefit was producing a deterioration in the service. Home visiting, the pride of National Assistance, was cut back. In social security offices some claimants still felt they received reasonable treatment, but others made more caustic remarks. A 1978 study produced the following comments, describing the SB offices and the treatment received:

Morbid. Very still, very stark, horrible room looked like a block of concrete. Everyone else sat around the room sniffing or moaning or groaning. Very hot, stuffy and very strong lighting.

It was like a sleazy cafe at about 3 o'clock in the morning.

He didn't give a damn. He asked you questions and you answered, and when you'd go to add something, he'd be on the next question; he was only interested in his questions.

He wasn't very helpful at all. He was a snob, he talked to you like dirt. The attitude was that it was his money he was giving away.

Very understanding; a very nice person, she was genuinely sympathetic; in fact, she made you feel quite at home, to be honest.

(Richardson and Naidoo 1978: 20–1)

A DHSS official who spent time in an inner-city office reported that new claimants got prompt attention and got their money within a few days. In quantitative terms the operation was fairly efficient, but the quality of service was often poor:

Long queues at the reception counter, brusque handling of telephone inquiries, inadequate attention to welfare and explanation of entitlement, abruptness, even discourtesy, in dealing with claimants or their representatives; all of these were fairly common occurrences.

(Laurance 1980)

POVERTY IN THE 1980s

The last published low-income figures using the 1964 definition were for 1985. In 1960, it will be recalled, there were 7.5 million people on low to very low income, including 2 million children. In 1985 there were 15.4 million people living at this level, including 3.4 million children. Even if the rise in the benefits that set the line is taken into account, the difference – for the worse – is substantial. And there were still 2.4 million people living on incomes below the basic Supplementary Benefit line (Department of Health and Social Security 1988). The numbers on SB by 1985 had grown to 4.1 million claimants – 7 million when dependents were included (Department of Health and Social Security, 1986) – swollen principally because of persistently high unemployment, but also by the growth in numbers of one-parent families. So where do we stand now on the five goals of the 1940s: rights, solidarity, adequacy, opportunities not coercion, and dignity? The answer is, not too well.

To begin with, there has been a strong push to replace solidarity with individualism. Under the attractive banners of self-help, personal responsibility, enterprise and initiative, the individual has been urged to go out and seize prosperity and future security for himself. Universal benefits, whether tax-funded or through National Insurance, have not been ended, but they are no longer discussed in terms of mutual aid or solidarity. Rather, they are presented as what the government is doing for you – at substantial cost. The government's aim is that social approval will be conferred on those who help themselves as individuals and who make the maximum use of the private sector to meet their social security needs, rather than on those who act collectively to sustain both themselves and others.

At the same time, during the 1980s the rights of poor people have been diminished. This loss of rights has not occurred through the large-scale repeal of social security and other programmes. Instead, there have been small and repeated changes, which cumulatively have added up to a steady loss of entitlements. To give some examples: rights under the Employment Protection Act, particularly for women, have been whittled away; and changes in the contribution rules for National Insurance have made it harder to qualify for benefit by right and reliance on means-tested benefits has increased accordingly. Rights that people believed they had acquired through contributions have gone, as a number of benefits have been abolished or converted to means-tested benefits. Benefit rights for 16 and 17 year-olds have been withdrawn. More generally, the policy emphasis has been shifted from benefits by right to a far greater stress on 'targeting' money on the poor, through means-tested benefits.

It is true that some other rights have been acquired. There are new rights for women in social security, though it has to be said that many of these have been forced upon a reluctant government through the operation of EC Directives and the European Court. And some of the rights conferred by government have benefited the 'haves', but have taken little note of the consequences for the 'have-nots'. The right to buy your council house, good in itself, was not balanced by giving councils either the right or the resources to replace the property. The homeless and those unable to climb on the home ownership bandwagon have been left out in the cold.

A notable feature of the 1980s was the return to coercion of the unemployed. There are many programmes aimed at opening up opportunities and offering support and guidance, but benefit sanctions now form a key part of policy for the unemployed, and these sanctions are markedly harsher than those of the 1930s. The actively-seeking-work rules are back, and so is training which is virtually compulsory, for both adults and young people.

Adequacy has also lost out – through removing the earnings relationship of the key long-term benefits, through the freezing of some benefits, for example, Child Benefit, and the failure to restore their full value when the freeze ended. Some groups have seen their position slightly improved, but as a consequence of a policy which has required that improvements to the benefits of the poorest must principally be paid for through losses in benefit by the not quite so poor. Adequacy of housing for low-income groups has been undermined by savage cuts in the housing programme for both new building and repairs. Homelessness increased inexorably during the 1980s.

The dignity of poor people was not – to say the least – a major concern of government during the 1980s. Indeed, shaming the poor has been an instrument of policy. Blaming the unemployed for their own unemployment was a favourite tactic of the early 1980s, to reduce the political fallout of the sharp rise in the numbers of the jobless. Periodic fraud campaigns with exaggerated claims of success have created an atmosphere of doubt and suspicion about the genuineness of the needs of people on benefit. A key emphasis has been on the need to root out the so-called dependency culture, with its implication that people on benefit are simply spongers on hard-working taxpayers. Long queues outside benefit offices returned in the 1980s, and conditions in inner-city offices in particular remain bad, though efforts at improvement are under way. And in the Social Fund – introduced in 1988 to replace cash grants with loans for special needs – we find echoes of Bessie Braddock's memories, as the local office runs out of money even to lend to people whose need is evident.

At the beginning of the 1980s, government attitudes seemed matched by public opinion – both hostile to the unemployed and dismissive of the poor. But at the beginning of the 1990s, there are signs that public attitudes have changed. There is serious public concern about the numbers of homeless people sleeping on our city streets. Policies that disadvantage the elderly arouse hostility. Any further damage to the NHS and what it is seen to stand for is unpopular. A new EC public opinion survey published in 1990 showed that only 21 per cent of those questioned thought that poverty was caused by laziness (Commission of the European Communities 1990), down from 43 per cent in 1977. It may be that there is now a sense that we have drifted too far from the goals of the 1940s.

To some extent, the Conservative government has responded to this shift of opinion. There is still a notable absence of any acknowledgement of the extent of poverty in the UK or of any clear intention to develop the anti-poverty policies needed to combat it. But there have been some new initiatives – additional benefits for some disabled people, a partial attack on homelessness, the end of the three-year freeze of Child Benefit are examples. Talk of rights has returned, through the Citizen's Charter. Citizens, as consumers of public services, are now to have the right to the full benefit of these services, provided at a good standard. This includes the service given to social security recipients, but without changes to the level of benefits or of the operating rules, including the strong element of compulsion. The language is softer, but for poor people the reality is little changed.

I shall end with two quotations that illustrate the difference between the goal of governments in the 1940s and the 1980s/90s. The first is from John Moore in 1987, when he was the Secretary of State for Social Security, speaking of what he called a culture of dependency on the state.

> This kind of climate can in time corrupt the human spirit. Everyone knows the sullen apathy of dependence and can compare it with the sheer delight of personal achievement. . . . The indiscriminate handing out of benefits not only spreads limited resources too thinly, it can also undermine the will to self help and build up pools of resentment among taxpayers who are footing the bill.
>
> (Moore 1987)

The second is from James Griffiths, Minister for National Insurance, introducing the 1946 National Insurance Bill. He said:

> to those who profess to fear that security will weaken the moral fibre and destroy self respect let me say this. It is not security that destroys, it is insecurity. It is the fear of tomorrow that paralyses the will, it is the frustration of human hopes that corrodes the soul. Security in adversity will, I believe, release our people from the haunting fears of yesterday and make tomorrow not a day to dread but a day to welcome.
>
> (House of Commons, 1946: 1758)

REFERENCES

Abel-Smith, B. and Townsend P. (1965), *The Poor and the Poorest*, London: Bell & Son.

Banting, K. G. (1979), *Poverty, Politics and Policy*, London: Macmillan.

Beveridge, Sir W. (1942), *Social Insurance and Allied Services*, Cmd 6404, London: HMSO.

Brown, J. C. (1983), *Family Income Supplement*, London: PSI.

Commission of the European Communities (1977), *The Perception of Poverty in Europe*, Brussels: Commission of the European Communities.

—— (1990), *The Perception of Poverty in Europe*, Brussels: Commission of the European Communities.

Deacon, A. (1977), 'Concession and coercion: the politics of unemployment insurance in the Twenties' in A. Briggs and J. Saville (eds) *Essays in Labour History 1918–1939*, London: Croom Helm, pp. 9–35.

Department of Employment, *Employment Gazette*, February 1978.

Department of Health and Social Security (1982), *Social Security Statistics 1982*, London: HMSO.

—— (1986), *Social Security Statistics 1986*, London: Department of Health and Social Security.

Department of Social Security (1988), *Low Income Families 1985*, London: Department of Social Security.

Golding, P. and Middleton, S. (1978), 'Why is the press so obsessed with welfare scroungers?', *New Society*, 26 October, pp. 195–7.

House of Commons Debates (1946), vol. 418, 6 February.

—— (1947), vol. 444, 24 November.

Laurance, T. (1980), 'Impressions of a local office', unpublished seminar paper, 25 June, under the auspices of the Supplementary Benefits Commission.

Ministry of Social Security (1967), *Annual Report 1966*, London: HMSO.

Moore, J. (1987), Speech to the Conservative Political Centre, 26 September.

National Assistance Board (1951), *Annual Report for 1950*, London: HMSO.

—— (1955), *Annual Report for 1954*, London: HMSO.

—— (1956), *Annual Report for 1955*, London: HMSO.

Richardson, A. and Naidoo, J. (1978), *The Take up of Supplementary Benefits: a Report on a Survey of Claimants*, London: Chelsea College, University of London.

Rowntree, B. S. (1941), *Poverty and Progress*, London: Longmans Green.

Rowntree, B. S. and Lavers, G. R. (1951) *Poverty and the Welfare State: A Third Social Survey of York, Dealing Only with Economic Questions*, London: Longmans Green.

Supplementary Benefits Commission (1977), *Annual Report 1976*, London: HMSO.

Townsend, P. (1957), *The Family Life of Old People*, Harmondsworth: Penguin.

Chapter 10

Aspects of education in post-war Britain

Robert G. Burgess

Education has remained constantly in the public eye in the post-war years. Indeed, education has been extensively discussed in the media. In the 1950s and the 1960s, debate focused on the structure of schooling, key issues being whether grammar schools should be abolished and the comprehensive school system adopted. At the same time, demands for a more scientifically and technically qualified workforce prompted calls for a new structure of higher education based on colleges of advanced technology, polytechnics and new universities.

As these structural changes began to be adopted by the end of the 1960s, the focus of debate shifted to the content of education. Discussions began to centre on what is taught, to whom and for what purpose. In the 1970s, teaching methods were under scrutiny in the Black Papers, which appeared between 1969 and 1977, and progressive teaching methods in primary schools were challenged through 'The William Tyndale Affair' (Gretton and Jackson 1976; Ellis *et al.* 1976). The advent of the National Curriculum, itself a by-product of this concern, has further focused debate on the content and shape of education. The associated Standard Attainment Tests have served to centre discussion further on educational standards and pupils' abilities in key curriculum areas, such as reading.

In the conclusion to an essay on 'Patterns and processes of education in the UK' (R. G. Burgess 1984), I commented:

> Since the end of the Second World War there have been numerous changes in the structure of state education provided in the UK. There have been changes in the provision of nursery education; 'new' methods have been adopted in the school system as project materials have been introduced into infant, junior and secondary schools; the selection system has largely been replaced by comprehensive schools; the school leaving age has been raised to sixteen; and more places are available for students to engage in further and higher education. As such, it would appear that there has been large scale educational change.
>
> (Burgess 1984: 118–19)

To this list of developments can be added the National Curriculum, testing and local financial management of schools, all of which have been introduced in the period following the 1988 Education Reform Act.

Much of the detail concerning the structure of education in England and Wales has come from educational legislation and in particular from the 1944 Education Act and 1988 Education Reform Act. The former was concerned with the promotion of education and the development of educational opportunity. Among the key elements of the 1944 Education Act were the abolition of the distinction between elementary and higher education, and the establishment of a unified system of free compulsory schooling from the age of 5 to 15 (which was subsequently raised to 16 in 1973). It also established a tripartite system of secondary education, which was to be the subject of much debate in the following years. In addition, the act extended the concept of education to include nursery schools and classes, and further education. It also formulated a relationship between county schools, on the one hand, and voluntary schools (usually provided by the churches) on the other. The act also made provision for two Central Advisory Councils for Education, for England and Wales respectively. These councils were important in the period up to 1967, as they initiated a major series of reports on the educational system. For instance, the 1959 Crowther Report on the education of 15 year-olds drew attention to the inadequacy of the education provided in secondary modern schools and the further education sector, particularly in the case of day-release provision for apprentices (Central Advisory Council for Education 1959). This was followed in the 1960s by reports on secondary, higher and primary education respectively. First, the 1963 Newson Report, *Half Our Future*, considered the education of 'less able' pupils, while the Robbins Report examined the requirements for higher education and the needs of the economy for qualified manpower (Robbins 1963). Finally, the 1967 Plowden Report examined primary schools and advocated patterns of primary practice that remain influential. The significance of these reports is well summarised by Williamson:

> Interwoven in the public, professional and political discussion of these reports was the work of sociologists exploring social class differences in educational opportunity and relating these to many features of the social and cultural organisation, both of education and of family life.
>
> (Williamson 1990: 137)

In this respect the 1944 Education Act and the Central Advisory Councils for Education stimulated consideration of the structure of education and the opportunities it provided. However, neither the 1944 act nor any of the reports laid down guidelines on the structure of the curriculum (apart from the teaching of religious education, which was required under the 1944 act).

With the passing of the 1988 Education Reform Act, the situation was very different, with curriculum matters taking centre stage. This act gave the Secretary of State the power to prescribe a common curriculum for pupils of compulsory school age in all maintained schools. In particular, a compulsory National Curriculum was prescribed, in core and foundation subjects. In primary schools most time was to be devoted to the core subjects (mathematics, English and science), while in secondary schools the core subjects were to be given approximately one-third of pupil time. Such a situation contrasts markedly with what had gone before, where schools and their teachers had considerable freedom to develop the curriculum. Their only constraints had been those of examination syllabuses and university entrance requirements. These examinations were the only major national tests that were provided in schools. Now, under the 1988 act, attainment targets could be set for each subject for pupils at the ages of 7, 11, 14 and 16. Finally, Local Education Authorities, school governors and headteachers were required to ensure that the National Curriculum was taught in all maintained schools.

The 1988 Education Reform Act also held implications for the structure and financing of schools. First, it allowed schools to opt out of Local Education Authority finance and control, and be given grant-maintained status. It also insisted that local authorities were to delegate responsibilities for financial management and the appointment of staff to school governing bodies. In these circumstances the position of local authorities was systematically weakened under the act, and the Inner London Education Authority was abolished from April 1990. Finally, as far as higher education was concerned, it removed polytechnics and some colleges of higher education from the control of Local Education Authorities, and established a new funding system for universities and polytechnics through the Universities Funding Council and the Polytechnics and Colleges Funding Council respectively. These were amalgamated into one council in 1992. Accordingly, the legislation had implications for the structure of the educational system as well as the control and the content of the curriculum.

THE STRUCTURE OF THE EDUCATIONAL SYSTEM

Within the United Kingdom there are three educational systems: for England and Wales, for Scotland and for Northern Ireland (for further discussion see Burgess 1984). The basic pattern of the educational system for England and Wales is shown in Figure 10.1.

Since 1945, two issues above all have provoked debate: the move to a comprehensive system of education and the development of higher education in general, and the new universities in particular. I shall examine each of these issues in the context of developments in Coventry, where debates about educational expansion, the structure of secondary education, and the

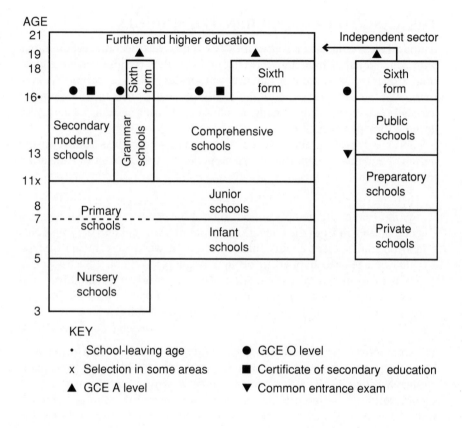

Figure 10.1 The educational system of England and Wales
Notes:
1 First and middle schools are not shown on this figure.
2 All schools may apply for grant maintained status.
3 Within the secondary sector a small number of schools take the title City Technology College.
4 Further and higher education includes colleges of further education, technical colleges, colleges of higher education, polytechnics and universities.
5 This figure is not intended to show the proportion of schools in the educational system; expecially as comprehensive schools are now the predominant form of secondary education.
Source: Adapted from R. Bell and N. Grant, *Patterns of Education in the British Isles*, London, Allen & Unwin, 1977, p. 212

development of a new university were all on the agenda in the post-war years.

THE CASE FOR COMPREHENSIVE SCHOOLS

Among Local Education Authorities, Coventry has become synonymous with educational change and experiment, as well as comprehensive education. Coventry was among the first authorities to build comprehensive schools in the early 1950s, with the result that many other local authorities adopted Coventry's plan with a physical house system, specifically designed for pastoral care.

The case for comprehensive education in Coventry was rooted in the notion of equality of opportunity, as explained by the Director of Education in a speech in 1940:

> There was no reason why children of between eleven and fifteen years of age in a senior elementary school should have less good amenities, less good provision from the educational point of view and less playing fields and special subject rooms than children between eleven and sixteen years of age who happen to be in a secondary school. 'We've got to get away from that false distinction which has really originated from old class distinction and which is now getting out of date', he said. 'Children of a nation as a whole must be looked at as a whole.'
>
> *(Coventry Standard* 1940)

The promotion of educational opportunity to ensure parity of esteem between pupils in secondary schools and grammar schools was paramount. Meanwhile the debate in Coventry was overtaken by the war, as school buildings suffered heavy damage from enemy bombing. After the war, the authority therefore needed to build new schools. In 1949, the authority took the historic decision that they should be built on the comprehensive principle, but as the local press explained, the reason for the decision had nothing to do with social equality:

> Coventry is to be one of the first authorities to build a new school of the 'Comprehensive' type. The idea is one favoured by the Ministry of Education. It is being brought forward because of the pressure on school accommodation now and to come. In Coventry the shortage is chronic and any scheme that will provide more and better classrooms is welcomed.
>
> *(Coventry Evening Telegraph* 1949)

These plans, however, had to be experimental so that, if necessary, they could be reorganised into separate grammar, technical and modern schools. The new schools carried a comprehensive label but did not mark a decisive break with the tripartite system.

Coventry is often referred to as a pioneer in the comprehensive revolution (Archer 1979; Benn and Simon 1972; Firth 1963, 1977; Pedley 1978). It did not create a comprehensive system overnight. In the early years, comprehensive schools always contained a proportion of pupils who had been allocated places on the basis of 'passing' the eleven plus. The process took a step forward in 1954, when two boys' comprehensive schools were established. But it took a further twenty-one years before the system was complete.

Comprehensive schools were often compared with grammar schools, so much so that in the 1960s Harold Wilson referred to comprehensive schools as 'Grammar schools for all' – a strategy that was designed to overcome the fears of the general public about the abolition of the grammar schools. Such a situation was mirrored in Coventry where the Chairman of the Education Committee was reported to remark that comprehensive schools

> Are both grammar schools and secondary modern schools. All eight of these (in the city) provide the same courses as those provided in grammar schools but in addition offer all the courses available in secondary modern schools and the additional advantage of the possibility of changing from one type of course to another within the same school as aptitudes develop.
>
> (Callow 1960)

They thus brought together under one roof a variety of courses that had previously existed in separate institutions under the tripartite system. The City Council meanwhile continued to purchase places for boys at the local direct-grant grammar school and itself ran two grammar schools for girls. The inherent contradictions in this situation came to a head in the early 1970s, when the two main political parties took opposing views of the future development of secondary education in the city. The Conservatives accepted the demand for comprehensive education but considered that grammar schools should be maintained, so as to preserve parental choice. The Labour group, however, wished to end selection and include the two girls' grammar schools in the comprehensive system. This view was endorsed by the Labour-controlled council, and by the then Labour government, with the result that by the mid-1970s Coventry had a completely comprehensive system at secondary school level. The issues in Coventry – equality of opportunity, the abolition of inequality, parity of esteem with grammar schools and overcoming the deficiencies in post-war secondary education – were the same as those dominating the debate on comprehensives throughout the country (R. G. Burgess 1985; Rubinstein and Simon 1972).

THE DEVELOPMENT OF HIGHER EDUCATION: THE UNIVERSITY SECTOR

Higher education was also an area of considerable debate. Since the publication of the Barlow Report (1946), it was argued that England required further provision of higher education places if it was to meet the demands of an advanced, technologically trained society. In the immediate post-war years, claims were made for former university colleges to become universities in their own right. In particular, Hull and Leicester were established as universities, and at a later date the University College of North Staffordshire became the University of Keele. The Barlow Report also encouraged the idea of establishing a technological university, which could be located in Coventry. There was much support for this idea in the city, especially as the Bishop of Coventry in 1942 had launched a call for the establishment of a university locally. In the early 1950s, the local Coventry newspaper, *The Coventry Evening Standard*, carried a leader entitled 'Why not a University for Coventry?' and a case was made for establishing an institution of advanced learning within the city. However, it was not until the early 1960s that a group championing the cause of a new university was set up (Shattock 1991), devoted to preparing a case for the kind of university that would be appropriate for a Midlands city, where industry might be more interested in applied, rather than pure science. The title of the new University of Warwick was suggested by the then Bishop of Coventry, Cuthbert Bardsley.

It was under Lord Rootes that a committee brought together a case, which was subsequently accepted by the University Grants Committee, for a new university to be established at Coventry alongside proposals for the establishment of new universities at Kent and Essex. Indeed, in the early 1960s, seven new universities were established on greenfield sites in England. Each of these universities developed in different ways. At Sussex it was argued by Asa Briggs (1964) that they were redrawing the map of learning. The basic academic unit there was the multi-subject school, where interdisciplinary work was developed and disciplines linked together. This became an important feature of new universities, where emphasis was placed on the breadth as well as the depth of study. This pattern was also taken up at East Anglia.

Another feature associated with new universities was the development of a collegiate system, which was put in place at Kent, Lancaster and York. Meanwhile at Essex, key developments were established through large departments (Sloman 1964). At Warwick the philosophy was to establish a university based on research, teaching and service to the community. Here, Jack Butterworth, the Vice Chancellor of Warwick, gave founding professors and their staff the opportunity to create the academic terrain.

Warwick has become identified with strong departments and a strong university centre. Many of the founding professors were opposed to multi-subject schools and collegiate systems, as they expressed a desire to establish strong subjects and strong departments. Indeed, the founding Professor of Economics remarked that he had decided to leave Oxford

> partly due to a certain dissatisfaction with Oxford's institutional structure. In my experience, the college system meant that (as far as humanities and sciences were concerned) college tutors were rather isolated in the same subject. It seemed to me that opportunities to discuss one's subject (in my case economics) with one's subject colleagues were particularly necessary at a time of rapid development and increasing specialization, and would be more likely to be found in a university which had a departmental rather than a collegiate structure.
>
> (Quoted in R. G. Burgess 1991: 101)

Such views resulted in the development of a strong subject base which focused on depth as well as breadth, where students would be required to learn technical competence, within a disciplinary framework. Similarly, in history the emphasis was upon subject specialism, as the local paper reported:

> The history syllabus will concentrate on breadth rather than on chronological completeness. The emphasis will be on Europe and America, and England will be treated as a European country and will not be given special treatment. The aim of the syllabus is to provide a sound and uninsular historical training which appeals to the imagination.
>
> (*Coventry Evening Telegraph* 1965)

This course was to include not only academic study but also periods of training in Europe and North America – a feature that was to distinguish the Warwick history course in subsequent years.

In the sciences, subject specialism was also evident. Indeed, in a paper to the professors-elect, the founding Professor of Engineering remarked:

> It is perhaps necessary at the outset to correct a few popular fallacies. Engineering courses are commonly expected to impart a miscellanea of useful facts which should enable an engineer to practise his profession. This may be true of medical training, but it should not be true of an undergraduate engineering science course. An engineering science school should aim primarily to produce in students an attitude of mind, a confident, critical, appraising and sometimes sceptical attitude towards physical situations in industrial practices which is based on a sound knowledge of fundamentals and an active imagination. We really ought to call our engineering school the 'school of well informed common sense'.
>
> (Quoted in R. G. Burgess 1991: 102)

Accordingly, engineering courses were designed to promote intellectual activity where students were involved in problem-solving.

Founding professors at Warwick were also concerned with developing subject areas which were research-led and which would have the potential to compete for staff and graduate students, nationally and internationally. Indeed, in mathematics it was argued by the founding professor that it was

> extremely important to set it [mathematics] up orientated towards research, as I had seen other new universities wait four years to get their own students for research degrees and by that time the whole department had solidified towards an undergraduate orientation rather than research. If you solidify towards a research orientation then the undergraduate orientation will happen anyway because you've got to teach undergraduates.
>
> (Quoted in R. G. Burgess 1991: 103)

Indeed, this development influenced the direction of the Mathematics Department at Warwick, which established a strong base in teaching and research, thus making it a leader, nationally and internationally. This close interrelationship between teaching and research was regarded as a key element of university life and was well illustrated by the Vice Chancellor's comments on the university video in the mid-1970s, when he stated:

> As Vice Chancellor, I can tell you something about the unique character of a university and how it differs from every other institution of higher and further education. Here you will undertake a three or four year course which will train you intellectually. Your mind, your intellect will be stretched by distinguished academic staff who are themselves working and researching at the limits of knowledge and because they will take you step by step to the very edge of the subject you are studying, you will be given the opportunity of improving your intellectual capacity. This is what a university is about and why it is unique.
>
> (Quoted in Burgess 1991: 109)

The growth of the higher education sector was partly driven by concern to improve the educational performance of the country. Evidence of continuing economic decline, however, suggested that this was not a universal panacea. Attention therefore, from the late 1960s onwards, increasingly focused upon the content, rather than the structure of education.

CURRICULUM CONTENT

One area of change has been in the primary school, where there has been a shift towards the teaching of special subjects in recent years, furthered particularly by the introduction of the National Curriculum. The common framework of the primary school day now is for subject areas to be taught in the mornings and other activities provided in the afternoon. Hilary Burgess (1989) describes how an infant teacher organised her class whereby subjects such as mathematics and language were provided during the mornings, while the afternoons were for 'messy activities'. Her field notes report the teacher saying:

> I love being messy with them as well. I like the messy activities which we do a lot of in the afternoon and I like to play with them in the Wendy House . . . they are desperately wanting to read when they come to school. To them it has just been a page of hieroglyphics until you actually introduce them to reading.
>
> (H. Burgess 1989: 22–3)

The children's progression towards the attainment targets laid down by the National Curriculum also has to be assessed on a regular basis.

Broadfoot *et al.* (1991) report that primary teachers now have to keep subject records in science, mathematics and English, with sub-divisions being provided in particular areas so that separate records on oracy and reading are maintained alongside a general English record. In particular, one of their respondents summed up the situation by stating: 'All these changes make you feel that unless you're good at documentation in the National Curriculum, you can't be a very good teacher' (quoted in Broadfoot *et al.* 1991: 160).

The impact of assessment has also been controversial in the area of secondary education. Since the publication of the Beloe Report (1960), it has been debated whether there is a place for teacher assessment in the public examination system. As Scott (1990) has reported, coursework and teacher assessment have gradually been introduced into public examinations, with the result that GCSEs involve elements of assessed work, including experimental skills, fieldwork, research skills, interactive skills, co-operative skills and so on (SEC 1987). The use of coursework assessment, which was an important element in the CSEs, the less prestigious of the two sets of examinations that GCSEs replaced, has however brought its own difficulties. Scott commented:

> Evidence from the case studies suggest that this close integration of assessment task and learning programmes is not being achieved. In English, teachers are reluctant to intervene in the completion of coursework assignments in case their contribution is considered to be unfair. Science and home economics teachers have found that conducting assessed practicals in ways in which their definition of examination comparability is satisfied has meant that they have had to make a number of artificial arrangements within their classroom – testing half

the class while the other half were given a nominal task to do. History teachers have argued that coursework should be completed under examination conditions so that they can genuinely sign the document that the work that is done is the work of the individual candidate and no one else.

(Scott 1990: 264)

But, as Scott reports, there is evidence that pedagogic practices are changing and assessment technologies are contributing to the change. These included reviewing pieces of work produced by a pupil, the drafting and redrafting of pupil's work, peer group critique and self-critique, especially in the study of English and the retaking of practical assessments in science. In addition, Scott reports that didactic methods of teaching appeared to be on the decline and there was more emphasis on the regurgitation of knowledge.

EDUCATIONAL PROCESSESS

Educational processes have considerable social impact. As Williamson has commented:

In post-war Britain, occupation and education were closely linked and the possession of educational qualifications was increasingly seen as what, above all else, made social difference legitimate. The idea of the meritocracy with its associated value of equality of educational opportunity, was widely endorsed even though there were major disagreements about what form of educational system would realise such goals.

(Williamson 1990: 135)

Education provides status and opportunity, yet research has shown that there have been marked inequalities in educational opportunity. In particular, much of the research in the 1950s and 1960s has pointed to the class inequalities that exist within the educational system. Indeed, Halsey *et al.* (1980) have indicated that in the post-war period there were significant gains in educational life-chances for those who participated in secondary education, with the result that there were real improvements in the educational life-chances of working-class boys. Educational processes seem to have had less impact upon the life-chances of girls and of children from ethnic minorities. Evidence from subject areas and from classroom encounters indicates that girls tend to be more widely represented in the arts and social sciences while boys are more involved in mathematics, scientific and technical subjects (R. G. Burgess 1986). This becomes a vicious spiral in secondary school entries for GCSE and 'A' level, with the result that this pattern continues through into higher education enrolments in particular fields of study, for instance the number of female entrants for engineering courses has climbed only slowly and still represents no more than 10 per cent of the total intake. Similarly, as far as ethnic groups are concerned, participation rates in higher education signal that little has changed in terms of social divisions. Indeed, as I have argued elsewhere (R. G. Burgess 1984), the overall pattern of education is based on distinct social divisions reinforced by social class, gender and race. So much so that the patterns established in the early years of schooling have an influence upon the routes that can be taken in secondary, further and higher education and in the opportunities that are available outside educational settings. In this respect, those engaged in the education service and who are associated with research in education need actively to consider ways in which equality of educational opportunity can be promoted and examined in the coming years.

REFERENCES

Archer, M. S. (1979) *The Social Origins of Educational Systems*, London: Sage.

Barlow Report (1946) *Scientific Manpower*, London: HMSO.

Beloe Report (1960) *Secondary School Examinations Other than the GCE*, London: Secondary School Examinations Council.

Bell, R. and Grant, N. (1977) *Patterns of Education in the British Isles*, London: Allen & Unwin.

Benn, C. and Simon, B. (1977) *Half Way There* (2nd edition), Harmondsworth: Penguin.

Briggs, A. (1964) 'Drawing a new map of learning', in D. Daiches (ed.) *The Idea of a New University: An Experiment in Sussex*, London: Andre Deutsch, pp. 60–80.

Broadfoot, P., Abbott, D., Croll, P., Osborn, M., Pollard, A. and Towler, L. (1991) 'Implementing national assessment: issues for primary teachers', *Cambridge Journal of Education* 21(2): 153–68.

Burgess, H. (1989) 'The primary curriculum: The example of mathematics', in C. Cullingford (ed.) *The Primary Teacher*, London: Cassell, pp. 16–36.

Burgess, R. G. (1984) 'Patterns and processes of education in the UK', in R. K. Brown and P. Abrams (eds) *UK Society: Work, Urbanism and Inequality*, London: Weidenfeld & Nicolson, pp. 58–128.

—— (1985) 'Changing concepts of secondary education: Coventry's comprehensive schools', in B. Lancaster and T. Mason (eds) *Life and Labour in a Twentieth Century City: The Experience of Coventry*, Coventry: Cryfield Press, pp. 288–320.

—— (1986) *Sociology, Education and Schools*, London: Batsford.

—— (1991) 'Working and researching at the limits of knowledge', in M. Shattock (ed.) *Making a University*, Coventry: University of Warwick, pp. 95–110, 115–16.

Callow, W. (1960) 'Schools: What the city plan means', *Coventry Evening Telegraph*, 22 March.

Central Advisory Council for Education (1959) *Fifteen to Eighteen*, London: HMSO.

Coventry Evening Telegraph (1949) 'Coventry experiment in education', 12 March.

—— (1965) 'Special supplement on the University of Warwick', 31 March.

Coventry Standard (1940) 'Address on educational training', 11 May.

Cox, C. B. and Dyson, A. E. (eds) (1971) *Black Papers on Education*, London: Davis-Poynster.

Ellis T., Haddow, B., McWhirter, J. and McColgan, D. (1976) *William Tynedale: The Teacher's Story*, London: Writers' and Teachers' Co-operative.

Firth, G. C. (1963) *Comprehensive Schools in Coventry and Elsewhere*, Coventry: Coventry Education Committee.

—— (1977) *Seventy Five Years of Service to Education*, Coventry: Coventry Education Committee.

Gretton, J. and Jackson, M. (1976) *William Tynedale: Collapse of a School or a System?*, London: Allen & Unwin.

Halsey, A. H., Heath, A. F. and Ridge, J. M. (1980) *Origins and Destinations: Family, Class and Education in Modern Britain*, Oxford: Oxford University Press.

Newsom. J. (1963) *Half Our Future*, London: HMSO.

Pedley, R. (1978) *The Comprehensive School* (3rd edition), Harmondsworth: Penguin.

Plowden, B. (1967) *Children and their Primary Schools*, London: HMSO.

Robbins, L. (1963) *Higher Education*, London: HMSO.

Rubinstein, D. and Simon, B. (1972) *The Evolution of the Comprehensive School* (2nd edition), London: Routledge & Kegan Paul.

Scott, D. (1990) *Coursework and Coursework Assessment in the GCSE*, Coventry: CEDAR, University of Warwick.

Secondary Examinations Council (1987) *School Based Assessment*, London: SEC.

Shattock, M. (1991) 'The pre-history of the university', in M. Shattock (ed.), *Making a University: A Celebration of Warwick's First 25 Years*, Coventry: University of Warwick, pp. 9–22, 113–15.

Sloman, A. E. (1964) *A University in the Making*, London: BBC.

Williamson, B. (1990) *The Temper of the Times: British Society Since World War II*, Oxford: Blackwell.

Chapter 11

Consumption

James Obelkevich

Post-war Britain often seems to be full of things that went wrong – the economy, industrial relations, policy towards Europe, to name only a few. But consumption is not on that list. It is one thing that went right.

The 1950s were the starting point. They saw the early stages of a long consumer boom that brought the biggest improvement in the material standard of living in Britain since the Middle Ages. What previously had been luxuries for the rich – cars, refrigerators, televisions, overseas holidays – now were enjoyed by the majority of the population. In the long haul from poverty to affluence, this was the great leap forward.

The impact of affluence was all the greater in coming after a long period of austerity. The 1930s had meant hardship for millions; rationing and shortages had been a fact of life not just during the war but for years afterwards. But when the economy recovered and the last controls were finally lifted, in the mid-1950s, the result was a long-delayed explosion in consumer spending – the first wave of what later would be called mass 'consumerism'. In 1957 Prime Minister Harold Macmillan claimed that 'Most of our people have never had it so good'; two years later, popular affluence was given the credit when the Conservatives won an unprecedented third consecutive general election victory. A new Britain seemed to be emerging – a modern, affluent society in which poverty and unemployment had been eliminated and class divisions were disappearing.

Decades later, it is clear that not all the hopes of the 1950s have been realised. Class divisions remain and in the last decade poverty has actually increased. Consumer spending itself, like the economy as a whole, has experienced wide fluctuations. Spending sprees, like the ill-fated boom of 1987–9, have alternated with periods of stagnation, notably after the 1973–4 oil crisis and during the recessions of 1980–2 and 1989–92. Mass consumption is nevertheless here to stay, one of the defining features of an advanced society.

Yet for all its impact on British life, post-war consumption has been curiously neglected by historians and sociologists. Even the classic *Affluent Worker* study (Goldthorpe, Lockwood *et al.* 1968–9) tells us surprisingly little about what the workers (and their wives) actually did with their affluence; most general works on class and stratification assume that 'social class has to do with how people get their incomes, not how they spend them' (Saunders 1990: 106). The result is that consumption is still a no-go area, with market researchers and journalists like Peter York and Jilly Cooper rushing in where sociologists fear to tread.

Why has consumption been ignored? One reason can be summed up in the phrase 'high thinking and plain living' – the view that what counts is the life of the spirit, and that consumer comforts, pandering to our lower nature, should be kept to the minimum. Masculine snobbery also plays a part. It sees consumption as trivial, domestic and inconsequential, a mere pastime for women. What really matters, it suggests, is the man's world of production, politics, power and the public sphere. That is why we have so many studies of, for example, car production, transport policy and industrial relations in the motor industry, but little on what people actually do with their cars and what cars mean to them.

In recent years this attitude has begun to change and consumption is being taken more seriously. In part this reflects the growing interest in women and women's activities. It may also reflect the growing fascination with style and consumption in the 1980s. In the realm of cultural theory, Baudrillard and others have (rather dubiously) highlighted consumption as the central activity of the postmodern era. Whatever the reasons, we are belatedly rediscovering the truth stated by Adam Smith two hundred years ago: that consumption is not a frivolous irrelevance but 'the sole end and purpose of all production'.

DEFINITION AND SOURCES

We can define consumption as the process in which goods and services are bought and used to satisfy people's needs. It excludes 'capital goods', used in the process of production, and in this chapter I have also omitted goods and services provided by the public sector, which deserve separate treatment. Consumption is closely related to supply-side matters such as marketing and retailing. But the main focus here is on its three primary aspects: the buying of goods or services; their uses; and, not least, their meanings and cultural significance.

It follows from this that consumption is not one activity but infinitely many. It varies from product to product and each has its own story: there is not much in common between the consumption of champagne and the consumption of shampoo. The best way to approach the subject is therefore not through grand theories of consumption in general but through detailed empirical research on a particular product or a particular group of consumers.

At this point it is often assumed that since we are all consumers ourselves, such research is unnecessary – that we know everything we need to know about consumption from our own experience of watching television commercials and shopping in Sainsbury's. If only things were so simple. Most of us know little enough about the consumer habits of the people next door, let alone those in another social class. Similarly with advertising: no matter how closely we examine a television commercial, we can never tell how other people have reacted to it, nor even what the intentions of the advertisers were.

There has in fact been a good deal of serious and detailed research on post-war consumption: most of it, however, has been carried out not by sociologists or historians but by market researchers. Since 1945 they have become an essential part of the marketing process, and their work, generally superior to comparable studies by academics, yields a wealth of information and insight on consumer tastes and habits. That most of this material is confidential and closed to outsiders is a matter of regret.

There nevertheless remains a great deal of evidence on consumption available to anyone willing to seek it out. Official sources include the indispensable Family Expenditure Survey and the National Food Survey. The published business and marketing sources include market reports and surveys such as *Retail Business* (1958–) and Mintel's *Market Intelligence* (1972–), and specialised works like the National Readership Survey (1957–). The trade press, probably richer and more extensive in Britain than in most other countries, is largely untapped; we have much to learn from journals like *Chemist and Druggist, Domestic Equipment Trader* and *DIY Superstore*.

TRENDS IN CONSUMPTION SINCE 1945

The remarkable growth in personal consumption since the war was made possible by the growth of the economy as a whole. Between 1950 and 1973, the boom period that came to an end with the first oil crisis, GDP increased at an average annual rate of 3 per cent – probably the highest growth rate in British history. (Of course Britain's competitors in western Europe and Japan were growing even faster.) Real disposable income per capita increased by about 30 per cent in the 1950s, 22 per cent in the 1960s and 30 per cent in the 1970s: a doubling of purchasing power in a generation. The people of Britain had more money to spend, and more things to spend it on, than ever before.

The effects of this affluence can be seen in the shifting pattern of consumer expenditure. Food had long been by far the largest item in the budget, and in the early 1950s it still accounted for a third of all consumer spending, a figure hardly changed since before the First World War. But in the following three decades its share fell sharply; the most recent data, for 1990, put it at 18 per cent. (It should be noted that since overall income was growing, the actual amounts spent on food, and on other 'declining' categories, in fact increased.) There was also a relative decline in spending on tobacco (mainly cigarettes); this was probably the result of a series of health warnings, notably in 1962 and 1971, about the links between smoking and cancer and other diseases. Clothing was the third item with a declining share of expenditure. But partly because clothes prices fell, people got considerably more for their money. The bulging wardrobes of today contrast with those of the clothing-poor 1940s, when rationing was in force: then working-class children often went without underwear and businessmen might wear the same white shirt to work all week.

Other items, notably housing and transport, took a larger share of the budget. People spent considerably more on housing as a result of the shift from renting to buying, with owner-occupation increasing from 29 per cent of households in 1950 to over 50 per cent in the early 1970s. The other growth area, transport, was due mainly to the spread of car ownership. In 1950 only 16 per cent of households had cars; this rose to 52 per cent in 1971 and 65 per cent in 1990.

The home

Overall spending patterns, however, tell only part of the story: we need to go beyond the statistics to the changing ways of life that lie behind them. And the one post-war trend that stands out above all the rest is the growing significance of the home. Thanks in part to the spread of the new 'consumer durables', people's homes became more convenient, more comfortable and more attractive as places in which to spend leisure time. By the end of the

Table 11.1 Consumer expenditure on goods and services as a percentage of total household expenditure

	1953/4	1970	1985
Food	33.0	25.7	20.1
Alcoholic drink	3.4	4.5	4.9
Tobacco	6.6	4.8	2.7
Clothing	11.8	9.2	7.3
Housing	8.8	12.6	16.4
Fuel, light, power	5.2	6.3	6.1
Durable household goods	6.8	6.5	7.2
Other goods	7.0	7.4	7.8
Transport	7.0	13.7	15.1
Services	9.5	9.0	12.0
Misc.	0.6	0.3	0.4
	100.0	100.0	100.0

Source: Department of Employment, 1986: Table 8

1950s what appeared to contemporaries a new way of life was emerging: affluent, modern and unprecedentedly 'home-centred' (Abrams 1959a).

As far as housing conditions are concerned, it takes an effort now to recapture the backwardness – so it seems to us – that prevailed after the war. Apart from a serious housing shortage, which forced couples to start their married life sharing a house with their in-laws, many households still lacked basic amenities. In 1951 over 10 per cent of households were still without electricity; more than a quarter of households either had only an outdoor toilet or had to share an indoor one; 38 per cent lacked a fixed bath and 7 per cent had to share. Most people took one bath a week; those without a bathroom had to take theirs in a tin bath in front of a coal fire, with water which had been heated on the range and which was ordinarily reused by other members of the family. For the millions of families in these circumstances, it was the first indoor bathroom and toilet, not the first washing machine, that marked the real breakthrough to a modern standard of living.

It was nevertheless the new appliances that attracted the most comment at the time. The very phrase 'consumer durables' was new (it was first recorded in America in 1951) and these now-familiar appliances made a deep impression on contemporaries. Technologically advanced, yet not too expensive – accounting for only a small percentage of total consumer spending – they soon passed from luxuries to necessities. By the 1970s the main durables – including fridge, washing machine, television and telephone – were standard equipment in the homes of the majority of the population. They remain among the prime symbols of the high-consumption way of life.

Today we tend to regard refrigerators and washing machines as functional and unexciting. But in the 1950s and 1960s they captured the popular imagination. The twin-tub, that peculiarity of the British, became for a time one of the icons of the age. Contrary to some feminist analyses, these

Table 11.2 Consumer durables: availability in households (percentages)

	1955	1975	1990
Vacuum cleaner	51	90	96
Washing machine	18	70	86
Refrigerator	8	85	98
Freezer	–	15	79
Television	35	96	98
Telephone	19	52	87
Central heating	5	47	78
Dishwasher	<1	2	12
Microwave oven	–	–	47
Video recorder	–	–	60

Sources: Family Expenditure Surveys and trade sources

'white goods', as they are called in the trade, have saved women untold amounts of time and labour in their shopping, cooking and housework. But the 'brown goods' – television, record players, etc. – are even more significant, bringing entertainment not only to women but to every member of the household. They have made the home what it had not always been before, the chief leisure centre for every member of the family.

Each of the brown goods or 'consumer electronics' has shown the same trend, starting as a heavy, expensive piece of equipment for family use and eventually becoming lighter, cheaper, more convenient and more adapted to individual use. At the end of the war even radios were fairly expensive (many households did not own one) and most were intended for family listening. But the advent of transistors, in the late 1950s, made possible the first inexpensive, truly portable and 'personal' models, the kind which teenagers, for example, could keep and listen to in their bedrooms. The cheap portable record player, which also appeared at this time, was similarly designed for use by the individual (or peer group) rather than by the family. Cassette players, launched in 1964 but only becoming popular in the early 1970s, were a step in the same direction, as was the Walkman, first marketed in Britain in 1980.

Television was another success story of the 1950s and early 1960s. When ITV started broadcasting in 1955, only about one household in three had a set, but by 1960 the figure had risen to 75 per cent. Colour was introduced on BBC2 in 1967 and on the main channels in 1969; colour sets were among the leading consumer acquisitions of the 1970s and were present in over half of British households by 1976. Watching television – or doing any of a variety of things with the television on – soon became by far the most popular leisure activity. By the end of the 1960s television had replaced newspapers as most people's main source of news and had cut deeply into the popularity of other media and forms of entertainment. Cinema attendances declined from a peak of 1.5 billion in 1946 to 70 million in 1985; professional football attendances in England and Wales fell from 41.2 million in 1948–9 to 18.8 million in 1987–8. (Pubs, however, fared much better. Starting in the 1960s they were invaded by growing numbers of young people, much to the displeasure of the older male regulars.) In the 1980s the advent of the video recorder, especially in households with more than one set, extended the range of choice and allowed individual viewing.

The new model home required one further ingredient: effective heating. In the 1950s most people still relied on open coal fires; even well-off people did not have central heating and many did not want it. Market research showed that many middle-class people, steeped in the traditions of high thinking and plain living, felt uneasy about being warm, as if it were self-indulgent or improper. So strong was this resistance that an advertising campaign for central heating around 1960 was built on the theme 'You don't have to be selfish to be warm'. Central heating was slow to spread and did not reach a majority of households until 1977. But the trend was towards warmer houses in any case. By 1970 the average living room was over 5 degrees (F) warmer than it had been in 1950 – in houses without as well as those with central heating (Hunt and Steele 1980: 5). Central heating, in turn, meant that in winter every room in the house could be used. Bedrooms were no longer only for sleeping; teenagers turned their bedrooms into living rooms, where they did homework, saw friends, listened to music on their audio equipment or, more recently, watched their own television sets, separate from the rest of the family.

Houses became not only warmer but cleaner. Open fires had produced so much dust, ashes and soot that keeping houses clean was a never-ending struggle. Vacuum cleaners helped, but it was new methods of heating that had the biggest effect. Housework was made easier, new cleaning products appeared, and cleanliness itself took on a new meaning. Traditional products (laundry soap, Vim, Domestos, for example) were strong, even harsh, with a strong smell to match, and promised war to the death against dirt and germs. The newer products (such as Jif or Frish or washing-up liquid) were 'mild' and 'gentle' and, above all, pleasant smelling, turning the cleaning process from a dirt-removal operation into a pleasurable experience. (Women often use Frish, a characteristic product of the 1980s, as an air-freshener.) To be clean was not just to be dirt-free but also to smell nice.

As this example suggests, the changes in post-war homes were not simply functional, a matter of new amenities and appliances. They also reflected new tastes. Houses were warmer, cleaner, more comfortable and fresher smelling. And as people equipped their rooms with more lamps (and used stronger bulbs), they also became brighter and better lit. Brown paint, the pre-war favourite because it didn't show the dirt, was replaced by white, the most popular paint colour for DIY decorating. Hard surfaces were replaced by soft, with linoleum, for example, giving way to carpets. Nearly every room of the house now was 'fitted', with decoration that 'matched'. Houses looked, felt, sounded and smelled different: they were transformed not just by new appliances but by a new aesthetic, a new sensory regime.

Nowhere were the changes more significant than in the homes of the working class. In the past, poverty had often made them a source of shame: they now became a source of pride. It has often been claimed that the new-style home isolated or 'privatised' its inhabitants, cutting them off from the outside world: but the evidence for this (leaving aside the minority in tower blocks) is scanty (Procter 1990; Devine 1992). Although working-class people now spent less time in the street and saw less of their neighbours, they seem to have more than made up for it by leading an active social life both within the home, entertaining relatives and other visitors, and outside it.

The post-war home did, however, tend to separate the members of the family from one another. Such trends as the expectation that each child should have his or her own well-equipped bedroom, and the decline of family meals and the rise of individual snacking or 'grazing', all point in the same individualistic direction. As households became better equipped, they became more dispersed, more 'cellular', more geared to individual gratification.

The body

If people in the post-war period took more trouble over their homes, they also did so over another significant area of consumption – their bodies. They used more cosmetics and toiletries and developed new washing and grooming habits; a more 'modern' set of attitudes towards the body emerged, among men as well as women.

Cleanliness was still basic. As facilities improved, people washed and bathed (and showered) more than their predecessors. And in the products they used on their bodies they also wanted more straightforward comfort – hence the success of soft toilet paper, introduced in the late 1950s, a luxurious contrast with the traditional hard, shiny paper and with the newspapers still used by many people in their outside toilets.

But increasingly people also wanted their bodies to smell nice – or to avoid smelling bad – and so demand grew for 'personal freshness'. Deodorant soon became a necessity for most women. In 1957 only 32 per cent of women between ages 16 and 64 were using it at all – mainly on special occasions and in the summer; by 1966 over 50 per cent were using it daily (Odhams 1966: 162). Men though resisted it, confident in the belief that their own body odours were natural, normal and even desirable. Artificial fragrance, by the same token, they rejected as unmanly – something for women or homosexuals. Indeed, apart from shaving requisites and hair cream, a male toiletries market hardly existed.

The turning point came in 1957, when Old Spice entered the British market and British men – and women – discovered the joys of aftershave. Women liked aftershave and bought it for men because it made them smell nicer; men were less enthusiastic, but accepted it because it had a functional justification (that it was 'good for the skin') and thus avoided the traditional male fragrance phobia. By 1969, after many Christmas presents and much prodding and encouragement from wives and girlfriends, aftershave was used regularly by over half the adult male population.

Usage of these and other toiletry products has often been interpreted in terms of self-absorption and narcissism; but other motives – self-expression, fear of offending other people, and the desire to please them – have been at least as important. It is men who have changed the most. Yielding to pressure from women, they have washed more, splashed on the aftershave and generally cleaned up their act; classic masculine pride in sweat and grime has largely been abandoned. At any rate the well-scrubbed, sweet-smelling body, male as well as female, has become one of the most characteristic emblems of post-war consumer culture.

SOCIAL CONSEQUENCES

Affluence was not just a matter of having more money in the pocket. Indirectly it changed society, giving new meanings to the basic categories of class, age and gender.

Class is perhaps the most obvious example. If defined in terms of the ownership of wealth and capital, then Britain has remained a very unequal society. But consumer goods are much more equally, or less unequally, distributed than wealth. They are more 'democratic' and many, like tele-vision, are essentially classless. One consequence was that many working-class people who in the past would have described themselves as 'poor' no longer did so. Some even claimed not to belong to any class at all; others said in effect that they were working class at work but middle class at home (Zweig 1961: 136). Although they did not usually acquire new durables before the middle classes did, in most cases they were not far behind. What is significant is not so much that they were catching up with the middle classes as that people in all classes were getting their first fridge or washing machine at much the same time. Affluence did not eliminate class differ-ences: but it significantly reduced them. What the middle classes had, the working classes wanted, and often got.

Age, one of the more neglected social variables, has also been redefined by the spread of affluence. If children today grow up earlier, it is partly because they have more money to spend and more freedom in spending it. And if teenagers since the 1950s have created 'youth cultures', it is for the same reason – not because they were alienated or rebellious (Abrams 1959b). Teenagers did not revolt: they spent money, treating themselves to clothes, records, audio equipment and entertainment on a scale that would have been unimaginable to previous generations.

It is gender where the links with consumption are closest. The cliché about men earning the money and women spending it obviously needs to be qualified, given the growing numbers of married women returning to work. But there is still a good deal of truth in it. Throughout the post-war decades women continued to be the main buyers and spenders, managing the money, doing the routine shopping and initiating the major purchasing decisions. Men's domain was limited to the car and audio equipment and to setting overall spending limits. Not only did women buy for themselves and for their children, they also often bought basic items – shirts, socks, underwear, shaving equipment, toiletries – for their husbands and boy-friends. If women faced any challenge to their role as the controllers of consumption, it came not from style-conscious men – a tiny, over-publicised minority – but from their increasingly affluent and demanding children.

INTERPRETATIONS

There has not been much academic research on consumption, but there are many myths, clichés, popular beliefs and other varieties of conventional wisdom. What light, if any, do they throw on the subject?

One recent example could be called the Thatcher myth – the claim that the 'consumer revolution' took place in the 1980s as a result of Thatcherite economic policies. This is easy to disprove. The crucial break with austerity, as we have seen, started much earlier, in the 1950s, and most families owned their own homes, as well as television and the other standard durables, before 1979. The novelties of the 1980s – micro-waves, videos, CDs, personal stereos – simply continued existing trends.

On the Left, attitudes towards post-war consumption have generally been critical. One of the most familiar claims is that the entire process was directed from above, by powerful manufacturers and retailers, and that consumers themselves were weak and helpless. Again the evidence suggests otherwise. What actually happened in the 1950s was the very oppo-site of this: the shift from a sellers' to a buyers' market took away the advantage from the producers and gave it to the consumers. Rationing and shortages ended; resale price maintenance, following legislation in 1956 and 1964, was abolished. Previously, manufacturers had shared out markets with one another and fixed prices with retailers, to the disadvantage of consumers; now such conspiracies became illegal in all markets except books and drugs. Competition increased and the notion of marketing began to be accepted. Instead of selling what they happened to produce, compa-nies now had first to find out what consumers actually wanted. With the rapidly expanding market research industry providing the vital information on consumers, the new approach caught on and in the course of the 1960s and 1970s became the norm in most of the main consumer-goods markets. Manufacturers, including the very biggest, listened to consumers as never before: they had to.

The big retailers make even less likely villains. It is true that the multi-ples have grown enormously since 1945 and have won large shares of many consumer markets; groceries are only the most familiar example of retailer concentration. But there is little evidence to suggest that this has been to the disadvantage of consumers. On the contrary, in the 1950s the grocery chains ended price-fixing (unless prevented by manufacturers) and intro-duced self-service, with the result that shopping became quicker, cheaper and less embarrassing. The losers were not the consumers but the manufacturers (and high-price small shopkeepers). By the early 1970s the grocery multiples had grown to the point where they had the whip hand over even the biggest manufacturers. They forced suppliers to cut their prices and to spend specified amounts on advertising – or risk having their products delisted; they also undercut manufacturers' brands by bringing out cheaper, own-label versions. The manufacturers' loss was the retailers' – and consumers' – gain. It was not in the West that producers dominated but in the consumer-unfriendly regimes of communist eastern Europe – where even basic necessities were in short supply and and where well-made Western goods were a privilege of the Party elite.

What then of the influence of advertising? There is a widespread belief that advertising has quasi-magical powers and that it determines all consumer spending. Consumers are seen as puppets, with clever and cynical advertisers pulling the motivational strings; if a product is successful, it must be because of the advertising.

The reality is that advertising is less powerful, and its influence more circumscribed, than is often supposed. It is true that advertising expenditure in Britain – less than half of which is devoted to television – has been high by European standards. There are occasional campaigns that produce spectacular results. But advertising is by no means indispensable. Great commercial success has been achieved, as Marks and Spencer (and The Body Shop) has demonstrated, with no advertising at all; other examples include such products as meat, potatoes, furniture – and hard drugs. Nor is advertising any guarantee of success. Every year new products are launched, advertised and, because of poor sales, withdrawn. British Satellite Broadcasting spent over £20 million on advertising and still went down.

The effects of advertising, as advertising people themselves admit, are hard to measure. Lord Leverhulme said that half the money he spent on advertising was wasted: the trouble was that he didn't know which half. Even now it is hard to separate the influence of advertising from that of other elements in the 'marketing mix' – the quality of the product, price, distribution, packaging, promotions – not to mention the actions of competitors. Many shoppers buy the cheapest brand, or switch for the sake of variety ('brand promiscuity'); few are loyal to a single brand. In any case the influence of advertising for a particular brand tends to be limited to sales of that brand: it usually has no effect on the size of the market as a whole – on whether people want to use the product in the first place.

Most people's responses to advertising are not those of naïve and helpless victims. (Young children are an exception.) As Stephen King of the J. Walter Thompson agency has argued, the question is not how advertising uses people but how people use advertising. Advertising is occasionally witty or entertaining, often boring, sometimes distasteful; what it is not is omnipotent. It is not the master key to consumer culture.

One fashionable version of the advertising myth is the belief that 'products don't matter' – that it's the images that count. Products are all the same, we are told, and their functions can be taken for granted. What people consume – a favourite argument of cultural theorists – is not the product but its images and meanings. Of course, image rules in fashion-driven markets like lager and among style-conscious teenagers. But products and functions do matter: cars, those notorious status symbols, are a good example. People stopped buying British Leyland cars not because of images but because of the poor quality and performance of the cars themselves.

A more general claim about consumption is that it is the dominant concern in contemporary life and that Britain, like other Western countries, has become a 'consumer society'. In such a society the priority is on the production of consumer goods rather than on capital equipment or military hardware; most people are no longer poor or 'sustenance driven' but have money for 'wants' as well as 'needs'; they are catered for by user-friendly shops with self-service, long opening hours, easily available credit, and price competition; and they are protected by government and by organisations like the Consumers' Association. On these criteria, we could agree that Britain has moved some way towards becoming a consumer society.

The notion of 'consumerism', however, is more ambiguous. Besides its neutral, descriptive sense, indicating a way of life involving the purchase of Western-style consumer goods, it has a second, more pejorative sense, and this is where doubts set in. 'Consumerism' in this sense is a term of abuse, implying (a) that people buy consumer goods in the belief they can buy happiness; (b) that such people have an insatiable desire to shop and spend and acquire possessions; and (c) that their relationships with these possessions are more important to them than their relationships with other people. Applied to the working class, this is the central argument of several well-known books by Jeremy Seabrook. Before the war, he suggests, working-class people were poor but happy; since 1945, they have become affluent but miserable, selling their socialist souls for a mess of consumerist pottage.

What is lacking is any evidence that consumerism in this negative sense was either new or particularly widespread. In fact, there have always been people who spend and overspend for show and effect: conspicuous consumption was not invented in the 1980s, nor in the 1950s. For the working class, it was probably more significant before the war than it is today. The traditional working-class parlour, rarely used by the family, was so arranged that the furniture and fittings could be seen by neighbours and passers-by – an entire room of the house devoted to display. But when television arrived, most families put the set in the front room and changed the purpose of the room from show to use, the very opposite of what we would expect from the 'consumerism' thesis.

Nor is there evidence that the numbers of those in the grip of consumerism in recent decades has greatly increased. In fact, most consumer spending is not selfish. It is not for the purchaser himself or herself, but for their families; most consumption takes place in a family context. A great deal is also spent on gifts, mainly by women, for friends and relatives. Full-blown consumerism in the negative sense probably did not extend far beyond the legendary tribes of yuppies and of Essex folk. Complaints about consumerism – like those about 'luxury' in earlier centuries – seem to be based not on evidence but on snobbery – the fear that someone, somewhere, is buying things which the speaker disapproves of and thinks they shouldn't have.

One of the most common assumptions about consumer culture is that it is shaped primarily by 'style leaders', especially those from the various youth cults. The result is a one-sided history of consumption, obsessed with street fashion and the like, which ignores the tastes and habits of the people who matter most, the vast non-trendy majority. As the popularity of flying ducks and patterned carpets suggests, the influence of style leaders is surprisingly limited. Studies of consumption in British society need to focus less on youth culture, more on 'doily culture'; less on designer T-shirts and Giorgio Armani and more on twin sets and Marks and Spencer.

There is finally the view that mass consumption has meant Americanisation. Of course American companies, products and advertising agencies have left their mark, and British consumer culture in this period has been much more deeply influenced by America than by Europe. No continental country has put up so little resistance to the American marketing invasion. And yet the transatlantic influence should not be exaggerated. Alongside Coca-Cola and Kellogg's Corn Flakes there is a long line of products successful in America which proved much less popular in Britain. The fate of designer jeans, cake mixes and frozen orange juice suggests that British tastes by and large remained reassuringly British.

CONCLUSION

Consumption matters for three reasons. Since virtually everything people do involves something they have bought, it can throw light on almost every aspect of life. It enables people to say things about themselves in their purchases and possessions that they might never put into words. And it embodies the basic categories of society itself.

We cannot say whether post-war affluence has made people happier. But it has brought them comforts and conveniences they had never known before; and, through travel and the media, it has opened the way to the wider world. Of the various forces undermining 'traditional' society since the end of the war, the welfare state is the favourite of the textbook writers: but none had a greater effect than affluence.

The 1980s saw consumerism at its most blatant. It also saw the growth of the ecology movement and the backlash against consumerism. Perhaps the 1990s will clear away some of the myths surrounding consumption and lead us to a deeper understanding of its role in British society.

REFERENCES

Abrams, M. (1959a) 'The home-centred society', *The Listener*, 26 Nov., pp. 914–15.
──── (1959b) *The Teenage Consumer*, London: London Press Exchange.
Central Statistical Office (1992) *Social Trends 22*, London: HMSO.
Department of Employment (1986) *Family Expenditure Survey 1985*, London: HMSO.
Devine, Fiona (1992) *Affluent Workers Revisited: Privatism and the Working Class*, Edinburgh: Edinburgh University Press.
Goldthorpe, J. H., Lockwood, D., Bechhofer, F. and Platt, J. (1968–9) *The Affluent Worker*, Cambridge: Cambridge University Press.
Hunt, D. R. G., and Steele, M. P. (1980) 'Domestic temperature trends', *Heating and Ventilating Engineer*, 54 (April), pp. 5–15.
Odhams Press (1966) *Woman and the National Market Cosmetics 1966*, London: Odhams Press.
Procter, I. (1990) 'The privatisation of working-class life: a dissenting view', *British Journal of Sociology*, 41, pp. 157–80.
Saunders, P. (1990) *Social Class and Stratification*, London: Routledge.
Zweig, F. (1961) *The Worker in an Affluent Society*, London: Heinemann.

Chapter 12

Food and nutrition in post-war Britain

Anne Murcott

The British diet is not what it was. All the evidence – including personal experience – confirms that there have been considerable changes in British eating habits since 1945. Some of these were due to government policy intended to improve nutritional standards. Others reflect economic, demographic and cultural changes which were independent of policy.

What follows is presented chronologically. The first period, 1945–54, was that of post-war food rationing. It was followed by a period (1955–76) of gradual change. The third period, 1977–90, saw renewed government activity, directed particularly at the role of diet in Britain's high rates of coronary heart disease.

FOOD AND NUTRITION IN BRITAIN: 1945–54

People's experiences of eating in the 1940s varied tremendously. Among a small number of retired couples interviewed in 1990 (Walford 1990), Mr A. recollected with a shudder:

> I don't want those times to return again. They were terrible. Fruit was scarce – there wasn't any to have. I mean, I like sugar in my tea but when there wasn't any, you couldn't have it. I take sugar now though.

Mr B. remembered that up to and around 1945 'it was a case of plenty of food cooked very badly. Never mind the quality, feel the weight'. But Mrs C. took a different view. Aged 11 in 1939, she considered herself a product of the war years, when

> in a way the working classes had never had it so good. You got your fair share of food and you got good bread too. Before the war my mother tended to cook white bread, and then we got national flour. It was sort of grainy and we all liked it. They grumbled in the shops about it, though.

Mrs D., however, recalled little:

When war broke out I moved home to my mother's with our eldest. I don't remember much about it. I gave our coupons to my mother and she did all that.

Her husband, also less involved, explained: 'Rationing didn't affect me very much. Of course I was in the Air Force and we were fed very well.'

It is not known whether part of Mr D.'s wartime service experience included exposure to the Army Education Directorate's series of booklets *The British Way and Purpose* (BWP). He might, then, have missed no. 13 of December 1943 whose Chapter 3 (BWP 1944) discussed wartime disturbances to family life, and reminded service personnel of the reasons for the government's food policy. Explaining the measures adopted to lessen these disruptions, BWP argued that the 'fair' distribution of food involved rationing, price control, provision for special groups, and arrangements for communal feeding, notably the British Restaurants.

Wartime food policy, designed to ensure equitable distribution of scarce supplies to safeguard the nation nutrionally, is well known (Burnett 1989; Drummond and Wilbraham 1958; Titmuss 1963; Adams 1982; Johnston 1977; Driver 1983). Less familiar is its corollary, the official monitoring of the nation's diet and food expenditure. It started in 1940 with an annual, household-based survey among the urban working class, reflecting a concern for low-income groups that was well established among nutritionists before the war (Orr 1936; Burnett 1989; Drummond and Wilbraham 1958) and among poverty researchers from the turn of the century. But in 1950 the National Food Survey (NFS) was expanded into a representative nationwide enquiry, and has been conducted annually ever since. Despite its limitations, it now provides a 40-year data set on domestic food purchasing that is regarded as one of the best of its kind in the world.

Though paying special attention to nutritionally vulnerable groups, wartime policy was firmly concerned with the population as a whole. It did not end in 1945: indeed, rationing became even more extensive after the war – bread, for example, was rationed between 1946 and 1948 – than it had been before. The policy continued until rationing itself was ended in 1954.

The success of food rationing was demonstrated just as the policy itself came to an end. A comparison between pre-war and post-war household expenditure on food (Hollingsworth 1985) showed that the social class gradient in nutrient intake had been reduced. The wartime experiment in social engineering – regulating the supply of food – not by trade interests, but according to 'the needs of the people' (MacCarrison 1944 in Driver 1983: 18) – had proved its worth.

It did not, however, change everything: many older habits were as strong as ever. In rural areas there was still a high degree of self-sufficiency in food supply, and it was still taken for granted that women were responsible for family meals and that their place was in the kitchen. But the immediate post-war years also brought signs of things to come. Bird's Eye began frozen food processing in 1945 and a year later bananas again became available. Self-service groceries appeared; by 1950 the pioneers in this new form of retailing, the Co-op, had 600 such stores in operation. Even among the urban poor in Liverpool a few families were found to have adopted the then 'foreign' dish of curry and rice. And in 1950 Raymond Postgate founded the Good Food Club and Elizabeth David published *A Book of Mediterranean Food* (David 1950).

FOOD AND NUTRITION IN BRITAIN: 1955–76

The immediate response to the end of rationing was a surge in demand for foods previously in short supply – meat, eggs, canned fruit and so on. Sugar consumption rose particularly rapidly, and by 1960 Britain had the fifth highest per capita intake in the world. But around this time dietary patterns settled into place and only changed gradually thereafter (Burnett 1989).

There was a good deal of continuity in other food-related areas as well. Although the government was no longer responsible for the nutritional status of the population as a whole,it still took an interest in particular vulnerable groups (Barnell *et al.* 1968). At the other end of the spectrum *The Good Food Guide*, edited by Raymond Postgate until 1969 and there-after by Christopher Driver, continued to help discriminating eaters find decent meals in Britain restaurants. Change in this period was gradual. The government began to be concerned about various nutritional and medical problems which were becoming more prominent in the post-war period, notably obesity. Social investigators 'rediscovered' poverty, even as Harold Macmillan was saying that 'You've never had it so good' (Townsend 1954; Lambert 1964; Coates and Silburn 1973), and it has remained on the agenda ever since.

Burnett (1979) has summarised key trends of this period. For the majority, the standard of living rose – partly as a result of a decline in the size of the average household, partly as a result of the low rate of unemployment and the increase in the number of women in paid employment. More households had refrigerators, consumption of frozen foods rose steadily, and the expression 'convenience food' entered the vocabulary. Eating out at restaurants saw a modest growth and, together with the expansion of holidays abroad, brought wider familiarity with 'foreign' cuisines.

Changes in rural areas remained slow. Echoing earlier studies, Emmett (1964) described a North Wales village economy of 1958–62 as one based more on exchange than money. Here, the cooking techniques women learned were more suitable for pre-war, farm-produced ingredients than for the newly available tinned produce that would have relieved the villagers' dietary monotony. And good shopping facilities were lacking.

Frozen food that could have helped, Emmett noted, did not become available in the area until 1960.

Class and regional variations were clearly evident. Although the overall proportion of total household expenditure on food went down (from the 33 per cent in 1953 to 24.8 per cent in 1975), there was still a wide gap between the proportion spent by the wealthiest (19.6 per cent) and that spent by the poorest (32.5 per cent). *British Tastes*, a compendium of market research evidence, revealed that home baking predominated in Yorkshire, while the Midlands diet was described as remarkable only for a 'stodgy unimaginativeness' (Allen 1968). But some shifts were evident in the apparently new-found home-centredness of affluent Luton car workers of the 1960s – shifts measured in terms of husbands' participation in shopping and washing up (Goldthorpe *et al.* 1969).

Policy analysts and commentators continued their work on poverty, which included attention to diet (Townsend 1954), and they were now joined by those documenting the effects of unemployment. Marsden and Duff, for example, reported that some workless men experienced loss of appetite or indigestion, or forsook their own food to ensure other family members did not go without (1975: 194).

Policy still focused on the nutritionally vulnerable (MAFF 1976; Darke 1977). Legislation in 1971 on the provision of welfare foods for infants and children earned Margaret Thatcher, as the minister responsible, the uncom- plimentary epithet 'milk snatcher'. Two new concerns appeared. Diet was identified as a possible risk factor in cardiovascular disease (DHSS 1974). And the reappearance of rickets in Britain, largely among the Asian population (though the peak of net annual Asian migration was already past), added them to the groups at nutritional risk (DHSS 1977).

Meanwhile, the transformation of the food industry was well under way. In 1972, as Britain entered the European Community, the French firm Carrefour opened the first hypermarket on an out-of-town site just north of Cardiff in Caerphilly. From the public's point of view, retailing could be described as 'extremely fluid' (Zackon 1970: 45); husbands were reported to be accompanying their wives to the supermarket.

Some of the changes in agriculture were discussed in Newby's (1977, 1983) study of East Anglian farm workers. The contrast with the studies of rural life of the 1950s is striking. The farmworker's self-sufficiency in food was much reduced, payment in kind was barely available, and the time- honoured perk of gleaning now took the modern form of gathering what was left after the harvesting of peas for Bird's Eye. As consumers, farm- workers were at a disadvantage. Prices at a local supermarket were 10–15 per cent higher than in urban stores in the same chain and 25–30 per cent higher in small family shops; a greengrocer's mobile van offered limited, expensive choice. But unlike working-class households elsewhere in the early 1970s, most owned a freezer.

Other things had not changed. Men were expected to have large appetites that needed regular stoking; providing meals for them (and for children) continued to form a key element of women's role and identity. Eating was recognisably 'British', with minimal dietary variation. There was no 'ethnic' food – no pizzas, pastas, rice or curries. (In Britain as a whole, by contrast, a Gallup survey only a year later reported that seven out of ten people were familiar with chow mein and sweet and sour pork, and eight out of ten knew about pizzas (Burnett 1979).

Concern for healthy eating was not uppermost in the public mind. In his account of changes in working-class culture since the 1920s, Hoggart observed that a 'good table' still meant one that was 'fully stocked' rather than one 'presenting a (nutritionally) balanced diet' (Hoggart 1957: 37). A market-related academic survey of housewives' meat-buying habits of the late 1950s (Marsh 1958) reported reasons for their choice as economy, leanness, flavour and ease of cooking – but no mention anywhere of nutrition or health. A similar study, on the 'behaviour, motivations and attitudes of housewives as food providers', found that the women put 'health consideration(s)' first, but only by a small margin, and they chose food that 'contained health nutrients' rather than looking for 'nutrients that happened to be contained in foods' (Sofer 1965: 196).

What people knew about nutrition – in some cases, not very much – was reported in a number of studies by social nutritionists and market researchers. This body of work continued to approach the subject by concentrating almost exclusively on the attitudes and beliefs of house-wives (Lynch 1969). A typical finding was that though awareness of specific nutrients was high, more detailed knowledge was often lacking. But such an approach came under increasing criticism from feminists and others, as a decontextualised judgement of women's failings.

A rather different approach was that of the influential anthropologist Mary Douglas. Her analysis of British meals suggested that attempts to engineer dietary change were likely to founder on deep-lying popular assumptions about the structure of the meal and about the suitability of particular foods in that structure (Douglas and Nicod 1974).

In the early 1970s the period of moderate change came to an end. Double figure inflation was imminent and by 1974 the economy moved into 'serious depression' (Burnett 1979: 334). Unemployment crept upwards. And growing concern about health led the government to a more activist stance in nutritional policy.

FOOD AND NUTRITION IN BRITAIN: 1977–90

The publication in 1976 of *Prevention and Health: Everybody's Business* (DHSS 1976) marked a turning point in government policy. Concern about coronary heart disease, hitherto largely confined to public health professionals, was now brought to the public's attention as one of the major health problems facing the nation. And among the risk factors in heart disease, which also included smoking and lack of exercise, it specifically mentioned improper diet. While recognising that the role of diet was still a matter on which experts disagreed, the document noted the possible advantages of reducing the consumption of sugar and animal fat. And in more general terms, it encouraged people to take responsibility for their own health.

In one sense this document – launched, incidentally, under a Labour government – marked a return to the wartime policy focus on the diet of the population as a whole. (Though concern for nutritionally vulnerable groups continued as before). But its method of putting the policy into effect was very different. Instead of the 1940s multi-pronged approach – regulation and control, as well as public education – it was limited to only the last of these. The government would not intervene, other than to provide the advice and education that would enable responsible individuals to make an informed choice of their own.

This attitude was also reflected in the government's change of policy on the diet of schoolchildren. In legislation in 1980 it released authorities from responsibility for the provision of school meals in the form provided for in 1944. This was not welcomed by all. A group of parents in Yorkshire were reported to regard chips or sandwiches as an inadequate substitute for 'proper' school dinners.

In 1976, when *Prevention and Health* was published, some of the patterns of food consumption associated with the 1980s were already apparent. The rate of sugar consumption was slowing. Bread consumption continued its long-term decline, though by 1977–8 this was confined to white bread, as consumption of brown bread was beginning to increase. Similarly, milk consumption declined during the 1980s, but low fat milk gained at the expense of whole milk. With over 80 per cent of households owning a fridge and 30 per cent a freezer, total expenditure on frozen food continued to increase and in 1974 had already reached £345 million. People ate out more often, while meals at home started to fragment, being replaced by what market researchers in the 1980s described as 'grazing'.

The public debate on healthy eating, triggered by *Prevention and Health*, 'took off' with the publication in September 1983 of what is known as the 'NACNE report' – *A discussion paper on proposals for nutritional guidelines for health education in Britain*. It was prepared for the National Committee on Nutrition (NACNE) – a body constituted in 1979 by the Health Education Council (HEC) and the British Nutrition Foundation (BNF). This alliance between a quango and an organisation set up by the food industry was in itself a source of controversy. The HEC was established by the government in 1968; in 1983 it was still funded by the government but was otherwise an independent body. The BNF, by contrast, was funded by its members – large corporations in the food industry – and received no income from the government. Founded in 1967, it provides a forum in which member companies join 'eminent scientists' that they may 'share common concerns with the scientific community about nutritional problems which affect consumers'. Their object, among other things, is to advance the 'education of the public in nutrition'. The HEC's independence from government and the BNF's funding sources were, in the eyes of lobbyists, policy commentators and journalists, responsible for a behind-the-scenes tussle for the text of the report.

Though never officially adopted, NACNE's recommendations for the population at large to reduce their intake of fats, sugar and salt, and to increase their intake of dietary fibre, were echoed in those of a second report of 1984. This was produced by a panel of the Committee on Medical Aspects of Food Policy (COMA), whose remit is to examine the relation between diet and heart disease (DHSS 1984). COMA's 'recommendations to the general public' subtly refined those of NACNE (17) (DHSS 1984). Public health education efforts to reduce Britain's high rate of mortality from coronary heart disease (higher in Scotland, Northern Ireland and Wales than in England) were formalised in major campaigns: 'Heartbeat Wales', the first, being followed in 1987 by 'Look After Your Heart' in England.

The furore caused by the publication of NACNE soon turned into a public debate about healthy eating amongst lobbyists, pressure groups and others. One notable participant was the London Food Commission (LFC), whose position is closely allied to investigative journalism such as Cannon's (Walker and Cannon 1984; Cannon 1987). From quite another political quarter, battle was joined by policy commentary in the form of a collection of papers by various scientists published by the Social Affairs Unit (Anderson 1986). This represented a counter to Cannon, the LFC and others in pointing out, for instance, that the aetiological relation between diet and coronary heart disease remained scientifically contentious. At around the same time, the editor, now in his capacity as columnist in *The Spectator* (Anderson 1987), coined the memorable expression 'Food Leninists' in his trenchant criticism of both current (Tory) government thinking on nutrition education and the leftish lobbies and the Labour Party food policy proposals (Labour Party 1986) alike.

Prevention and Health, together with a companion booklet *Eating for Health* (DHSS 1978), did much to make people more aware of the links between health and nutrition. By 1987 'the phenomenon of healthy eating' was widely recognised. Market researchers reported that 'the healthy eating movement had strengthened its hold on the public's imagination in general' (DMB&B 1987: 1). It was promoted by a wide variety of propaganda material, ranging from HEC leaflets in doctors' surgery waiting rooms, to Tesco and Sainsbury's leaflets and pamphlets at supermarkets, to product labelling and advertising. There was even a gourmet version, in the massively labour-intensive *nouvelle cuisine* and *cuisine minceur*. And there was a contribution from the ecology movement, with its concern for the health of the planet and for the health of the people; its attention to food habits and food production was also shared by various radical groups and journalists on the left.

Food was news, both in journalism and in the electronic media. In 1976 there was a series on BBC Radio 3, with an accompanying publication that offered a guide to 'sensible' eating; a little later there were brief messages promoting healthy living on Radio 1. But it was not long before healthy eating had triggered a veritable explosion of media coverage: television programmes, articles in newspapers and women's magazines, and special healthy eating periodicals.

When market researchers looked at what people understood by healthy eating, however, they found that in the face of 'much conflicting advice and activity' (DMB&B 1987: 2) there was a good deal of confusion. And what healthy eating meant in practice was unclear. Market research now enquired not only into housewives' nutritional knowledge but also into the broader question of attitudes towards food and health among both men and women. There was a similar shift in focus, from knowledge to attitudes, in research by social nutritionists. Work by sociologists came to the same conclusion: that the connection between healthy eating propaganda and people's actual eating habits and attitudes was by no means simple. A study of women in South Wales found that women were alert to the messages encouraging healthy eating. But they felt that there was a conflict between what was good food in terms of health and what was good food in terms of personal taste and preference. And they normally put their husbands' preferences first, accepting without question that it was part of their duty as wives to provide 'a cooked dinner' (Britain's infamous 'meat and two veg'). This finding was confirmed by Charles and Kerr's study in North East England. There too, women's role and identity as family food provider meant privileging the tastes and preferences of children and, especially, husbands. And as elsewhere, the experts' understanding of such terms as 'balanced diet' and healthy food was quite different from that of the housewives themselves (Charles and Kerr 1988).

A similar approach was taken by Graham in her analysis of infant feeding, part of a study of the 'transition to motherhood' in a northern town at the end of the 1970s. Mothers during the first six months of the babies' lives typically abandoned the 'medically preferred methods' (i.e. breast feeding) and introduced mixed feeding before the age of four months). Her conclusion was that there was a conflict between what the doctors recommended and what the family was willing to put up with: the women's culturally defined responsibilities for providing for the whole family and maintaining domestic harmony gave them 'good' social reasons for 'bad' nutritional habits (Graham 1980). As with Charles and Kerr, the question of diet was linked with a feminist analysis of women's role.

Public controversy over diet has not always been concerned with nutrition. It has also been provoked by ethnic and religious divisions. A school in Yorkshire with a predominantly Asian roll was boycotted by non-Asian parents amidst rumours that Muslim and Hindu festivals were being celebrated in the school and that halal meat was served at lunch. As it turned out, the school was Church of England and the school dinners included fish fingers and steamed pudding: but the episode reminds us yet again that the significance of food is emotional and cultural as well as nutritional.

This chapter is a preliminary account of post-war changes. Whether they can teach us any lessons, and help in the effort to improve the nation's diet, is a challenge for future study.

REFERENCES

Adams, P. (1982) *Health of the State*, New York: Praeger.

Allen, D.E. (1968) *British Tastes*, London: Hutchinson.

Anderson, D. (ed.) (1986), *A Diet of Reason*, London: Social Affairs Unit.

Anderson, D. (1987) *The Spectator Book of Imperative Cooking*, London: Harrap.

Barnell, H.R., Coomes, T.J. and Hollingsworth, D.F. (1968), 'Some aspects of the implementation of food policy', *Proceedings of the Nutrition Society* 27, pp. 8–13.

Burnett, J. (1979) *Plenty and Want*, London: Scolar Press.

——— (1989) *Plenty and Want*, London: Routledge.

BWP (1944), *The British Way and Purpose*, London: Army Education Directorate.

Cannon, G. (1987) *The Politics of Food*, London: Century.

Charles, N. and Kerr, M. (1988), *Women, Food and Families*, Manchester: Manchester University Press.

Coates, D. and Silburn, R. (1970), *Poverty: the Forgotten Englishmen*, Harmondsworth: Pelican.

Darke, S.J. (1977), 'Monitoring the nutritional status of the UK population', *Proceedings of the Nutrition Society*, 36, pp. 235–40.

David, E. (1950) *A Book of Mediterranean Food*, London: John Lehman.

DHSS (1974) *On the State of the Public Health*, Annual Report of the Chief Medical Officer, London: HMSO.

——— (1976) *Prevention and Health: Everybody's Business*, London: HMSO.

——— (1977) *On the State of the Public Health*, Annual Report of the Chief Medical Officer, London: HMSO.

——— (1978) *Eating for Health*, London: HMSO.

——— (1984) *Diet and Cardiovascular Disease*, Report on Health and Social Subjects 28, London: HMSO.

DMB&B (1987) *The DMB&B Healthy Eating Study: II*, London: D'Arcy Masius Benton and Bowles.

Douglas, M. and Nicod, M. (1974) 'Taking the biscuit: the structure of British meals', *New Society*, 30, pp. 744–7.

Driver, C. (1983) *The British at Table 1940–1980*, London: Chatto & Windus.

Drummond, J.C. and Wilbraham, A. (1958) *The Englishman's Food*, London, Jonathan Cape.

Emmett, I. (1964) *A North Wales Village: a social anthropological study*, London: Routledge and Kegan Paul.

Goldthorpe, J.H., Lockwood, D., Bechhofer, F. and Platt, J. (1969), *The Affluent Worker in the Class Structure*, Cambridge: Cambridge University Press.

Graham, H. (1980) 'Family influences in early years on the eating habits of children', in Turner, M. (ed.), *Nutrition and Lifestyles*, London: Applied Science Publishers.

Hoggart, R. (1957) *The Uses of Literacy*, Harmondsworth: Penguin.

Hollingsworth, D.F. (1985) 'Rationing and economic constraints on food consumption in Britain since the Second World War', in Oddy, D.J. and Miller, D.S. *Diet and Health in Modern Britain*, London: Croom Helm.

Johnston, J.P. (1977) *A Hundred Years' Eating*, Dublin: Gill and Macmillan.

Labour Party (1986) *Food Policy: A priority for Labour*, Consultative Paper London: Labour Party.

Lambert, R. (1964) 'Nutrition in Britain 1950–60', Occasional Papers on Social Administration.

Lynch, G.W. (1969) 'Nutrition in the home', in *Getting the Most out of Food*, London: Van den Berghs.

MacCarrison, R. (1944) *Nutrition and Health*, London: St Catherine Press.

MAFF (1976) *Manual of Nutrition*, London: HMSO.

Marsden, D. and Duff, E. (1975) *Workless*, Harmondsowrth: Pelican.

Marsh, A.A. (1958) *Meat Buying Habits*, Leeds: University of Leeds.

Newby, H. (1977) *The Deferential Worker*, London: Allen Lane.

—— (1983) 'Living from hand to mouth: the farmworker, food and agribusiness', in Murcott, A. (ed.), *The Sociology of Food and Eating*, Aldershot: Gower.

Orr, J. Boyd (1936) *Food, health and income*, London: Macmillan.

Sofer, C. (1965) 'Buying and selling: A study in the sociology of distribution', *Sociological Review*, 13, pp. 183–209.

Titmuss, R. (1963), *Essays on the Welfare State*, London: Allen and Unwin.

Townsend, P. (1954) 'Measuring poverty', *British Journal of Sociology*, 5, pp. 130–7.

—— (1979) *Poverty in the United Kingdom*, Harmondsworth: Pelican.

Walford, E. (1990) 'Women as nurturers', MSc (Econ) dissertation submitted to the University of Wales.

Walker, C. and Cannon, G. (1984), *The Food Scandal*, London: Century Arrow.

Zackon, D. (1970) 'Family food behaviour and attitudes', London: Queen Elizabeth College mimeo.

Chapter 13

Religion in post-war Britain: a sociological view[1]

Grace Davie

INTRODUCTION

This chapter has two sections. The first is relatively short and assumes a chronological approach. It suggests three periods in the religious life of this country since 1945. These are (a) a period of reconstruction (1945–60); (b) a decade and a half of 'relevance' (1960–75), characterised by a tendency to minimise the distinction between the sacred and the secular; and (c) (from the mid-1970s onwards), a re-emphasis on the sacred as a distinctive category, both within and outside the mainline denominations.

The second section looks at the post-war period from a different perspective. It examines three topics – the role of women within the churches, the ecumenical debate and the European question (ecumenism and Europe are closely linked) – within the following framework: what has happened, is happening, with respect to these issues (among others) was unthinkable, unimaginable even, forty years ago. What, then, with hindsight, can we say about such changes? Why have they occurred? Do they, primarily, reflect shifts in society – including global society – rather than in the churches? If so, how can the churches accommodate the consequences? Or have the churches themselves been able to initiate societal shifts as well as respond to these? To what extent is the latter tendency likely, given the supposedly secular nature of British society in the late twentieth century? But, most important of all, is it correct to assume that our society will, necessarily, become more rather than less secular as the year 2000 approaches? In other words, are the sociological assumptions of the last forty years – to a large extent dominated by the secularisation debate – still helpful as we try to understand the nature and form of these complex and sometimes unexpected developments?

Bearing the predominance of the secularisation debate in mind, it is hardly surprising that Wallis and Bruce (1989) use this theme as a pivot in their recent review of the British contribution to post-war sociology of religion. In so doing, they indicate the variety of approaches and the range of data that this type of thinking encompasses. The secularisation thesis is far from straightforward; it is complex, nuanced and at times contradictory (Martin 1978; Wilson 1982). It has, however, provided an effective way forward, a framework for ordering a wide range of ideas and information about religion in contemporary society, particularly in its north European forms. On the other hand, it is undeniable that significant weaknesses in the sociology of religion in this country derive, at least in part, from too great a dependence on this approach. Conspicuous among these weaknesses have been the relative lack of attention paid to the mainline churches (too readily assumed to be in irreversible decline) and the tendency to regard more diffuse patterns of religiosity simply as Christian 'residues'. In contrast, a great deal of work – some of it excellent – has been done on sects and new religious movements, groups that involve a relatively small proportion of the population. With respect to minorities more generally, more attention needs to be paid to the growing other-faith communities in this country and to the proper foundations of a truly pluralist society. The Rushdie controversy has revealed all too clearly the rather facile assumptions of a live-and-let-live approach to religious toleration, an approach not unrelated to the preconceptions of secularisation.

Thompson's rejoinder to Wallis and Bruce (Thompson 1990) indicates a more fundamental weakness not only in the sociology of religion, but also in the review article itself. There exists in both an explicit and worrying atheoretical bias associated with a failure to relate contemporary patterns of religious life to more general sociological thinking. This chapter is written with Thompson's rejoinder in mind. The first section concludes by reviewing the confused and conflicting data concerning the nature of British religion within a broader discussion of modernity, a debate which necessarily questions certain aspects of the secularisation thesis. The second part considers the three topics selected for particular study primarily in relation to wider social processes; more especially in relation to changing gender roles in contemporary society and to the gradual emergence of a greater European identity in the post-war period.

A CHRONOLOGICAL APPROACH

Clearly, any attempt to introduce chronological divisions into post-war history must, to some extent, be arbitrary. There are always alternative sets of dates that can be argued equally well. Nor are such divisions – however decided upon – tidy or self-contained units. The thread of events will always be continuous despite changes in mood and emphasis. We can take just one example. It is clear that the liturgical changes within the Church of England set in motion by the desire for relevance characteristic of the 1960s do not just come to an end in the 1970s; on the contrary, they continue to work themselves out but in the rather different atmosphere of later decades. The result is both sad and paradoxical. What started as a genuine attempt to provide forms of worship accessible to the man in the street has ended in liturgical chaos. Congregations select from the bewildering variety on offer to create their own particular, often rather exclusive, styles. Worship has become less rather than more accessible for the great majority of people.[2]

Bearing this example and the arbitrary nature of the task in mind, we can, none the less, outline some characteristics of the periods suggested in the introduction.

Six years of war left Europe, never mind Britain, in ruins. Not only was the need for material reconstruction obvious, there was, in addition, the task of reconstituting the whole fabric of political, economic and social life. The material task was daunting enough. In the diocese of London, for example, only seventy out of 700 churches remained unscathed after the bombing and many had been completely destroyed, quite apart from the need to provide new church buildings and personnel to keep pace with post-war housing programmes. Faced with the challenge the churches, the Church of England included, managed pretty well: the mood of the 1950s was, in ecclesiastical terms, relatively optimistic as reconstruction proceeded. But the emphasis lay essentially in what the word reconstruction implies: that is, in an attempt to put back what had been destroyed and to rebuild the institutions of the past. The assumption that this might be possible conveys better than anything else the mood of this decade and a half. Hastings sums up such feelings – perilously close to complacency – in the following:

> By the middle of the 1950s it may well have seemed that the Church was right after all to dodge any more radical measure of post-war reform. It had not been needed. The leadership had re-established confidence quite effectively without it. The Captain of England's cricket team in 1954 was ordained in the Church of England in 1955 – David Sheppard, a bright young product of the old Cambridge Evangelical stable. It was a most satisfying moment, symbol of what the fifties seemed all about.
>
> (Hastings 1986: 447)

It was not to last. The gradual realisation that the old order could not be rebuilt and that a majority in the nation remained very largely indifferent to religious organisations of whatever kind required a different type of response.

The churches were, inevitably, in for a bumpy ride through the 1960s. The world into which they appeared to fit so well was being challenged on every front. Profound changes in society prompted radical reactions in the churches, not least in the Church of England. Controversial restatements of the Christian faith, new views about morality, the extensive revision of church services, the demand for reorganisation in the parochial system, and debates about the nature of ministry dominated the agenda. All might still be well if the Church could shake off its image of belonging essentially to the past. A modern, up-to-date and, above all, relevant church must be shaped to face the future.

A good example of the changes that were taking place can be found in the career of David Sheppard – that bright young product of the Cambridge Evangelical stable – who, by this time, was hard at it in Canning Town and coming to terms with some radical shifts in perspective. Clearly, there was no room for complacency:

> When we went to the Mayflower Family Centre, church life had largely collapsed. There were six regular communicants. Twenty might come to a special service. It was plain that we should give the lion's share of our time to our neighbours, who were right outside the life of the Church, and to the life of the community in Canning Town. That meant being ready to listen to what was important to people whose social and economic experience of life was enormously different.
>
> (Sheppard and Worlock 1988: 25–6)

By any standards, the Mayflower Centre in Canning Town was an impressive undertaking. It – and a number of similar ventures – should not be underestimated; they represented a real effort to make contact with working-class people. But membership figures, together with almost any other indicator of religiosity in the 1960s, reveal all too clearly the Churches' continuing inability to stem the growth of religious indifference in Britain. Relevance *per se* was not going to solve the problem.[3] Important and lasting shifts had, none the less, occurred within the churches, which would never be quite the same again. Changes in the Church of England and in the Free Churches must, however, pale into insignificance compared with the transformation in Roman Catholicism brought about in this period by the Second Vatican Council. Vatican II altered the framework of ecclesiastical life on a global scale for all Christians – Protestants and Roman Catholics alike – in a wide variety of ways and in a remarkably short space of time. It was, Hastings argues (1986: 525), the most important ecclesiastical event of the century, never mind of the 1960s[4].

A new image for the churches, free from the shackles of the past, expressing its relevance (not to mention its worship) in the language of the people, was one reaction to the complacency of an earlier period. As we have seen, its results failed to include a widepread return to church-going. A second reaction (as the 1960s gave way to a rather less confident decade) took a very different turn. Amongst a minority – if not in the population as a whole – religious life was, it seems, proving increasingly attractive, though not always in ways that people either expected or approved of. Controversies surrounding what have become known as new religious movements provoked angry headlines in the popular press (Beckford 1985; Barker 1989; Wilson 1990); house churches began to multiply at a

phenomenal rate (Walker 1985); and immigrant communities – a significant section of the population – retained their own forms and styles of
religious life, resisting pressures to adapt to British ways of thought, not
least to its markedly understated religiosity (Knott 1988). But even within
the mainline churches there was evidence of growth and renewal amongst a
minority, notably the evangelical parishes of the Church of England. The
evidence about religious life becomes, therefore, curiously contradictory:
on the one hand, widespread indifference persists (usually in the form of
Christian nominalism), but on the other, there are signs of change. The
stress begins to lie increasingly on the distinctiveness of the sacred as
religious boundaries are reaffirmed. For significant groups of people,
church membership becomes sought after and chosen, rather than
something that may be assumed or taken for granted.[5]

In many respects, these confusing tendencies reflect underlying shifts in
society though they have been differently interpreted. For some commentators they are associated with what has become known as late capitalism; a
post-industrial or post-modern society quite different in mood from the
optimistic certainties of the 1960s (a shift in emphasis ushered in by the oil
crisis of the early 1970s). The concept of post-modernism remains, however, controversial. For it is equally possible to argue that the re-emphasis
on this kind of religious life both within and without the mainline churches
is an ongoing part of modernity, rather than a post- or anti-modern reaction
to this. For all its optimism and creativity, modernity has – and always will
– engender a whole range of unsolved moral, ecological and, surely,
religious problems. The religious dimension must, therefore, be considered an essential part of modernity, though its shapes and forms may
be widely diverse (Hervieu-Léger 1986). Both views – obliged to take the
religious dimension into account – challenge the assumptions of the
secularisation thesis. So, too, does the rather unexpected prominence of
the British churches – as supposedly declining institutions – in the political
debates of the 1980s. We shall return to this point in the concluding section
of this chapter.

THEMATIC APPROACHES

The role of women in the churches: with special reference to the ordination of women within the Church of England

There can be no doubt that the role of women, both lay and ordained,
within the British churches has been transformed in the post-war period. It
is equally true that this shift reflects – rather than determines – changes in
the wider society. Had the revolution in gender roles not taken place in the
Western World (both in Britain and elsewhere), the debate about women's
ordination simply would not be happening. The churches, in this instance,

are operating as reactive rather than proactive institutions, exemplifying a phenomenon about which they are – as sacred institutions – understandably ambivalent. For beneath this debate lies a fundamental tension: it can be summarised quite simply. Churches claim to embody an unchanging and, many would say, unchangeable message. They have, none the less, to exist – like any other human institution – within particular societies and cultures. And societies and cultures shift and adapt over time. Birth rates, for example, rise and fall; patterns of family life alter; structures of employment change; values and attitudes evolve correspondingly. Exactly how far the churches are free to respond to these (and other) shifts remains, and will always remain, a source of tension. Or, to put the question in a different way, are the promptings of the secular world seen by the churches as the hand of God (and so a source of enlightenment), or as distractions from the truth (to be avoided at all costs)? Answers to this question are complex and varied: we have seen how the pendulum can swing between a desire for relevance and a greater emphasis on the distinctiveness of the sacred.

This is not something peculiar to the post-war period in Britain. It is a more or less permanent tension for all churches in all places and at all times. Why, then, has the issue of the ordination of women within the Church of England caused such prolonged and acute anxiety? Is there something particular about the reappraisal of gender in post-war Britain, about the changing role of women in British society? Or do the tensions derive primarily from the nature of Anglicanism, and more especially of the Church of England? My conclusion tends towards the latter explanation. After all, most Protestant denominations in Britain have handled this shift relatively easily (Langley 1989).

The issue of women's ordination has been particularly painful for the Church of England in that it calls into question the wider, unresolved – possibly insoluble – issues of authority both within the English Church and within the Anglican Communion itself. Who, for example, has the authority to decide changes of such magnitude? How are such decisions to be enforced, always assuming that they can be arrived at in the first place? What happens if episcopal and synodical expressions of authority come into conflict in the Church as a whole, or in any particular diocese? Which of these will take precedence? How can the Catholic and Protestant ideas about priesthood be reconciled with respect to this debate? Is the Anglican Communion still a Communion if its bishops cannot mutually respect one another's authority? These, and many other delicate questions about authority, follow from the issue of women's ordination as night follows day. They cannot be dismissed lightly.

The emergence of synodical government and its implications for the debate about authority within the Church of England should be noted as a major development of the post-war period. The General Synod was opened by the Queen in November 1970, since when synodical matters have come to dominate Church affairs and to provide an ethos noticeably different from that of earlier decades. Like all such innovations, the system has its good points and its bad, but the uneasy compromise of the Bishop(s)-in-Synod as the locus of Anglican authority is bound to prove problematic in practice. What happens, for example, at diocesan level, if the Bishop wants one thing and his diocesan synod votes for another? Is it really possible not only to maintain two decision-making processes within one institution, but also to justify these theologically (Habgood 1983: 115ff.)? It is; but not without cost.

Beneath these painful debates, however, there is evidence of a decisive shift in public opinion with respect to the ordination of women. Both within the Church and outside it, there is a growing acceptance of both principle and practice. It is, it seems, an idea whose time has come. Moreover, positive opinion towards the ordination of women maintains itself despite an awareness that such a decision might have negative consequences for relationships with the Roman Church. What was unthinkable forty years ago may well be commonplace before the end of the century.[6]

The ecumenical debate[7]

When David Sheppard (already consecrated Bishop of Woolwich) moved from London to be Bishop of Liverpool in 1975, his first congratulatory telegram came from the Roman Catholic Archbishop of Liverpool, Andrew Beck (Sheppard and Worlock 1988: 39). That gesture proved a foretaste of things to come, for Sheppard's partnership with Beck's successor, Archbishop Derek Worlock, has become nationally, indeed internationally, famous. Liverpool, a city dominated by sectarianism well into the post-war period, is now at the forefront of practical ecumenism. The religious life of Liverpool (indeed its political life as well) is *sui generis*, and it would be dangerous to deduce any general trends from this most Irish of British cities (Davie 1987). None the less, one factor amongst many that have enabled such an outstanding Christian partnership in Liverpool has undoubtedly been the transformation in the ecumenical climate of the country as a whole. What was totally impossible in Liverpool in the immediate post-war decades was very nearly impossible everywhere else.

Sociologists differ in their interpretation of ecumenism. Is this a sign of strength on the part of the churches; that they have the confidence to engage in dialogue? Or is it a sign of their weakness; all churches now have their backs against the wall, so they may as well co-operate in their efforts to stave off disaster? That two plausible, yet mutually contradictory, explanations exist reflects the confusing nature of the data that we noted in the first part of this chapter. Either way, however, the shift from mutual hostility towards active co-operation – never mind toleration – has been remarkable. How has it come about?

In some ways the answer to this question is paradoxical. On the one hand, there has been more than one false start – notably, the failure of the Anglican–Methodist Unity Scheme (1972) and of Covenanting for Unity (1980); on the other, the gradual *rapprochement* of the various Christian churches has continued, despite – rather than because of – these organisational initiatives. Indeed it could be argued that the whole thing begins to take off precisely when organisational schemes cease to dominate the agenda. Left to itself, the centre of gravity gradually, but irrevocably, begins to shift, away from the separate identity of individual churches – still prevalent in the immediate post-war period – and towards an awareness that there are different ways of expressing what is essentially a common message. The change occurs at different times in different places, but a decisive moment arrives when the minority who have always looked for ecumenical opportunities turn themselves – almost imperceptibly – into a majority. As in the case of women's ordination, the middle ground has shifted. In consequence, those who resist begin to look curiously out of place, nowhere more so than in Liverpool.[8] This change in perspective is crucial to the ecumenical process, but we need to be clear about its implications. One of these is only too apparent: relatively successful ecumenism does not imply unanimity among British church people. Far from it. Many issues – for example, the split between those who feel that the churches have a part to play in political and social affairs and those who resist this trend – continue to divide Christian thinking in this country. Controversies remain; sometimes they are heated. But they result, for the most part, in splits that lie across rather than between the major denominations.[9]

The position of the Anglican Church in the ecumenical process remains distinctive. Clearly this catholic yet reformed church has a part to play in the *rapprochement* of Christians more generally. The Orthodox, for example, can find some common ground with Anglicans: common ground that just does not exist in their contacts with other Protestant churches. On the other hand, the Anglicans lie outside the ancient Orthodox/Roman divide. (The Orthodox are, moreover, one of the few Christian churches currently experiencing growth in Britain.) So much is relatively positive. More negative is the lack of clarity within Anglicanism – not least unresolved questions about the ordination of women within the Church of England – that has bedevilled many an ecumenical scheme. The Church simply cannot decide which way it is facing, and no creature that attempts to walk in several directions at once is going to get very far.

If Anglicanism has a distinct part to play in the ecumenical process, the transformation in the Roman Church provides, once again, the key factor. Vatican II – the 'protestantisation' of the Roman Church – not only permitted the Catholics to take part in ecumenical initiatives, it altered the whole context in which such initiatives took place. To exemplify, from an English point of view, the change in mood that had taken place between 1962 and 1965 (the years of the Council's deliberations) Hastings (1986) compares the visits to Rome of two English Archbishops. In 1960 Fisher paid a highly significant, yet private – almost furtive – visit to Pope John XXIII. Six years later, Ramsey made a similar journey. This time, though, the visit was an immensely public occasion, including a jointly led ecumenical service in St Paul's Basilica in Rome. Hastings offers the following comment: 'Here was both a deliberate example of prayer in common and a degree of mutual recognition which would have seemed unimaginable a decade earlier' (Hastings 1986: 530–1). Visits to and from Rome have become almost commonplace. Indeed it is difficult to persuade the younger generation that there was anything all that extraordinary in the Pope's arrival in Britain for the first time in history (1982). After all, they had seen on television that he was going everywhere else, so why not Britain?

There remains in this country, however, a curious ambivalence in popular thinking about the Pope. And what for the most part remains dormant in the national consciousness can from time to time reassert itself powerfully. The Archbishop of Canterbury's visit to Rome in the autumn of 1989 provoked just such a reaction. A not very well-worded press release spoke on this occasion of a universal primacy: a rather hypothetical notion of a single church united under the (undefined) jurisdiction of the Pope (*The Times*, 2 February 1989). Outraged headlines in the popular press revived memories of papal domination. Whatever sympathies British people had acquired for individual Catholics, indeed for the Catholic Church as a whole, there were still lines to be drawn – and this was one of them. We must protect our independence, not least the position of the Queen as supreme governor of the Church of England. Such resistance has political parallels in the debate about sovereignty within the new Europe. Indeed, the whole notion of Europe as a kind of secular ecumenism is not entirely inappropriate: ecumenism and Europe are connected at a whole variety of levels.[10]

The European framework

In 1945, Europe had come close to self-destruction for the second time in a century. The idea of European unity was barely conceivable as individual nations struggled to rebuild the fabric of their devastated societies. Surprisingly quickly, however, the seeds of a European Community began to germinate in the form of Coal and Steel Agreements, embodying the principle that the weapons of war themselves should be subject to supranational control. Since the mid-1950s, Europe has moved inexorably if not very steadily towards a greater common identity. The religious factor within this identity is of considerable significance, not least in relation to the somewhat ambivalent attitude of Britain to what is going on; a point all too often ignored by the churches themselves, never mind by the scholars who study them.

Let us start with the position of a Northern Irish Catholic who exists within a minority in Northern Ireland, within a majority in a United Ireland, within a minority in the British Isles and within a majority in Western Europe, indeed in Europe as a whole. His or her status depends entirely upon the unit of analysis in question. This example, taken from a situation so dominated by, and so conscious of, minorities and majorities, brings into a sharper focus a much wider phenomenon. If we are to take the European dimension seriously, this is bound to affect our perceptions about religious life in Britain. Big fish may not look quite so big as the size of the pond alters.

Amongst the British churches, there are two groups that stand to gain as the European framework begins to assert itself. Both the Roman Catholics and the Reformed Churches have their origins in Europe and may well find it easier than the rest of us to re-establish effective links with continental thinking. The position of Scotland within Europe merits particular attention from this point of view, in that a very large part of the Reformed community in Britain is located within Scottish Presbyterianism. The Church of England, on the other hand, together with the Methodists (essentially an offshoot of Anglicanism which had little to do with continental reformers) find themselves in a rather different position. Instead of going home to Europe, they will form a rather peripheral minority right on the edge of the continent. This is certainly true from a geographical or statistical point of view, and may well be so in other ways too. A lot depends on how these churches react to the changing situation. Indeed, a lot depends on whether these churches – whether all the British churches – are prepared to take the plunge and become proactive, rather than reactive, in the European debate. The issues are necessarily emotive and require the greatest possible clarity of thought. We have already seen, for example, that anti-papalism, if not anti-Catholicism, remains an exploitable factor. The more so if Europe is perceived as an essentially Catholic entity, as indeed it is on the basis of numbers.

What, then, can the more English of our churches do? Faced with a very rapidly evolving situation, there are a number of options. At its most negative, the Church of England could find itself providing both legitimation for and recruitment to a rather narrow-minded nationalism; it could become the spiritual arm of a movement motivated primarily by resistance to Europe. At its best, however, it could use its unique historical resource far more creatively; not only in the formation of public opinion more understanding of Europe (by stressing a common Christian identity), but by establishing positive connections with all European churches (Protestant, Catholic and Orthodox), bearing in mind that the East European dimension needs, increasingly, to be taken into account. There is, how-ever, a parallel – and potentially problematic – set of questions to be asked about the Church of England and its position at the centre of the Anglican Communion. The Anglican Communion is anything but European in either its history or its activity. Its centre of gravity lies in the New Common-wealth and in the English-speaking dominions of North America and Australasia. One of the greatest challenges facing the contemporary Angli-can Communion is to think through the implications of this worldwide community in relation to a rapidly altering political context. Is it possible to turn the Church of England towards a new European future without jeopardising too many of these former loyalties? Will the structures built up over four centuries of Anglican life – never mind four post-war decades – prove sufficiently flexible to take on the European dimension? One possible way forward may be to disconnect the primacy of the Church of England from that of the Anglican Communion, thus allowing the former greater freedom of movement on the European front. If some sort of reconciliation between the old and new loyalties of the Church of England proves possible, the Communion may well provide a unique series of links between Europe and the Third World. If the project fails, a certain degree of bitterness and disillusionment seems inevitable. Whatever the case, the entire agenda has been transformed since 1945.

CONCLUSION

Quite clearly, the churches – British and otherwise – are operating within a global framework quite different from that which emerged in the immediate aftermath of the Second World War. The framework, more-over, continues to shift in radical and unpredictable ways. The sheer speed of events in 1989, for example, took everyone by surprise; so, too, did the Iraqi invasion of Kuwait (August 1990) and the collapse of the Soviet Union (December 1991). Very few sociologists now deny that the religious dimension is an increasingly important factor in these shifts and in the subsequent reactions of international diplomacy. The politico-religious aspirations of the Islamic countries are perhaps the most obvious example of this shift, but it is by no means limited to the Muslim world. What Robertson calls the politicisation of religion and the religionisation of politics is a global phenomenon (Robertson 1989).

Such conclusions have serious implications for the secularisation thesis; implications which must, first of all, prompt a degree of questioning concerning the inherent Eurocentrism embodied in this perspective. It is no longer possible to assume that Europe's religious behaviour today will become everyone else's tomorrow. This simply isn't the case (Martin 1991). But we also need to look more closely at some aspects of religious life within Britain itself, not least at the rather unexpected prominence of the British churches in the political debates of the 1980s. For even here there has been some politicisation of religion and religionisation of politics.

Up to a point, it is possible to explain this phenomenon in terms of the immediate political context; the churches – and the established Church in particular – filled a conspicuous void in the absence of effective political opposition through much of the Thatcher period (Davie 1990a). The churches were, moreover, not only prominent, but undeniably effective in bringing particular social and economic issues to public attention and sustaining a significant level of political debate. A growing awareness of the effects of government policy on the most deprived areas of British society (*Faith in the City* 1985) was the most obvious example of ecclesiastical pressure in this respect. The problem remained intractable, but the *concept* of an urban priority area could no longer be ignored. The political void explanation was, however, only part of the story. For the continued prominence of religious issues in, for example, the Rushdie affair, in education (notably the content and aspirations of religious education), in medical ethics, in ecological issues, and in the tragically unresolvable Northern Irish question, must, surely, lead to a more fundamental reappraisal of the role of religion in contemporary British – and indeed European – life. Society's attitudes towards religion are undoubtedly very different in the 1990s compared with the immediate post-war period. Such attitudes remain, none the less, central to some of the most significant issues facing contemporary Britain, not least to those problematic of a truly pluralist society.

An adequate reappraisal of the religious factor in modern, or post-modern society has become a priority for the sociologist. It requires imaginative thinking and new frames of reference. The emphasis will, necessarily, be different from that which has dominated the subdiscipline in recent years. Not only does the sociology of religion require an improved theoretical input (Beckford 1989; Thompson 1990), it needs, above all, to overcome its conviction that secularisation is an inevitable consequence of modernity.

NOTES

1   Several themes within this chapter have been developed and expanded in G. Davie, *Religion in Britain since 1945*, Oxford, Blackwell, 1994. The book forms part of the Institute for Contemporary British History's series on *Making Contemporary Britain*.
2   The advertisement columns of the *Church Times* exemplify this tendency towards exclusiveness. We should also remember the sizeable minority of Anglicans (and indeed others) who continue to oppose the new forms of worship on aesthetic just as much as theological grounds.
3   A variety of sources exist for religious statistics in the UK. For the later post-war decades, these are gathered together in the series of *UK Christian*

Handbooks published by the MARC Europe Foundation (latterly reconstituted as the Christian Research Association), under the direction of Peter Brierley. Material for the earlier periods can be found in Currie, Gilbert and Horsley (1977).

4 For more detail about developments and changes in postwar Catholicism in Britain, see Hornsby-Smith 1985, 1990 and 1991.

5 This point is explored further in Davie 1993a, a discussion which builds on to two previous articles (Davie 1990a and 1990b). The three articles should be taken together. Davie 1994 contains a chapter concerned almost exclusively with religion and modernity.

6 This chapter, drafted for the conference at the London School of Economics in 1990, was revised for publication in 1994, just after the first ordinations of women to the priesthood in the Church of England. The intervening years were critical for this debate whose outcome remained unpredictable until the day of the final synodical vote (11 November 1992). A crucial stage in the process came, however, a few years earlier, when women were ordained to the diaconate; a move which enabled many parishioners to have their first, and clearly formative, experience of a woman's ministry.

7 A careful distinction should be made between the ecumenical debate and interfaith discussions. The latter are a crucial part of post-war religious thinking but are not the focus of this particular section.

8 No one who has taken part in the Whitsunday processions from one cathedral to another in Liverpool can doubt this point. Protestant demonstrators will still be there, complete with banners and bibles, but they look both out of date and out of touch. Their last effective protest took place in March 1982 when the Archbishop of Canterbury was prevented from speaking in Liverpool Parish Church. The Archbishop had just announced the forthcoming visit of the Pope to Britain. In Northern Ireland, of course, the situation remains very different indeed.

9 The parallel with political life is obvious. The major political divisions now lie across the major political parties rather than between them.

10 A key term in the European debate is 'subsidiarity'; a term which has its origins in Catholic social teaching. Thought not related directly to ecumenism, it provides an interesting example of transfer from religious to political discourse. The term has acquired some different connotations in the course of this metamorphosis (*The Independent*, 1 May 1990).

REFERENCES

Barker, E. (1989) *New Religious Movements. A Practical Introduction*, London: HMSO.

Beckford, J. (1985) *Cult Controversies. The Societal Response to New Religious Movements*, London and New York: Tavistock.

——— (1989) *Religion and Advanced Industrial Society*, London: Unwin Hyman.

Currie, R., Gilbert, A. D. and Horsley, L. (1977) *Churches and Churchgoers: Patterns of Church Growth in the British Isles Since 1700*, Oxford: Clarendon.

Davie, G. (1987) 'Paradox behind a united voice', *The Times*, 20 June 1987.

——— (1990a) ' "An Ordinary God": the paradox of religion in contemporary Britain', *British Journal of Sociology*, 3, pp. 395–421.

——— (1990b) 'Believing without belonging: is this the future of religion in Britain?', *Social Compass*, 37, pp. 455–70.

—— (1993a) 'Religion and modernity in Britain', *International Journal for Comparative Religion*, 1, pp. 1–11.
—— (1993b) ' "You'll Never Walk Alone": the Anfield pilgrimage', in A. Watter and I. Reader (eds) *Pilgrimage and Popular Culture*, London: Macmillan.
—— (1993c) 'Believing without belonging: a Liverpool case study', in *Archives de Sciences Sociales des Religions*, 1, pp. 79–89.
—— (1994) *Religion in Britain since 1945*, Oxford: Blackwell.
Faith in the City (1985), London: Church House Publishing.
Habgood, J. (1983) *Church and Nation in a Secular Age*, London: Darton, Longman & Todd.
Hastings, A. (1986) *A History of English Christianity 1920–1985*, London: Collins.
Hervieu-Léger, D. (1986) *Vers un nouveau Christianisme?*, Paris: Cerf.
Hornsby-Smith, M. (1985) *Roman Catholics in England*, Cambridge: Cambridge University Press.
—— (1990) 'The Roman Catholic Church in Britain since the Second World War', in P. Badham (ed.) *Religion, State and Society in Modern Britain*, Lampeter: Edwin Mellen Press.
—— (1991) *Roman Catholic Beliefs in England*, Cambridge: Cambridge University Press.
Knott, K. (1988) 'Other major religious traditions', in T. Thomas (ed.) *The British. Their Religious Beliefs and Practices 1800–1986*, London: Routledge.
Langley, M. (1989) 'Attitudes to women in British churches', in P. Badham (ed.) *Religion, State and Society in Modern Britain*, Lampeter: Edwin Mellen Press.
Martin, D. (1978) *A General Theory of Secularization*, Oxford: Blackwell.
—— (1991) 'The secularization issue: prospect and retrospect', *British Journal of Sociology*, 3, 465–74.
Robertson, R. (1989) 'Globalization, politics, and religion', in J. Beckford and T. Luckmann (eds), *The Changing Face of Religion*, London: Sage.
Sheppard, D. and Worlock, D. (1988) *Better Together*, London: Hodder & Stoughton.
Thompson, K. (1990) 'Religion: the British contribution', *British Journal of Sociology*, 4, pp. 531–5.
Walker, A. (1985) *Restoring the Kingdom*, London: Hodder.
Wallis, R. and Bruce, S. (1989) 'Religion: The British Contribution', *British Journal of Sociology*, 3, pp. 493–520.
Wilson, B. (1982) *Religion in a Sociological Perspective*, Oxford: Oxford University Press.
—— (1990) *The Social Dimensions of Sectarianism. Sects and New Religious Movements in Contemporary Society*, Oxford: Clarendon Press.

Chapter 14

The arts, books, media and entertainments in Britain since 1945

Arthur Marwick

Should anyone claim not to understand my title, let them repair immediately to the pages of the posh newspapers: what they manifestly mean by
these signifiers is what I also mean by them. This title has been chosen
deliberately to avoid that contentious substantive, 'culture', and to allow
me to address directly the two questions posed by the editors of this
collection: first, how far (if at all) have political authorities influenced
the production and reception of cultural artefacts?; second, what other,
perhaps more fundamental, influences must we consider?

Let me at once state my basic premise, together with a number of crucial
assumptions. My premise is that in all societies there is a human need for
colour, for stories, for dance, for song, for, in brief, the elements embraced
in my title (my 'media' heading excludes news reporting and political
comment). My assumptions are: that some individuals are more talented
than others in producing cultural artefacts; that, therefore, a division of
labour will prevail in which some will be brilliant television producers, and
others merely bus drivers or boring professors; and that one can make valid
distinctions between complex art forms designed to deeply enrich human
experience, at the top of the scale and, at the bottom, cultural products
merely designed to exploit an easy commercial market. Finally, I take it
that cultural production is closely related to, though not determined by,
class structure: it is important to be precise about the exact forms of British
class structure, 1945–90 and not, using the Marxist mantra, simply make it
up. From my own researches (Marwick 1990: 254–379), I am clear that
despite certain changes in the relationships between classes and in the
balance of forces within classes, Britain continues to have the following:
an upper class (often, though in my view erroneously referred to as the
'upper-middle class') – an amalgam of landed, commercial, industrial and
high professional elements, still deriving much of its ethos from an
enduring aristocratic core; a working class, those in manual occupations;
and, in between, a much less homogeneous middle class, variegated in
composition, background, education and outlook.

THE POST-WAR SCENE, 1945–57

The performing arts and broadcasting

The vital question at any time is: how are the arts financed? Without any doubt, British political authorities in this period of what might be termed the 'cultural welfare state' made a greater contribution to financing the arts than ever before. Behind that process lay the experience of the war, the sense that Britain was fighting for what was best in civilisation, the sense of pride in British culture, the sense that the best in that culture should be more widely shared. Early in the war, in a joint initiative between the government and the private Pilgrim Trust, the Council for the Encouragement of Music and the Arts (CEMA) had been established as a funding body to ensure that cultural activities continued through even the most stressful and straitened phases of the war. The Labour Party, winning 47.8 per cent of the popular vote, and returned with a substantial parliamentary majority, was strongly committed to maintaining the collectivist innovations of the war. Hence in 1946 CEMA was established on a long-term basis as the Arts Council, an autonomous body, but one whose level of funding would be determined by the government of the day, and whose general policies would be shaped by the ethos of that government. Conservative governments after 1951 effectively maintained the principle that government and local authority subsidy of the arts was a good thing, while at the same time keeping such expenditure subordinate to more material needs, and confined, on the whole, to fairly traditional projects. In the national perspective, the spheres in which the Arts Council played its most significant role were the very ones in which Britain had lagged far behind other advanced societies: opera and ballet. Before the war the Royal Opera House, Covent Garden, had been a commercial venue playing host to top international operatic companies; during the war it had actually been used as a dance hall. In January 1947, Britain's first state-sponsored company, the Royal Opera (funding, of course, was channelled though the Arts Council) gave its gala opening performance of *Carmen*. Already the Sadler's Wells Ballet (founded by private initiative) had transferred to the Royal Opera House, becoming the state-sponsored Royal Ballet.

Born of Victorian municipal pride, a fine tradition of local authority funding of free art galleries, free libraries, and great orchestras, did exist. The Labour government sought to extend this tradition through Clause 132 of the 1948 Local Government Act, which empowered local authorities to raise sixpence in the pound on the rates in order to support local cultural enterprises. Actually, the initiative towards establishing municipally funded theatres began during the war (Bristol Old Vic), extending through the 1950s and into the 1960s (Belgrade Theatre, Coventry, Crucible Theatre, Sheffield, Nottingham Playhouse). Theatre as a whole (which basically meant West End theatre and companies touring the provinces) remained in the hands of commercial impresarios, together with a few distinguished actor-managers. All complained that the Labour government's prolongation of the wartime entertainments tax was anti-cultural. However, the government granted relief from the tax for plays with an educational purpose, thus, in effect, giving considerable encouragement to Shakespearean and other classical productions. Internationally, Britain's most famous theatre was that at Stratford-upon-Avon, dedicated to the works of Shakespeare and run by a private trust; Britain still had no state-sponsored National Theatre.

The realms on which government impinged most directly, though in very different ways, were broadcasting and film. Film had low status among the British upper class: hence British governments, unlike French ones, did not directly finance film-making. At the same time, the American predominance was a matter of concern. The quota system, introduced in 1937 and strengthened by the Labour government, was intended to ensure that 30 per cent of feature films exhibited were British. The 'Eady Levy' on cinema receipts (voluntary in 1950, compulsory after 1957) was intended to give some financial support to British film-makers, but in practice tended to be distributed more to the richer established companies than to poor pioneering ones. Funding from the National Film Finance Corperation, established in 1949, was in the form of loans not grants. The British film industry was an interlinked and overlapping network of production companies, distribution companies and chains of exhibitors, overwhelmingly dominated by one British figure, J. Arthur Rank, and otherwise by the various American companies. Most films were actually *made* by small production companies, but even if the difficult task of raising the production finances was surmounted, the problem of securing distribution was, in a highly monopolistic environment, a potentially crippling one. Films were subject to the government-approved, though technically independent, British Board of Film Censors; local authorities could exercise a separate censorship if they so wished. No play could be performed till the text had been approved in advance by the Lord Chamberlain; improvisation on stage was not permissible. With all other spheres being governed by Victorian obscenity laws, one can see that there was in this sense quite strict political control of culture, although arguably censorship as applied was a fairly accurate indicator of public *mores* of the time.

Broadcasting, through the autonomous British Broadcasting Corporation, was a state monopoly, financed by licence fees paid by holders of radio and television sets. Its management, composed at the very top of 'the great and the good' (i.e., mainly upper-class figures) and, in practical terms, of professional broadcasters, broadly shared the 'cultural welfare state' ideas of the Labour government. As dispenser of patronage, supporter of major orchestras and, perhaps most important of all, a visitor into practically every household in the land, the BBC was a major force in British cultural life. At the end of the war radio services were reorganised into three: the Light Programme, the Home Service Programme and the Third Programme. The audience research, which the BBC had pioneered shortly before the war, treated the audiences for these three services as synonymous with working class, middle class and upper-middle and upper class, respectively. The Third Programme played an important part in the musical renaissance (the phrase is justified) after 1945; but much of its output was characterised by a mannered pedantry and a distinctive academic parochialism. The most significant phenomenon was the success of 'Saturday Night Theatre' on the Home Service, with an audience at the end of the 1940s equivalent to one-third of the entire adult population. Here was the precursor of the hegemony of television soon to come: drama and entertainment at the touch of a switch.

Television broadcasting, only just beginning at the end of the 1930s, had been brought to an end by the war; it grew again only slowly in the postwar years, though by the early 1950s there were 5 million television viewers. In order that television might not become an addiction nor distract children from their studies nor adults from their duties, television broadcasting was confined to a limited number of hours per day – also very much in keeping with the BBC ethic. Political ideology and activism does then intrude. In 1954 free-market Conservatives, much against the convictions of senior party members, managed to get the 1954 Act passed, which led to the setting up of a separate television channel, to be financed by advertising. However, this channel, run by different companies in different parts of the country, was very tightly supervised by the Independent Broadcasting Authority. Although (especially in the early days) commercial television was responsible for some pretty vulgar products (particularly game shows), in overall terms the high standards of British broadcasting were maintained, and a great stimulus was given to the BBC to reconsider some of its rather hide bound conventions.

Architecture

A number of forces, some of them contradictory, governed architectural production, something which impinges quite directly on most people. War damage to the built environment was considerable: the greatest need and most urgent concern of the electorate was housing. With a government committed to public initiatives and public control, it was not surprising that there was a marked movement of architects from private practice to public service. There was a very lively younger generation sympathetic to the ideals of the Labour government, and very much under the spell of Le Corbusier and his notion of the Unité d'Habitation.

The main emphasis to the mid-1950s was on building houses and schools. Their style was what Reyner Banham called 'People's Detailing', described by Charles Jencks as 'the English version of Socialist realism' (Banham 1966: 11; Jencks 1973: 245). The first generation of new towns, started in the 1940s, also catered to the traditional tastes for low-rise housing set in a reasonable space, while at the same time adopting some of the tenets of the international functionalist style. Industrial techniques for building schools were pioneered in Hertfordshire, then, in 1948, were taken up by the Ministry of Education. Several of the schools won international reputations. Major public building was less successful: government regulations limited building volume (and therefore height) – thus such public buildings as did begin to go up, the most notorious example being the Shell Centre on London's South Bank, were not only oppressively boring, but often had an ungainly squat appearance.

For the out-and-out modernists most scope seemed to offer itself as the local authorities in the big cities decided that lengthy housing lists and shortages of urban land could only be overcome through building multi-storey estates.

The first great break from the needs of home, family and children towards the need for public spectacle came with the preparation of the bombed-out South Bank site for the 1951 Festival of Britain. Appointed Director of Architecture, Hugh Casson designed the entire exhibition area in the modernist idiom of a single concept linking together spaces and buildings: the major temporary constructions were the Dome of Discovery, designed by Ralph Tubbs, and the Skylon designed by J. H. Moya. The Royal Festival Hall was really a London County Council project, designed by their chief architect, Robert Matthew, and would have been built anyway, festival or no festival.

The parochial age: 1945–59

If one had to find one label to cover British cultural production between the end of the war and the end of the 1950s, that label would have to be 'parochial'. This manifested itself in the delicate romanticism of John Piper and the formalised landscapes of the St Ives School; in the art of the London bohemia (later called the London School); in the bombastic poetry of Dylan Thomas; in the well-made, and not very radical, West End problem plays of Terence Rattigan; in the quaint film comedies of local custom and idiosyncrasy made by Ealing Studios; and their poetic analogue, the works of John Betjeman, who from 1948 eclipsed Thomas as Britain's best-selling poet. It must be added that neither of these came close in stature to T. S. Eliot, whose poetry attained its highest reputation at this time. Yet, the war had provoked a certain internationalism, though largely dormant till stirred into life in the 1960s: most important were the Matisse–Picasso exhibition held at the Victoria and Albert Museum in the winter of 1945–6, and the exhibition mounted ten years later entitled *Modern Art in the United States*, which culminated in examples of abstract expressionism.

If there was any kind of cultural revolt in the 1950s, it was a very British storm in a very British tea cup. If anything, the protagonists of 'The Movement' (in literature and poetry), the provincial artists of the Kitchen Sink School, and the 'angry young men' were even more parochial than the bohemians of the 1940s. The three key literary works were: the first novel by Movement writer Kingsley Amis, *Lucky Jim* (published in January 1954); *Look Back in Anger* by the unknown playwright John Osborne, presented at the Royal Court theatre on 8 May 1956; and *The Outsider* (published on 28 May 1956) by 24 year-old unknown writer Colin Wilson, neither novel nor drama, but an erudite study of lonely, perceptive 'outsiders'. Though lower-middle class, Amis was Cambridge educated. Perhaps it took such eyes to spot the comic potential of the provincial universities.

The brilliant, dedicated theatrical director George Devine had founded the English Stage Company at the Royal Court Theatre in order to present new plays that would break through the suffocating West End embrace. It was Devine who gave Osborne his chance and it was Devine who kept *Look Back in Anger* going, greatly assisted by a wildly enthusiastic *Observer* review by Kenneth Tynan, even though the play was not at that time paying its way commercially. Rather oddly, it was Colin Wilson's *The Outsider* which achieved overnight success – also assisted by an *Observer* review, by Philip Toynbee. Then, almost by accident, the Royal Court Press Officer produced the notion that Osborne was 'a very angry young man'. 'Angry young men', particularly Wilson and Osborne (whose play now began to make serious money for the English Stage Company as well as himself), but also the 'new' novelists and many associated with the Movement, became the centre of media attention. *Look Back in Anger* is marvellous theatre, if often in a rather conventional way. Most of the anger is directed against the conventions and complacencies of society. There is certainly no coherent 'alternative ideology'; indeed Osborne attacked those who looked for profound meaning in the play's most famous line, 'There aren't any good, brave, causes left', explaining it as merely an expression of 'ordinary despair' (John Osborne in Maschler 1957).

THE CULTURAL REVOLUTION, 1958–75

The apparent paradox of the 1960s is that there was a substantial increase in state patronage of the arts and, at the same time, the growth of 'an alternative culture' whose artefacts were often vigorously critical of established society; many of these artefacts in fact came to be subsidised by the Arts Council. The critical alternative culture began in the dying days of the

Conservative governments of Harold Macmillan and then Sir Alec Douglas-Home; the expansion of state subsidies was a function of the Labour government elected in 1964, confirmed in power in 1966. The major stages were the transfer in 1964 of the source of Arts Council funding from the Treasury to the Department of Education, the appointment of Jennie Lee as Minister for the Arts, and the publication in 1965 of Jennie Lee's government paper *A Policy for the Arts*. A nice case study is provided by the history of the Traverse Theatre in Edinburgh. The Edinburgh International Festival of Music and Drama had been set up in 1947, in part at least a result of local authority initiative, and Arts Council support. It had quickly attracted around it a 'fringe' of small pioneering theatrical companies. The Fringe provided a context within which the American Jim Haynes and the Italo-Scot Ricky Demarco founded the Traverse Theatre in early 1962, with the financial support of certain young Edinburgh lawyers and accountants. The Traverse secured only distinctly modest grants from the Edinburgh town council, many of whose members were shocked by its avant-garde productions; but by the later 1960s the main source of subsidy was the Scottish Arts Council. (I am indebted to the Traverse Theatre for allowing me to study their own private papers; see also Macmillan 1988).

Increased state patronage is important, but the crucial influences governing cultural developments of the 1960s were: a new openness to international influences; a relaxation in censorship (an Act of 1958 made literary quality a defence against prosecutions for obscenity in literature; film censorship began to relax at the same time; and in 1968 the Lord Chamberlain's powers over the theatre were abolished); and expansion in all levels of education (which, for example, produced both new audiences for opera, and a crop of sophisticated feminist writers). Earlier educational reforms came to fruition at the beginning of the decade, with the emergence of such working-class writers as Alan Sillitoe, David Storey, Shelagh Delaney and Dennis Potter. All are important for producing novels and plays, but, more important, their works then provided the basis for films and television programmes.

Almost all cultural artefacts, when taken in conjunction with their processes of production and reception, offer some insights into aspects of the society within which they were produced; some, of course, more than others. The film *Room at the Top* (released in January 1959) is one of those occasional products that illuminate a whole moment of change, and is, indeed, in itself a component of change. Absolutely crucial is the way in which, by condensing the ambiguities of John Braine's novel, the film presents two major preoccupations (or 'meanings'): class power, class rigidities and the possibility of social mobility; and sex, frankly presented and still more frankly discussed.

Much of the film is redolent of the narrow, stuffy world of the post-war era (in which, somewhat shakily, it was set). It is very British, parochial even. The import of Simone Signoret to play Alice is ambivalent in this respect. *Room at the Top* stands only at the threshold; a comparison of Signoret's role with that of Lesley Caron in *The L-Shaped Room* (1962) is instructive (pregnant, Caron tries to determine her own destiny; Signoret is tragically passive though often bitingly critical of Joe – played by Laurence Harvey). Some of the other films that followed have strong female characters; most dealt in an increasingly explicit and mature way with questions of sex and class. British films (one thinks of *Saturday Night and Sunday Morning* (1960), *A Taste of Honey* (1961), *Darling* (1965) *Alfie* (1966)) became an international fashion, and thus, until the mid-1970s, when studios began to be closed down, British film-makers sailed triumphantly along on a tide of American investment.

Up until the renewal of franchises in 1967, the reputation of the independent TV companies remained much lower than that of the BBC. Now new companies were formed, often associating themselves with individuals thought to have high cultural status. Meantime a couple of critical changes had taken place at the BBC: in 1960 Sir Hugh Greene, an upper-class figure, but one sensitive to changes taking place in society, became Director General; in April 1964 the BBC's second channel, designed to develop the BBC's more serious output, came on the air. *The* new development on BBC was the satire show of which the original was *That Was The Week That Was*. By the later 1960s the cultural revolution had located itself within the BBC's *Wednesday Night Play*, often highly explicit and socially very aware (examples are Nell Dunn's *Up The Junction*, Dennis Potter's *Vote, Vote, Vote for Nigel Barton* and Jeremy Sandford's *Cathy Come Home*). Internationally, what created the almost mythic status of British television was the BBC's last black-and-white drama series *The Forsyte Saga* (1967), adapted from the distinctly middle-brow novels of John Galsworthy, but with a brilliant cast of actors. The BBC also distinguished itself in the arena of the 'sit com', from the pungent, shocking, *Till Death Us Do Part*, to the nostalgic but unsentimental *Dad's Army*, first presented in 1968. The zany *Monty Python's Flying Circus* (beginning in 1969), widely popular, achieved a cult following in America. In 1971 London Weekend Television broadcast the first episode of *Upstairs Downstairs*, a series based on the careful delineation of the hierarchy existing within an aristocratic Edwardian household, and, in international fame, the true successor to *The Forsyte Saga*. In 1975 Thames Television put on the ninety-minute play *The Naked Civil Servant*, based on the autobiography of eccentric, but determined homosexual Quentin Crisp, with John Hurt in the lead role. A play in which one laughed, and indeed sided, *with* such a character was a true sign of the maturity of British television and a clear indication that it was preserving its own characteristics in the face of

American imports. In the mid-1970s came the first serious attempts of programmes catering for minority communities.

The story of the rise of British pop/rock music has been told so often that perhaps one can economise a little on detail here; the story is basically correct in identifying this music, and all the practices associated with it, as the central cultural phenomenon of the time. The origins of this music lay in black America, in part transmitted by such white performers as Elvis Presley, but given a highly distinctive quality by the working class and lower-middle-class young people performing it before live audiences at the end of the 1950s. One reason for the quick establishment of British pop/rock music and the curious eminence it achieved internationally was that, given the complete nullity of British popular music in the 1950s (Marwick 1991), there was an empty vessel waiting to be filled – and it was filled to overflowing. There is a very fresh and involving quality about the early songs (The Beatles first entered the British Top Twenty of recordings in December 1962, assumed a predominant position in 1963, and conquered the American market in early 1964). For national and international fame the only rivals were the London-based rhythm and blues group The Rolling Stones, who had a stronger anti-establishment and altogether wilder image than The Beatles. Perhaps the other musician most worthy of mention is Jimi Hendrix, actually a black American, whose career was launched in London – such was the charisma of the British pop/rock scene.

Such was the penetrative and involving power of rock/pop that it did help to break down some of the barriers between elite music and popular music. (As is well known, this is symbolised on the sleeve of The Beatles' complex and imaginative LP *Sergeant Pepper's Lonely Hearts Club Band* (1967), where among the famous personages in the photographic montage is the composer Stockhausen (Griffiths 1988: 80).) In the remodelling and transmission of culture at this time, an important role was occupied by the art colleges, in popular music as well as in innovative painting and sculpture.

One of the most influential figures in the British art world is Anthony Caro (b. 1924), who himself went through something of a 'personal revolution' at the beginning of the decade. Educated at upper-class Charterhouse and Christ's College Cambridge, Caro subsequently studied at the (much lower-class) Regent Street Polytechnic and the relatively classless Royal Academy school. His apprenticeship as a sculptor was served between 1951 and 1953 as an assistant to Henry Moore. Then in 1959 he visited the United States, where he fell under the influence of the critic Clement Greenberg, the apostle of abstract expressionism. Back in Britain the following year, Caro manifested a radical reaction against the monumentality of Moore in his *Twenty-four Hours* – an abstract construction in painted sheet metal, which consciously attempted to replicate the flatness of the kind of painting Greenberg was promoting. The first public exhibition of his welded metal constructions, sometimes covered in brilliant household paint, took place at the Whitechapel Gallery in 1963. Caro had a two-day-a-week teaching post at the St Martin's School of Art, Central London, where he exerted a very powerful influence. A kind of transition point may be detected in 'Sculpture: open air exhibition of contemporary British and American works' at Battersea Park in 1963. Among the American exhibitors was the leading exponent of abstract assemblages, David Smith.

In the international art world there developed the notions of Conceptual Art, Earthwork and Arte Povera. What happened, in fact, was that as well as an explosion in what was considered to be art, there was also an abandonment of the distinction between 'sculpture' and 'painting'. 'Pop Art' also became an international movement, but, very definitely, the origins of the British version lay in 1950s Britain.

In the world of music – which includes concert hall, radio (in 1964 a daytime music programme was adjoined to the evening Third Programme, the two in 1970 becoming Radio 3, supreme purveyor of classical music) and records – non-British works continued overwhelmingly to dominate the market. The native giants continued to be Benjamin Britten and Michael Tippett, the significant development being that in the early 1960s the latter began to achieve the recognition that had previously eluded him, while around 1970 there was a positive upsurge of enthusiasm.

Of British poetry in this period, it could be said that it was more ambitious, the limited subject matter and the formalism of the Movement being pushed to the side, and that it involved more people, both as practitioners and as audience. It is instructive to look at developments in Scottish poetry. What happened in the 1960s was that the wider Scottish society (traditionally governed by strongly puritan tenets), or at least parts of it, was brought into a closer alignment with the long-standing Scottish bohemia, while the poets themselves developed a new self-awareness and confidence. Analogous developments, involving such poets as Dannie Abse, took place in Wales. One cannot speak of direct political influences but certainly the renewed cultural energy was paralleled by active phases in both Scottish and Welsh nationalism.

Many left-wing commentators have perceived in the 1960s the definite formation of an alternative society, which somehow failed to displace existing society. Actually, there is no evidence that such dialectical processes operate in history, and a better analysis would suggest that the new cultural practices in fact permeated existing society, bringing about considerable changes, and setting the cultural agenda for the rest of the century. Architecture and house construction was the blackspot; here one can certainly blame misguided local government polices, hell-bent on redevelopment, cheap provision of housing, and facilities for private motor transport.

CONTINUING REVOLUTION AND CONSERVATIVE REACTION

Many of the new developments of the 1960s accelerated through the 1970s and even on into the 1980s. New liberties (or new licence, as some saw it) could not be taken back. Small experimental theatre groups continued to be founded; the cultural welfare state reached its apogee with the establishment of the three-stage National Theatre on its South Bank site in 1976. What was different by the end of the 1980s was the changed way in which the arts were funded, and the changed way in which they were regarded by government. The new approaches were encapsulated in the slim but glossy prospectus published by the Arts Council in 1985, entitled *A Great British Success Story*, which spoke of the arts as a productive investment, and of the productivity and efficiency of the British 'Arts industry'. The Council itself was no longer dispensing money so lavishly and had been turned by the Conservative government into a much more direct instrument of government policy. Everything now had its market value. The trend was towards commercial sponsorship. But it certainly could not be said that the Arts were pervaded by Conservative influences. Some commentators have noted the return on the part of some sculptors to figuration and traditional materials – Barry Flanagan's *Leaping Hare* of 1981 being perhaps the most famous example – but this was by no means a universal trend. It is true that Sir Anthony Caro turned towards figurative work, but the experimentation partly initiated under his inspiration continued. Where there was most obviously a new style to match the so-called 'enterprise culture' of Thatcherism, it was in architecture, as buildings in the eclectic, 'post-modernist' style began to appear everywhere.

Arguably, British literature in the later 1970s and 1980s was actually more innovative than at any time since the 1920s. Admiration for the non-naturalistic satire of Martin Amis, the imaginative feminism of Fay Weldon and Angela Carter, the magic realism of Salman Rushdie, and for the experiments with the time dimension of Peter Ackroyd could, of course, be combined with concern over the way in which formerly independent British publishers were being swallowed up by international conglomerates. The retailing of books began to take on more and more of an American character.

Fashion in poetry fluctuated more sharply than it did with drama (where leftist influences remained strong). The newest poetry of the 1980s was characterised by a flight from the intimately personal and the absence of any strong political commitment: a slightly paradoxical phenomenon (and that must continue to be my basic point) given that, by general consent, the most important and influential poet of the period is Seamus Heaney, whose poetry evidently has roots, however deeply they delve, in the troubles of Northern Ireland. Actually, the most single pronounced influence in drama was that of feminism. The doyenne of feminist playwrights, Caryl Churchill (b. 1938), had found in the 1960s that the best creative outlet for an overburdened housewife was the writing of radio plays. Her first stage play, *Owners*, was presented at the Royal Court Theatre Upstairs in 1972. Blockbusting commercial success eventually came with *Serious Money*, a satire on the stock market of 1980s' yuppiedom, which made absolutely no concessions, employing the fluent notions of sexuality and the other non-naturalistic devices she had pioneered in her earlier plays (all the same, the suspicion remained that her cash-paying audiences contained a large proportion of yuppies).

British television continued to enjoy a high reputation, while the film industry ran down (no government had ever given the industry much support; the Thatcher government removed what little there was). The film which comes nearest to *Room at the Top* in signalling a transition point in British society is *The Long Good Friday* (released 1981). Brilliantly cut and highly exciting, utterly uninhibited in language, the film captures the moment when collapsing consensus is being replaced by the bombastic claims of 'enterprise culture'; it suggests that Britain is a banana republic, the IRA invincible.

The sources of artistic creation are many. There are forms of artistic production, and modes of artistic consumption (in art galleries, for example), which cannot be self-financing. The evidence of recent years suggests that commercial sponsorship, even if it were completely unproblematic, is unlikely to be sufficient. State and local authority patronage remains an important issue; but within a liberal democracy such as Britain the extent of political influence on the arts, books and entertainment is not great, though at times sins of omission (as in regard to the film industry) may be devastating. Where political power is most directly relevant is in the realm of the media. The decision to establish commercial television (under, it must be stressed, careful supervision) in 1954 was, as it eventually proved, probably a wise one. There are reasons for fearing that new government policies initiated in the 1980s, effectively limiting the resources available within BBC or IBA channels for high-quality productions, will have damaging effects.

REFERENCES

Banham, R. (1966), *The New Brutalism: Ethic or Aesthetic*, London: Architectural Press.

Griffiths, P. (1988), 'Music' in Boris Ford (ed.) *The Cambridge Guide to the Arts in Britain since the Second World War*, Cambridge: Cambridge University Press, pp. 48–83.

Jencks, C. (1973), *Modern Movements in Architecture*, Harmondsworth: Penguin.

Macmillan, J. (1988), *The Traverse Theatre Story 1963–1988*, London: Methuen Drama.

Marwick, A. (1990) *Class: Image and Reality in Britain, France, and the USA since 1930* (2nd edition) London: Macmillan.
——— (1991) 'Britain 1951: society and culture', *History Today* 41, pp. 5–11.
Maschler, T. (1957) *Declaration*, London: MacGibbon & Kee.

Chapter 15

Gender inequalities in leisure and sport in post-war Britain

Celia Brackenridge and Diana Woodward

INTRODUCTION

In the popular mind both sport and leisure are essentially minor issues – 'optional extras' which may enrich people's lives, but matter less than earning a living or raising a family. Academics have by and large shared this view. There have been a few degree courses in Sports Science and Leisure Studies for over a decade now, but mainstream social science courses pay little attention to these topics in comparison with industry and the economy, or the welfare state.

In reality, both sport and leisure have major social, political and economic significance in contemporary society. The average adult now has around 2,600 hours per year available for leisure (Henley Centre 1982, cited in Sports Council 1983), and over 30 per cent of total consumer spending goes on it (Gratton and Taylor 1987). £6.9 billion was spent on sport alone in 1985 (Henley Centre 1986, in Sports Council 1988). Nearly 400,000 people were employed in sport and physical recreation in 1989, attracting £4,400 million in consumer spending and contributing £2,400 million in taxation (Sports Council 1989).

Apart from clearly being 'Big Business', sport and lesiure merit analysis for their role and meaning in people's lives. The social divisions based on class, gender, age and region which preoccupy social scientists in their study of other social institutions apply equally within sport and leisure. Indeed, such divisions are constructed and reproduced within this arena. Young people's behaviour in pubs and clubs, for example, is not just a matter of enjoying oneself; to the sociologist it is concerned with socialisation into gender-appropriate adult identities and securing peer group acceptance.

In this chapter we shall examine changes since the Second World War in the resources available for people to spend on sport and leisure. We shall also consider how these changes have influenced their use of free time.

Throughout the chapter, gender is used to illustrate the impact of social divisions on people's recreational experiences. We have chosen to take this approach to redress the balance of sport and recreation research literature which is almost exclusively, until recently, a male view. That view has tended to be, moreover, from one particular male perspective, that of the 'rugged heterosexual'. As we mention later, feminist research has opened up new ways of looking at and thinking about leisure and sport, including challenges to conventional notions of masculinity and femininity. In the second half of the chapter a series of issues within sport are taken as case studies, exemplifying the processes by which gender divisions have been created and perpetuated, or challenged and changed.

RESOURCES FOR LEISURE IN POST-WAR BRITAIN

Since Britain's emergence from the era of post-war austerity in the mid-1950s, its population has benefited from significant increases in the resources needed to enjoy leisure, more free time, higher real incomes, and improved access to leisure-enhancing equipment such as the motor car, the television set and the washing machine. However, as we shall see, this affluence of time and money has affected different sections of the population unevenly. The growing importance of the family as a unit of leisure consumption and the home as its site for all but teenagers and young adults, together with married women's increased participation in the labour force, have brought conflicting and contradictory changes for women's and men's lives (Clarke and Critcher 1985).

Time

Turning first to changes in the time available for leisure, a number of commentators have predicted the advent of a 'leisure society' made possible by increased industrial productivity, leading to a reduction in working hours (Jenkins and Sherman 1979, 1981; Handy 1984). In fact, over the past century and a half legislation has played a minor part in reducing maximum working hours and introducing paid holidays. Employees' increased productivity has been a more significant factor, bringing greater prosperity, a shorter working week and longer holiday entitlements for people in employment, and generating the funding for social benefits for the non-employed population, including extended educational provision and pensions (Veal 1987; Glyptis 1989).

However, these benefits have affected men and women differentially. Gershuny and Jones's study of time budget data shows a 10 per cent fall in employed men's working hours between 1961 and 1984, compared with only a 4 per cent fall for employed women, and no decrease at all for women in part-time jobs (in Horne et al. 1987). These factors, with others of a more contradictory nature such as increased longevity but more years of compulsory education, have contributed to an increase of 70 per cent since the beginning of the century in the amount of non-work time available to the average male worker during his lifetime.

Women have shared in these gains as their life expectancy has increased and their fertility has decreased, but despite the now widespread ownership of labour-saving domestic equipment, women with both domestic responsibilities and paid employment have profited less than others from the 'leisure revolution'. Women's participation in the labour force has increased steadily during the century, with married women being the fastest-growing group. Post-war census data show a steady increase in women's employment rates (from 27 per cent of the female population in 1951 to 33 per cent in 1981), a quadrupling of women's part-time employment (from 3 per cent to 13 per cent in the same period), and a significant decline in men's employment (from 66 per cent of the male population in 1951 to 53 per cent in 1981) (Carr-Hill and Lintott 1989). The estimated loss of 2.5 million full-time jobs between 1970 and 1990, and the associated increase in unemployment, needs to be set against the increase in part-time work to one in four of the employed population, most of them married women (Beechey 1987).

The inroads into women's time associated with their higher rates of employment have been partly counterbalanced by men's greater participation in domestic labour, but the burden of it is still mainly borne by women. Employed men's domestic labour increased by a third from an average of 74 minutes per day in 1961 to 98 minutes per day in 1984, but employed women still spend a further hour per day on it (Gershuny and Jones 1987). Although there has been some redistribution of housework to men, no studies suggest that women have given up overall responsibility for shopping, cleaning and childcare, nor that anything like equality exists between women's and men's domestic contributions (Green, Hebron and Woodward 1987, 1990; Shaw 1985, 1988).

'Affluence'

The general population has not only enjoyed an increase in the time potentially available for leisure; it has also become far more affluent during the post-war period – although, again, certain sections of the population derived much more benefit than others from this increased prosperity. Real disposable income almost doubled between 1951 and 1974 (*Social Trends* 1980). Whereas it took on average 15 hours' work to buy the average household's weekly food bill at the time of the Coronation in 1953, and 4 hours' work to pay for its housing, by 1981 this figure had fallen to under 9 hours to buy food, but had risen to over 6 hours to meet housing costs (Carr-Hill and Lintott 1989). The increase in real wages, compounded by easier access to consumer credit, contributed to a transformation of the typical household economy. Car ownership expanded from under 4 million vehicles in 1956 to 15 million in 1982 (Sports Council 1983). In 1961 fewer than one-third of households owned a car; by 1985 two-thirds had at least one car, including 18 per cent with two or more (Glyptis 1989). Over 97 per cent of homes now have a television whereas virtually none did in 1951, and an average of twenty-five hours a week is spent watching it. Whereas only 8 per cent of homes had a refrigerator in 1951, by 1985 95 per cent had one and two-thirds of homes had freezers. Washing machine ownership quadrupled between 1956 and 1985, and the same trends can be seen for vacuum cleaners, tumble driers, dish washers and microwave ovens (Young and Willmott 1973; Glyptis 1989). The clear social class differences in patterns of ownership evident until the 1960s have also become much less marked.

LEISURE ACTIVITIES

Some of the time freed from domestic drudgery has helped women to combine housekeeping with employment, and some has merely enabled housekeeping standards to be raised. However, the application of technology to housework has certainly liberated some time for leisure, which is primarily spent at home. Turning again to Gershuny and Jones' data, not only employed men but also employed women and housewives experienced a significant increase in their leisure time between the 1961 and 1984 surveys, amounting to half an hour per day or more.

For most people the majority of their free time is spent at home, and women's and men's favourite home-based leisure activities are not markedly different. The spread of television ownership has been accompanied by a steady increase in viewing, especially by women, and a decline in radio listening. Viewing rates have risen from 88 per cent of the population in 1961 to 98 per cent a quarter-century later. Reading, relaxation, crafts and hobbies remain popular home-based pursuits, but knitting and sewing have both declined since 1961. According to the *General Household Survey*, gambling, dancing, gardening and participation in voluntary associations are popular with both women and men but, predictably, they appeal to different age groups (*General Household Survey* 1985).

Over two-thirds of adult leisure time is spent at home. Outside the home, travel, playing sport, and visits to pubs, clubs and restaurants have grown considerably in popularity, but cinema attendance (until recently) and watching sport have lost ground. In 1951 nearly 26 million cinema admissions per week were recorded, a figure which fell to below 1 million in 1984. However, despite high rates of home video ownership, there has recently been a revival in the popularity of the cinema, fuelled by the growth of multi-screen cinemas. Spectator sports, especially football, have also declined in popularity. Football League attendances peaked at 41.3

million in the 1948–9 season, since then falling fairly consistently to below 10 million in the mid-1980s (Gratton and Taylor 1987).

Underlying these trends are such factors as the reduced attractiveness of some forms of commercial leisure away from home: elderly women on low incomes stop going to bingo because of physical infirmity, poverty, or fear of leaving home (Dixey and Talbot 1982; Green *et al.* 1990), and football fans economise during times of recession and high unemployment by watching matches on television rather than going in person.

Also, the home has become a more attractive place to spend free time since the 1950s, with improved standards of furnishing and heating associated with higher rates of owner-occupation, and a sophisticated range of leisure equipment (Glyptis *et al.* 1987).

SPORTS PARTICIPATION

Sport can be seen as exemplifying many of the social processes that differentiate people's experiences of leisure. Some 21.5 million adults and 7 million children participate every month in some form of organised sport or physical recreation. The number of women taking part in sport has risen steadily since the official formation of the Sports Council in 1972 but Britain still has one of the lowest sports participation rates for women of any equivalent developed nation. Approximately one-third of women take part in organised physical recreation compared with about half of men (*General Household Survey* 1985), but these gross figures obscure huge differences by age, class and race and other significant factors such as disability or urban/rural location. Nor can descriptive statistics give us an understanding of the gendered nature of sport and the pervasiveness of male control over the spaces, times and activities of women's sports.

Sport is not only a significant economic force, as we have seen, but also has an unavoidable impact on most people's consciousness. It is public, competitive and socially exclusive, reflecting the race, class and sex inequalities of the wider society. Sport celebrates 'masculine' qualities, whether in males or females, and thus embodies an approach derived from the nineteenth-century public school tradition (John Hargreaves 1986), but it denies the 'feminine' except in strictly prescribed forms. The division of sports between those prescribed and those proscribed for women is based on notions of appropriate behaviour derived from Victorian beliefs about female fragility and reproductive capacity. Feminine-appropriate sports include, for example, ice dance, rhythmic gymnastics and synchronised swimming, which reward grace, balance and poise as against aggression, strength or bodily contact (Jennifer Hargreaves 1989). At the personal and emotional level, sport helps to shape body image and sexual identity, whether negatively or positively. As an exhibition of the body, sport exemplifies narcissism but is still viewed as a more acceptable activity for males than females.

For Asian women, participation in sport and physical recreation is also mediated by powerful cultural and religious influences. However, for Asians and other black minorities, it is all too often the case that researchers fall into the trap of assuming homogeneity and making dangerous generalisations (Lyons 1989). Very little research has been focused on black and Asian women (for an overview on race and sport, see the Sports Council's *Sport and Leisure* magazine, Nov./Dec. 1991) and even classic texts on race and sport like Cashmore's *Black Sportsmen* (1982) have been criticised for omitting women and ignoring gender issues.

Although women have increased their participation over the last twenty years in terms of the numbers engaging in sport and the diversity of those sports, this has not been matched by a corresponding rise in women's leadership roles, in coaching, management and administration (Brackenridge 1987; West and Brackenridge 1990; White *et al.* 1989; Sports Council 1990). Many women's sports are now organised and coached by men, and mergers of men's and women's sports organisations, such as the Men's and Women's Squash Rackets Associations, have not always safeguarded the interests of women participants and, indeed, some would argue that they have proved to be a retrograde step for women.

At the elite end of the spectrum of participation in sport, the evidence suggests that women, whilst increasing their proportionate representation, also remain marginal in terms of power sharing.

THE FEMINIST CRITIQUE OF SPORT

Women's experience of sport in the post-war period has been characterised by struggle, gains and losses: feminism as a social movement has both assisted and hindered women's attempts to break into this essentially male institution. There remains a tension, however, between the desire of some women to claim their entitlement to a full part in the sporting life of the nation, and the anxiety of the majority that sport somehow defeminises women and challenges the basis of 'normal' social relations. Not surprisingly, liberal feminists have sought institutional and legal redress through reforms, from the late 1960s onwards, such as their constitutional right to use facilities or to exercise their votes in the voluntary sector. During the same period, radical feminists tended to ignore sport as something made by and for men, which was seen as much less important than issues such as health, disarmament, housing or poverty. Consequently there was very little in the way of a radical feminist critique of sport in this country during the era of 1970s feminism.

Table 15.1 Representation in British Olympic sport

Year	Participants %		Officials %	
	Men	Women	Men	Women
1960	82	18	88	12
1964	79	21	89	11
1968	78	22	84	16
1972	76	24	84	16
1976	76	24	86	14
1980	68	32	86	14
1984	NA	NA	NA	NA
1988	64	36	75	25

Sources: White and Brackenridge 1985; Brackenridge 1987; Sports Council 1990.

Academic feminists have also turned their attention to women's sport within the past decade, drawing upon the emerging body of literature from leisure studies. Large-scale research investigations such as Green, Hebron and Woodward's study (1987) of gender and leisure in Sheffield and Wimbush's work (1986) on women, health and well-being in Edinburgh provided a platform for the critical analysis of gender inequalities in sport and physical recreation. It might be argued that the feminist critique of leisure and sport has actually prompted both theoretical and policy advances. Feminism has also begun to nudge the institution of sport towards an uncomfortable recognition of racial and sexual exclusivities.

CASE STUDIES

Gender and physical education

For most, the first experience of sport comes through physical education (PE) classes at school. The female tradition in PE is a strong one: 'The assumptions regarding sport, femininity and heterosexuality were rarely questioned by physical educators' (Lenskyj 1986: 84).

Desite female domination of the PE profession in the 1950s and 1960s, women have lost ground more recently since the merger of previously sex-segregated specialist colleges and the widespread male takeover at senior level of the former women's colleges (Fletcher 1984). The curriculum in most schools has always been, and remains, rigidly sex segregated despite attempts by some curriculum reformers to develop mixed PE, and this mediates girls' experiences of sport in a highly restrictive way (Leaman 1984; Scraton 1986).

The content and the delivery of the girls' PE curriculum was designed to develop poised, conforming young ladies, with a close association between health, posture and sport in the 1950s and 1960s. Notwithstanding regular curriculum reviews by the Department of Education and Science and the professional PE agencies, the sporting diet for girls in school is little different today from that on offer in the immediate post-war years. Team games have long dominated the curriculum, largely because of the persistent Victorian belief in their moral educational benefit, with gymnastics, athletics, swimming and dance all claiming their place (Kane and Layson 1974; Hendry 1978). Girls who choose to deviate from this diet must seek outlets beyond the school. The impending National Curriculum holds few promises for radical change in girls' PE and may even serve to reinforce the traditional culture of gendered subservience unwittingly fostered by many female PE teachers (Sports Council 1988; Inner London Education Authority 1988).

Teenage culture

Scraton (1989) highlights the relationship between PE and young women's subcultures and shows how, far from being biologically determined, girls' subcultural experiences and resistances are structured by their social relations and mediated by class, race and gender. She notes that sociological studies of subcultures in the 1970s largely ignored young women, focusing instead on 'the lads'. According to her research, girls were objectified and appreciated only for their sexuality, so that their own choices of leisure, including sport, were influenced and constrained by what was considered socially and sexually acceptable to their potential male partners.

For teenage girls in the 1970s, competitive sports existed within the confines of the school team system and, to a limited extent, in voluntary sector clubs. Female subcultures, especially for working-class girls, were based in private rather than public spaces and the display of physical prowess through sport was construed by both girls and boys as a direct challenge to 'proper' womanhood. For girls with aspirations towards marriage, PE – even for those who enjoyed it – was a mere irrelevance. Relatively few, bar a steady stream of intending PE teachers, went on into the competitive sports system.

The 'Wolfenden Gap' (the youth 'drop out' from sport after leaving school) is as much in evidence today as it was when first identified in 1960. For girls, to 'drop out' from sport signified dropping into other roles (White and Coakley 1986), notably the sequential roles of man-hunter, partner, wife and mother – none of which left much time for sport. Post-school participation rates in sport are still much lower than school-age children's rates, and have led to repeated campaigns by the Sports Council and other agencies anxious to try and 'bridge the sporting gap'.

The Law

Schoolgirl Theresa Bennett made history as a sporting test case for the Equal Opportunities Commission when she was banned from playing soccer in an Under 11's team, Muskham United, in 1978. In the High Court the Football Association, with the help of Lord Denning, successfully overturned a ruling that she should be allowed to take part.

The British legal system does little to help women seeking equality in sport since sport is excluded from the Sex Discrimination Act (1975) both in private clubs and where strength or power are determining factors. So when golf or angling clubs choose to exclude women from membership rights or to restrict their access to facilities for play, there is nothing in law that women can do to challenge their exclusion. Hundreds of letters of complaint each year to the Equal Opportunities Commission have brought pressures to bear for legal changes, but a proposed Equal Treatment Act, which would bring Britain into line with continental Europe on sex equality matters, remains in draft form on the Home Secretary's desk.

State intervention

From the mid-1970s onwards, the state has co-operated with the voluntary sector in offering a series of short-term schemes and projects to facilitate the involvement of more women in sport, from the community level upwards (Brackenridge 1987). Whilst these have been relatively successful in terms of their numbers of participants, they have often failed to secure permanent funding or to mount an effective challenge to the social, political or economic bases of gender inequality. Thus their effects have been only marginal and ephemeral. Henry (1990b) explains how state funding was made available in the 1970s to ameliorate concerns about youth unemployment and civil disorder, but even these examples of welfare reformism provided for males rather than females (since the moral panic arose over male public violence) and failed to challenge fundamental racial and sexual inequalities.

Sexuality

In the interests of securing 'fairness' in competition, the Sex Test (now erroneously labelled as Feminity Verification) was introduced at Olympic level in 1968 (Parry 1990) to confirm the physical basis for female performance. Male doctors had, since the nineteenth century, controlled the medical validation of womanhood and the introduction of the Sex Test reinforced the close relationship between medicine, sport and patriarchy. Critics of the test have since argued against its degrading procedures rather than the test as such, since the sporting world tacitly accepts that 'real' women must be protected from sexual cheats or deviants.

Other visually dramatic practices used to validate womanliness by athletes themselves include the wearing of overtly feminine clothing, hair accessories and jewellery and the flaunting of heterosexual attractiveness, epitomised by Florence 'Flo Jo' Joyner at the 1988 Seoul Olympics. These 'apologetics' are used by female athletes to signify to both spectators and themselves that their sexual identity is intact and is not jeopardised by their sporting activity. This strategy has long been adopted by women athletes, whose socialisation has very effectively led them to internalise the values of 'proper' womanhood.

Sport sociology has yet to resolve the difficulty of explaining how sport can be, at the same time, both liberating and constraining – how women can appear to be challenging the patriarchal practices of sport and yet also becoming incorporated into them (see Jennifer Hargreaves 1989).

ACKNOWLEDGEMENTS

Thanks to Eileen Green for her contribution to the work that underpins this paper.

REFERENCES

Beechey, V. (1987) *Unequal Work*, London: Verso.

Brackenridge, C. (1987) 'Women and community recreation in the UK', paper presented to the International Congress on Movement and Sport in Women's Lives, University of Jyväskylä, Finland, Aug. 17–21.

Carr-Hill, R.A. and Lintott, J. (1989) 'Monitoring the quality of life: which activities are worth it?', paper presented at the Leisure Studies Association Annual Conference, Leeds.

Cashmore, E. (1982) *Black Sportsmen*, London: Routledge & Kegan Paul.

Clarke, J. and Critcher, C. (1985) *The Devil Makes Work: Leisure in Capitalist Britain*, Basingstoke: Macmillan.

Dixey, R. and Talbot, M. (1982) *Women, Leisure and Bingo*, Leeds: Trinity and All Saints College.

Fletcher, S. (1984) *Women First: The Female Tradition in English Physical Education, 1880–1980*, London: Athlone Press.

General Household Survey 1973 (1975) London: HMSO.

General Household Survey 1983 (1985) London: HMSO.

Gershuny, J. and Jones, S. (1987) 'The changing work/leisure balance in Britain: 1961–1984', in J. Horne, D. Jary and A. Tomlinson (eds) *Sport, Leisure and Social Relations*, London: Routledge & Kegan Paul.

Glyptis, S. (1989) *Leisure and Unemployment*, Milton Keynes: Open University.

Glyptis, S., McInnes, H.A. and Patmore, J.A. (1987) *Leisure and the Home*, London: Sports Council/Economic and Social Research Council.

Gratton, C. and Taylor, P. (1987) *Leisure in Britain*, Hitchin: Leisure Publications.

Green, E., Hebron, S. and Woodward, D. (1987) *Gender and Leisure: A Study of*

Sheffield Women's Leisure Experiences, London: Sports Council/Economic and Social Research Council.

Green, E., Hebron, S. and Woodward, D. (1990) *Women's Leisure, What Leisure?*, Basingstoke: Macmillan.

Handy, C. (1984) *The Future of Work*, Oxford: Blackwell.

Hargreaves, Jennifer (1989) 'The promise and problems of women's leisure and sport', in C. Rojek (ed.) *Leisure for Leisure: Critical Essays*, Basingstoke: Macmillan.

Hargreaves, John (1986) *Sport, Power and Culture*, Cambridge: Polity Press.

Hendry, L.B. (1978) *School, Sport and Leisure: Three Dimensions of Adolescence*, London: Lepus Books.

Henley Centre for Forecasting (1982) *UK Leisure Markets*, London: Henley Centre.

Henry, I. (1990a) 'The development of sports policy in post-war Britain', *Coaching Focus* 12, autumn: 9–11.

—— (1990b) *Management and Planning in the Leisure Industries*, Basingstoke and London: Macmillan.

Horne, J., Jary, D. and Tomlinson, A. (eds) (1987) *Sport, Leisure and Social Relations*. Sociological Review Monograph 33, London and New York: Routledge and Kegan Paul.

Inner London Education Authority (1988) *My Favourite Subject: A Report of the Working Party on Physical Education and School Sports*, London: ILEA.

Jenkins, C. and Sherman, B. (1979) *The Collapse of Work*, London: Eyre Methuen.

—— (1981) *The Leisure Shock*, London: eyre Methuen.

John, G. (1990) 'Participant and spectator sports facilities', paper presented at a seminar on 'Leisure: The Only Growth Market?', Royal Institute of British Architects, London.

Kane, J. and Layson, J. (1974) *Physical Education In The Secondary School*, London: Schools Council.

Leaman, O. (1984) *Sit on the Sidelines and Watch the Boys Play: Sex Differentiation in PE*, Harlow: Longman.

Lenskyj, H. (1986) *Out of Bounds: Women, Sport and Sexuality*, Toronto: The Women's Press.

Lyons, A. (1989) *Asian Women and Sport*, Birmingham: West Midlands Sports Council.

Parry, J.S. (1990) 'Women, sport and Olympism', *Sport and Leisure*, July/August: 24–5.

Scraton, S. (1986) 'Images of femininity and the teaching of girls' physical education', in J. Evans (ed.) *Physical Education, Sport and Schooling*, London: Falmer Press.

—— (1989) 'Boys muscle in where angels fear to tread', in F. Coalter (ed.) *Freedom and Constraint: the Paradoxes of Leisure*, London: Comedia/Routledge.

Shaw, S. (1985) 'Gender and leisure: inequality in the distribution of leisure time', *Journal of Leisure Research* 17: 266–82.

—— (1988) 'Leisure in the contemporary family: the effect of female employment on the leisure of Canadian wives and husbands', *International Review of Modern Sociology* 18: 1–16.

Social Trends (1980), London: HMSO.

—— (1990), London: HMSO.

Sports Council (1983) *Leisure Policy for the Future*, London: Sports Council.

—— (1988) *Into the Nineties: A Strategy for Sport 1988–1993*, London: Sports Council.

—— (1988) *Annual Report 1987/88*, London: Sports Council.

—— (1989) *Sport in Society Fact Sheets*, London: Sports Council.

—— (1990) *Women and Sport: Taking the Lead*, report of a Council of Europe Seminar at Bisham Abbey, London: Sports Council.

—— (1991) 'Sport and Race', *Sport and Leisure* November/December.

Veal, A. (1987) *Leisure and the Future*, London: Allen & Unwin.

West, A. and Brackenridge, C.H. (1990) *Wot! No Women Sports Coaches? A Report on the Issues Relating to Women's Lives as Sports Coaches in the UK 1989–90*, Sheffield: Pavic Publications.

White, A. and Brackenridge, C. (1985) 'Who rules sport? Gender divisions in the power structure of British sports organisations from 1960', *International Review of Sport Sociology* 20/21, spring: 95–107.

White, A. and Coakley, J. (1986) *Making Decisions: The Response of Young People in the Medway Towns to the 'Ever Thought of Sport?' Campaign*, London: Sports Council, Greater London and South East Region.

White, A., Mayglothling, R. and Carr, C. (1989) *The Dedicated Few: The Social World of Women Coaches in Britain in the 1980s*, Chichester: West Sussex Institute of Higher Education.

Wimbush, E. (1986) *Women, Leisure and Well-Being*, Edinburgh: Centre for Leisure Research.

Young, M. and Willmott, P. (1973) *The Symmetrical Family – A Study of Work and Leisure in the London Region*, London: Routledge & Kegan Paul.

Index